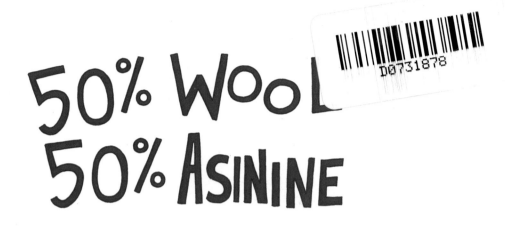

50% WOOL
50% ASININE

50% WOOL 50% ASININE

An *Argyle Sweater* **Collection by Scott Hilburn**

Andrews McMeel
Publishing, LLC

Kansas City • Sydney • London

The Argyle Sweater is distributed internationally by Universal Uclick.

10 11 12 13 14 WKT 10 9 8 7 6 5 4 3 2 1

ISBN-13: 978-0-7407-9154-3
ISBN-10: 0-7407-9154-0

Library of Congress Control Number: 2009938771

www.andrewsmcmeel.com
www.theargylesweater.com

ATTENTION: SCHOOLS AND BUSINESSES

Andrews McMeel books are available at quantity discounts with bulk purchase for educational, business, or sales promotional use. For information, please write to: Special Sales Department, Andrews McMeel Publishing, LLC, 1130 Walnut Street, Kansas City, Missouri 64106.

To Maddie and Emma

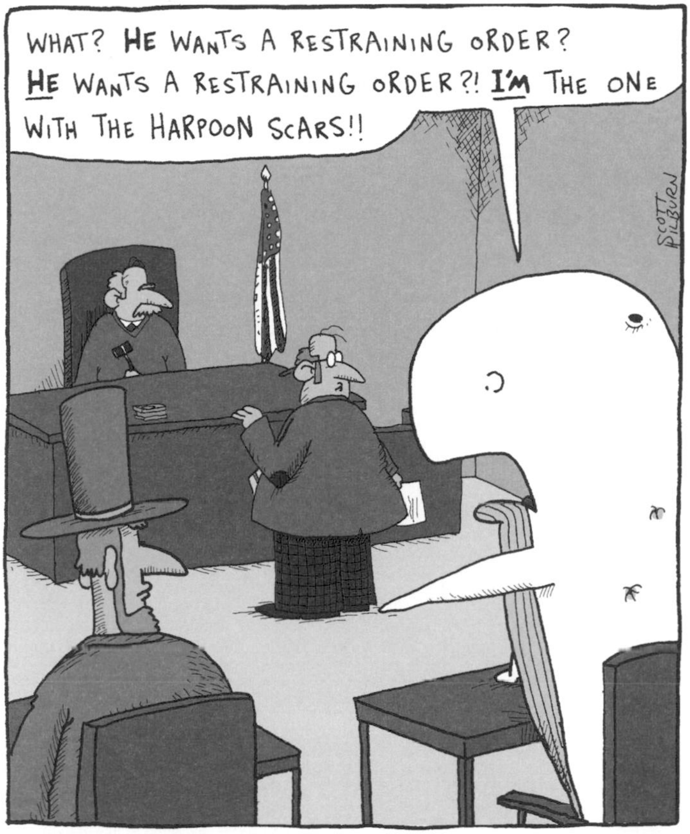
WHAT? HE WANTS A RESTRAINING ORDER? HE WANTS A RESTRAINING ORDER?! I'M THE ONE WITH THE HARPOON SCARS!!
SCOTT HILBURN

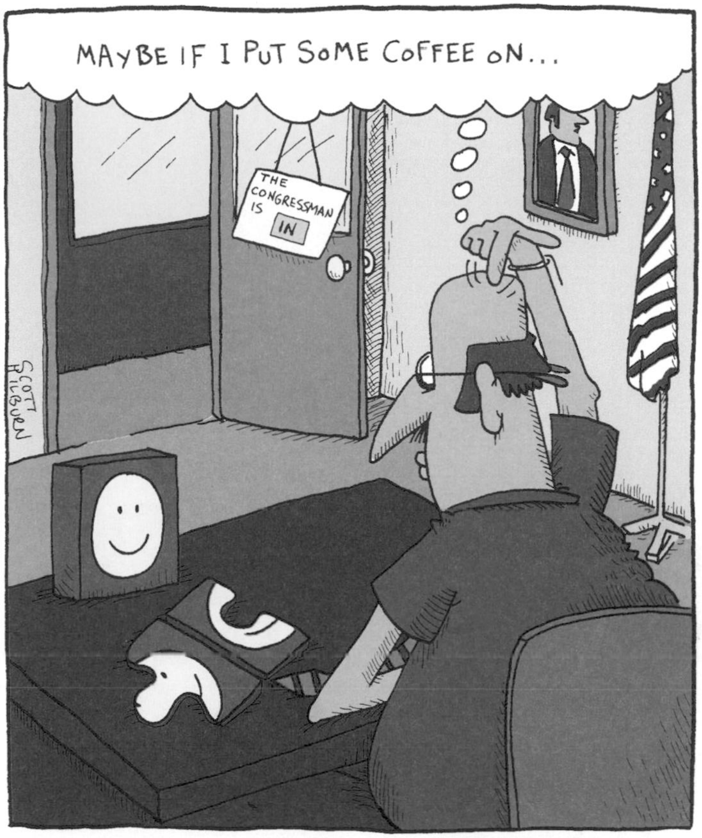
MAYBE IF I PUT SOME COFFEE ON...
THE CONGRESSMAN IS IN
SCOTT HILBURN

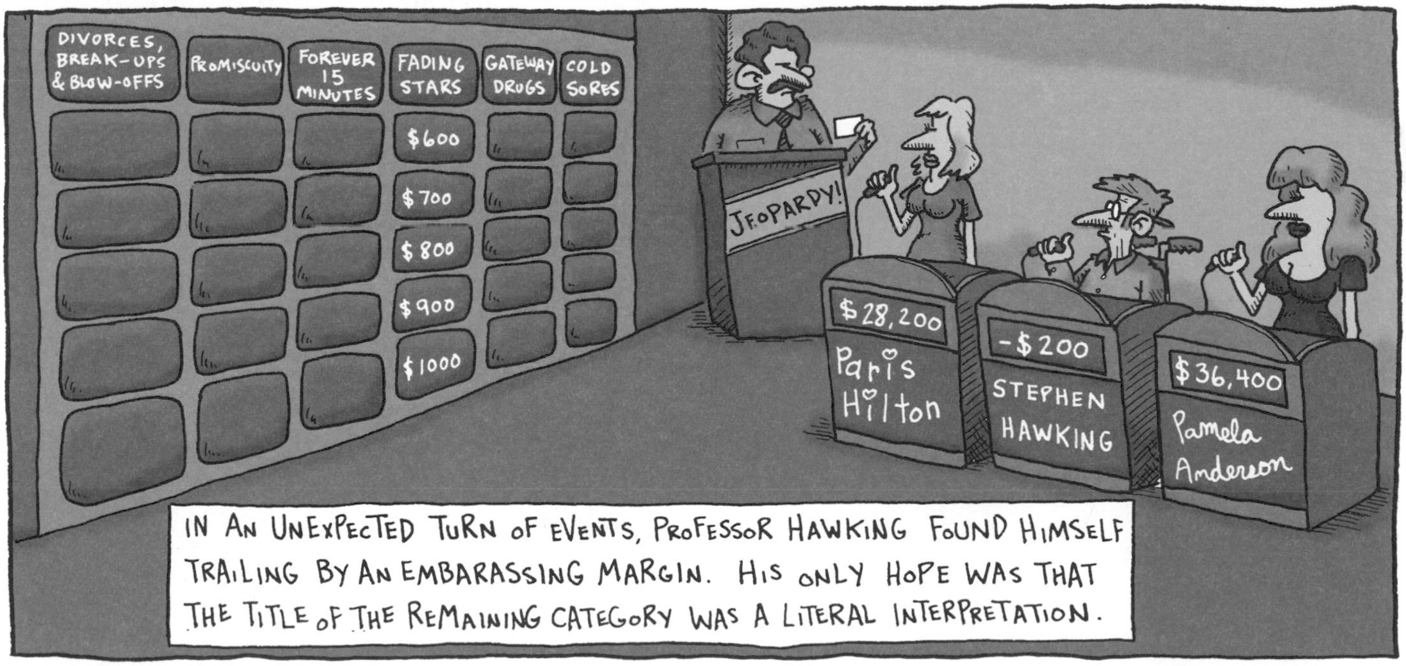
DIVORCES, BREAK-UPS & BLOW-OFFS
PROMISCUITY
FOREVER 15 MINUTES
FADING STARS
GATEWAY DRUGS
COLD SORES
$600
$700
$800
$900
$1000
JEOPARDY!
$28,200
Paris Hilton
-$200
STEPHEN HAWKING
$36,400
Pamela Anderson
IN AN UNEXPECTED TURN OF EVENTS, PROFESSOR HAWKING FOUND HIMSELF TRAILING BY AN EMBARASSING MARGIN. HIS ONLY HOPE WAS THAT THE TITLE OF THE REMAINING CATEGORY WAS A LITERAL INTERPRETATION.

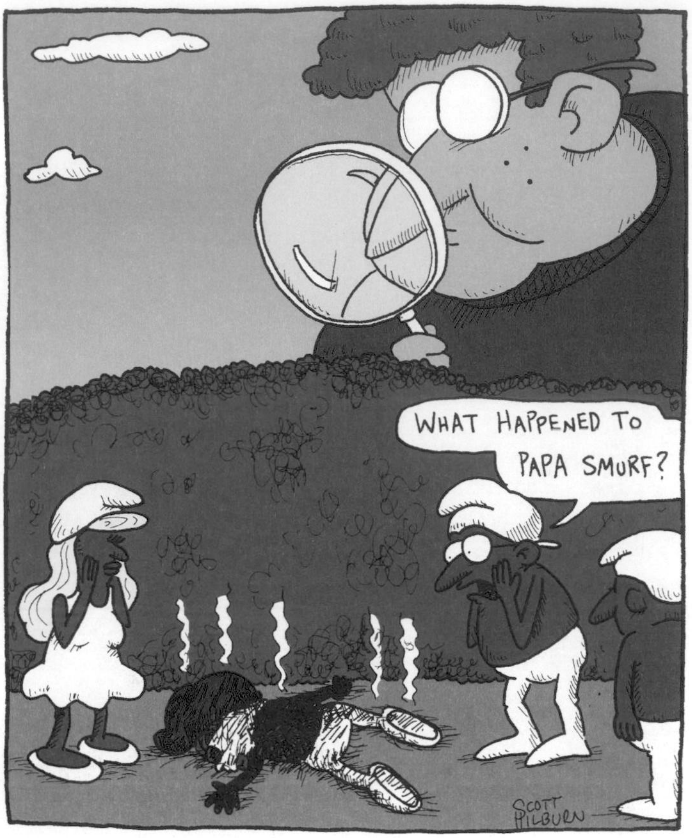
WHAT HAPPENED TO PAPA SMURF?
SCOTT HILBURN

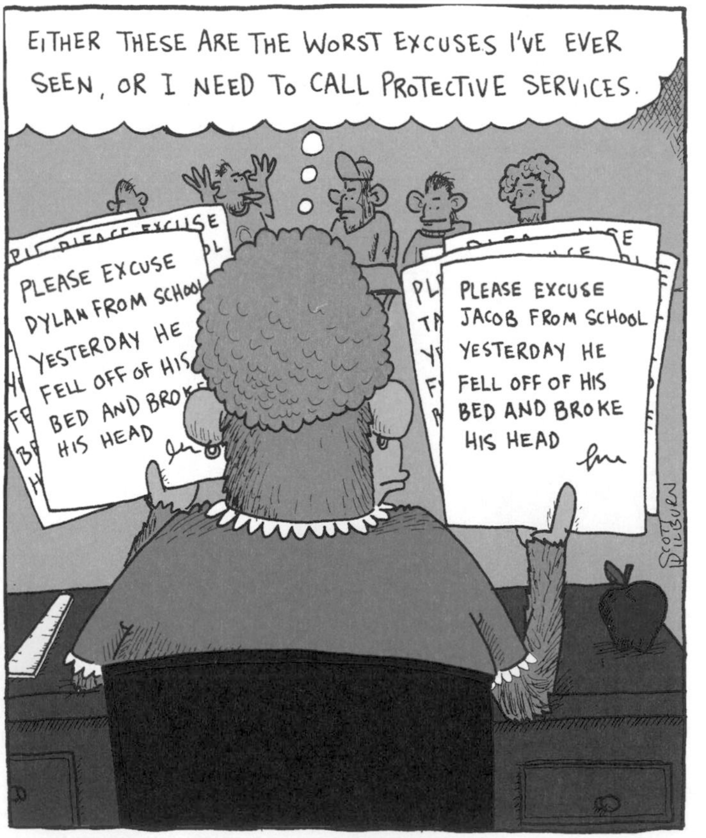
EITHER THESE ARE THE WORST EXCUSES I'VE EVER SEEN, OR I NEED TO CALL PROTECTIVE SERVICES.
PLEASE EXCUSE DYLAN FROM SCHOOL YESTERDAY HE FELL OFF OF HIS BED AND BROKE HIS HEAD
PLEASE EXCUSE JACOB FROM SCHOOL YESTERDAY HE FELL OFF OF HIS BED AND BROKE HIS HEAD
SCOTT HILBURN

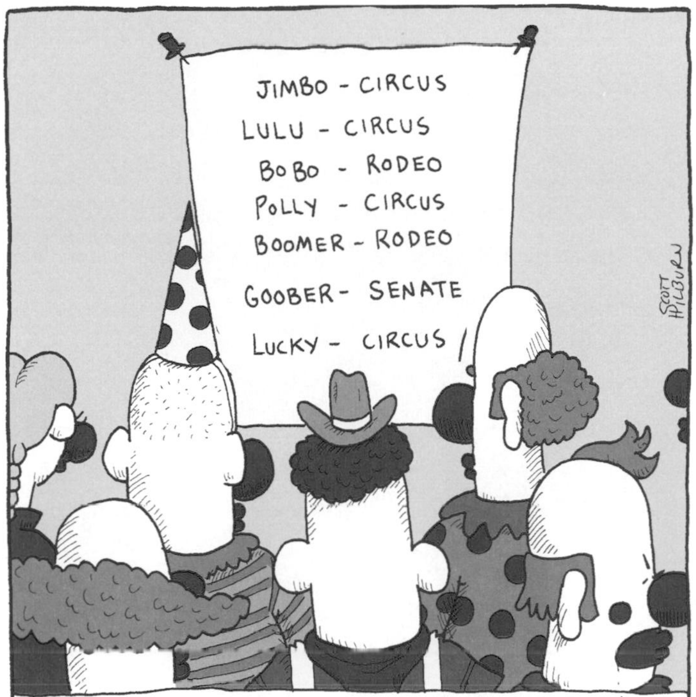
JIMBO - CIRCUS
LULU - CIRCUS
BOBO - RODEO
POLLY - CIRCUS
BOOMER - RODEO
GOOBER - SENATE
LUCKY - CIRCUS
SCOTT HILBURN

UPON GRADUATION, ALL OF THE CLOWNS WOULD GATHER TO FIND OUT WHERE THEIR ASSIGNMENTS WOULD BE.

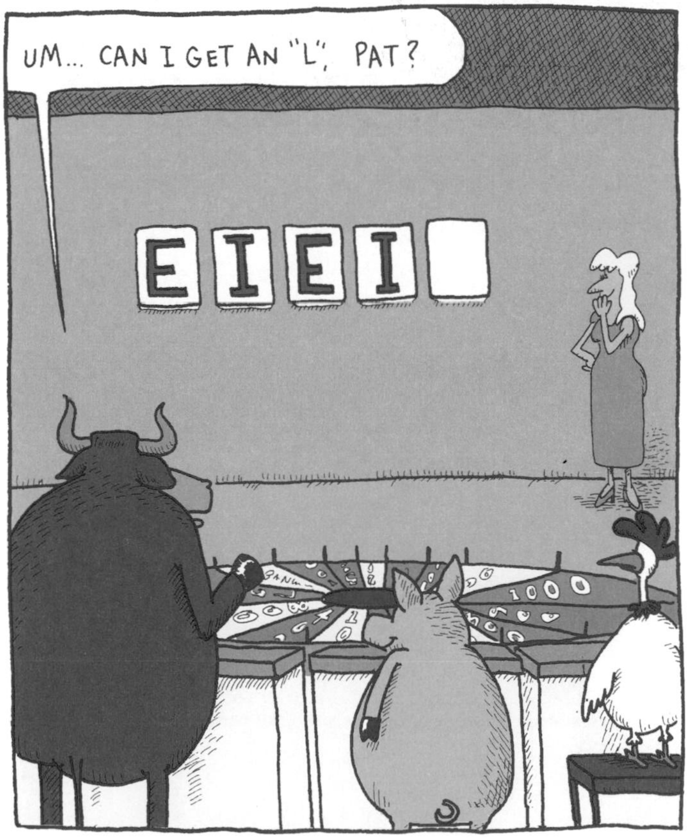
UM... CAN I GET AN "L", PAT?
EIEI

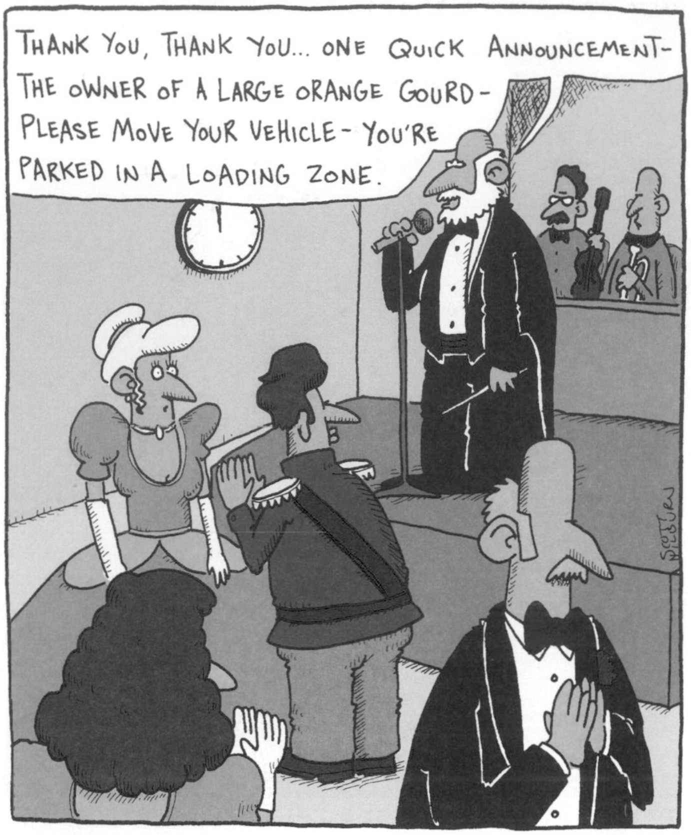
THANK YOU, THANK YOU... ONE QUICK ANNOUNCEMENT- THE OWNER OF A LARGE ORANGE GOURD- PLEASE MOVE YOUR VEHICLE- YOU'RE PARKED IN A LOADING ZONE.

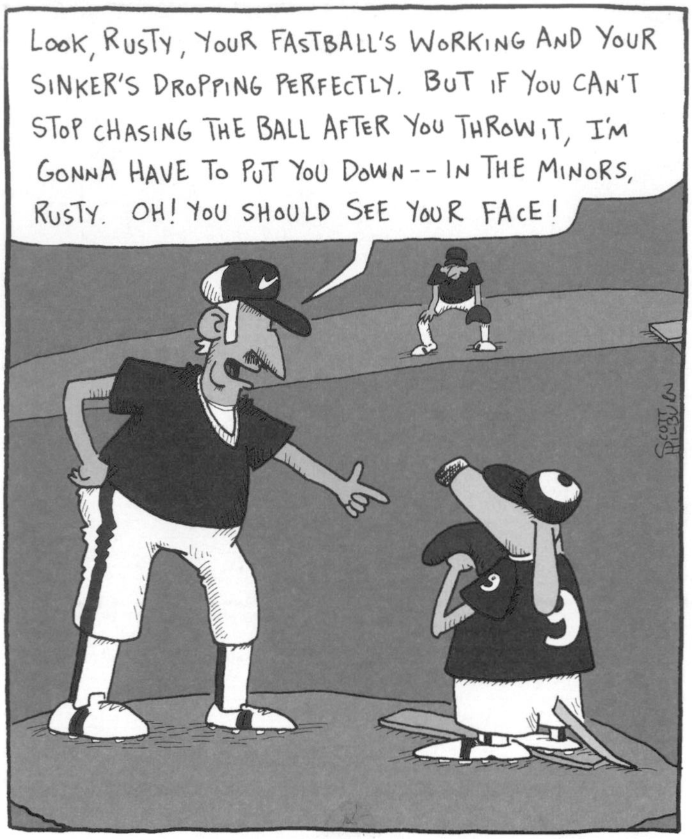
LOOK, RUSTY, YOUR FASTBALL'S WORKING AND YOUR SINKER'S DROPPING PERFECTLY. BUT IF YOU CAN'T STOP CHASING THE BALL AFTER YOU THROW IT, I'M GONNA HAVE TO PUT YOU DOWN-- IN THE MINORS, RUSTY. OH! YOU SHOULD SEE YOUR FACE!

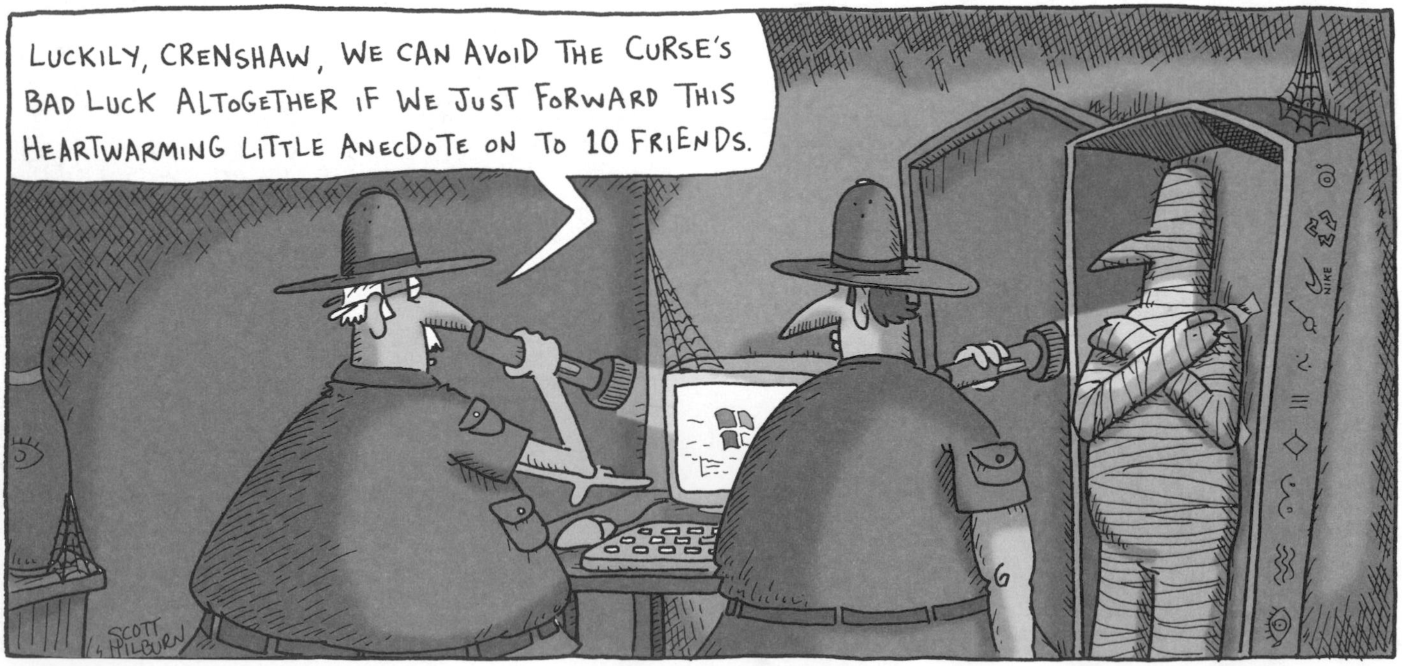
LUCKILY, CRENSHAW, WE CAN AVOID THE CURSE'S BAD LUCK ALTOGETHER IF WE JUST FORWARD THIS HEARTWARMING LITTLE ANECDOTE ON TO 10 FRIENDS.
SCOTT HILBURN

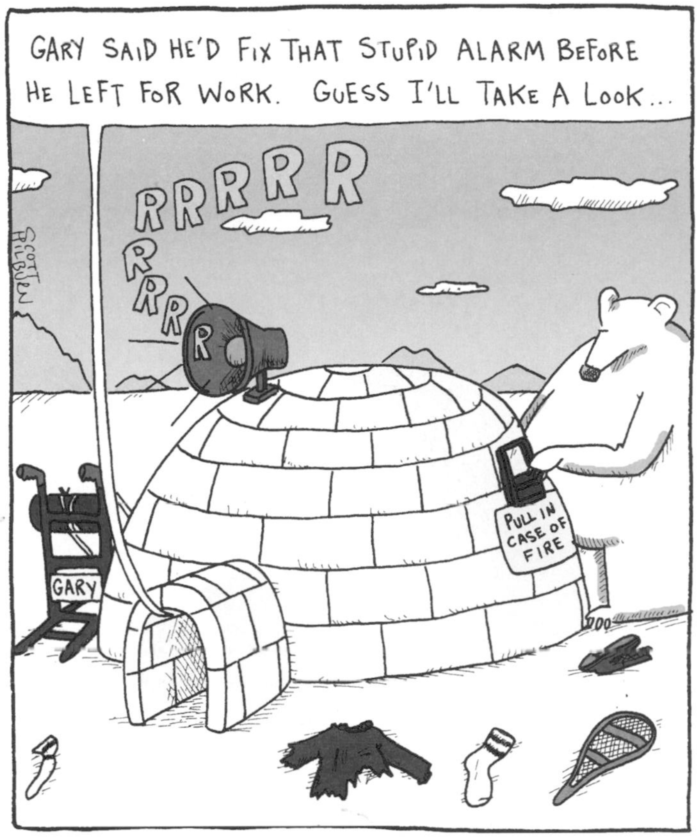
GARY SAID HE'D FIX THAT STUPID ALARM BEFORE HE LEFT FOR WORK. GUESS I'LL TAKE A LOOK...
RRRRR
RRRR
PULL IN CASE OF FIRE
GARY
SCOTT HILBURN

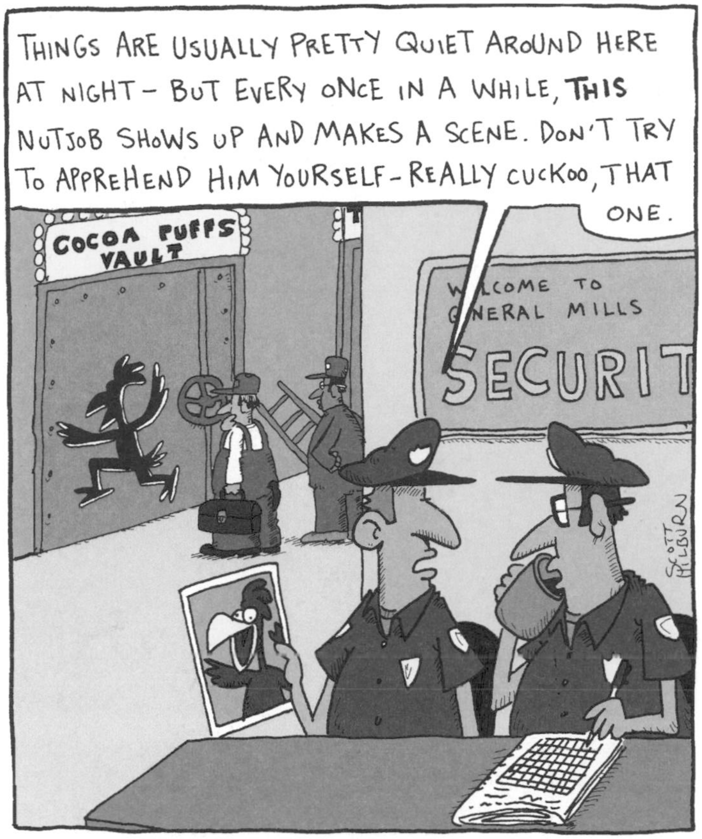
THINGS ARE USUALLY PRETTY QUIET AROUND HERE AT NIGHT – BUT EVERY ONCE IN A WHILE, **THIS** NUTJOB SHOWS UP AND MAKES A SCENE. DON'T TRY TO APPREHEND HIM YOURSELF – REALLY CUCKOO, THAT ONE.
COCOA PUFFS VAULT
SECURIT
SCOTT HILBURN

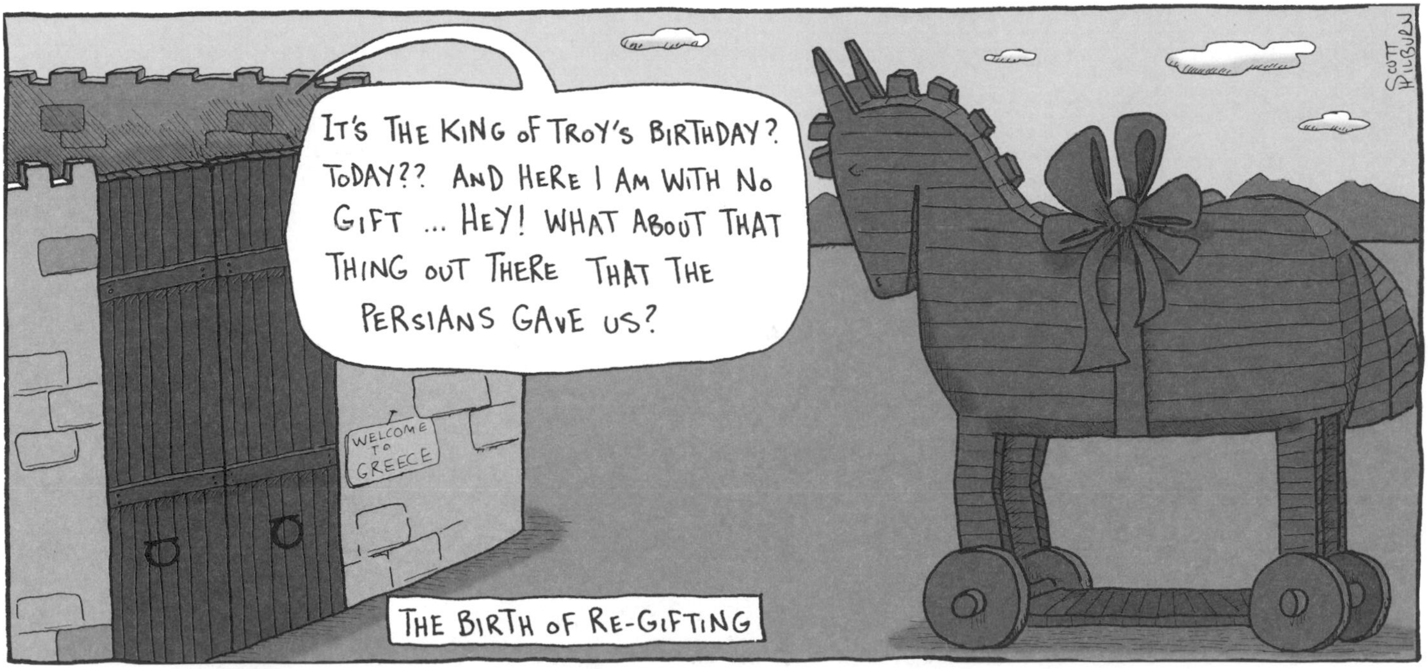
IT'S THE KING OF TROY'S BIRTHDAY? TODAY?? AND HERE I AM WITH NO GIFT ... HEY! WHAT ABOUT THAT THING OUT THERE THAT THE PERSIANS GAVE US?
WELCOME TO GREECE
SCOTT HILBURN

THE BIRTH OF RE-GIFTING

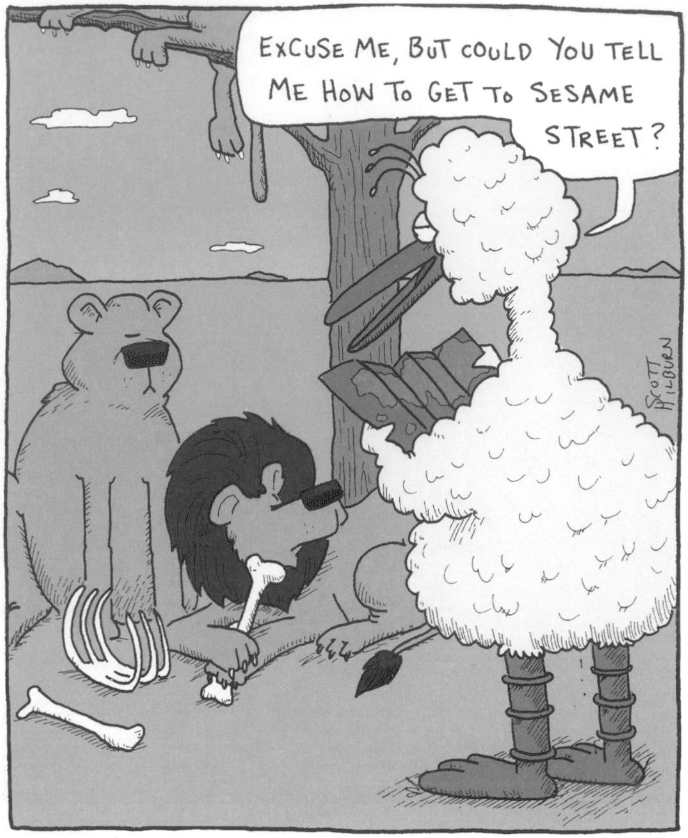
EXCUSE ME, BUT COULD YOU TELL ME HOW TO GET TO SESAME STREET?
SCOTT HILBURN

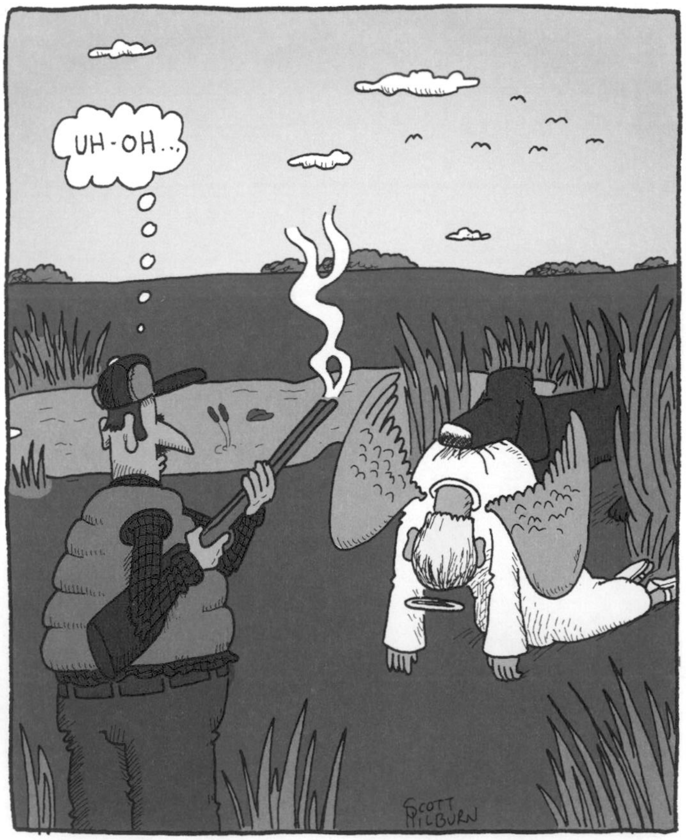
UH-OH...
SCOTT HILBURN

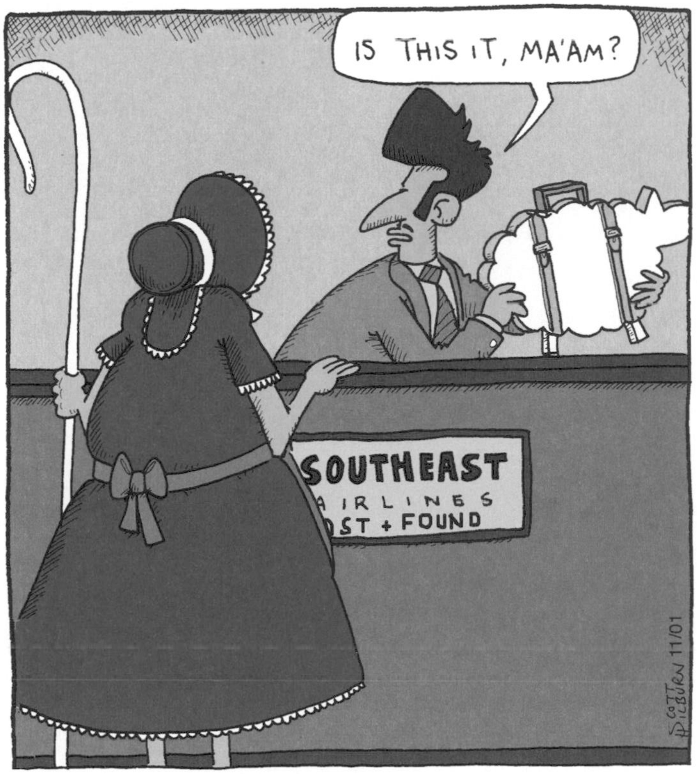
IS THIS IT, MA'AM?
SOUTHEAST
AIRLINES
OST + FOUND
SCOTT HILBURN 11/01

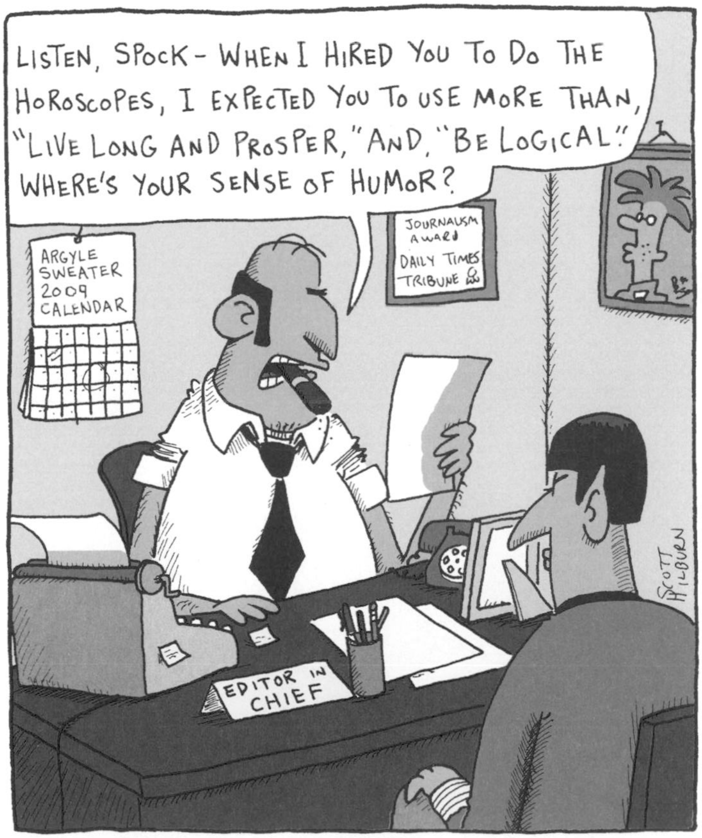
LISTEN, SPOCK- WHEN I HIRED YOU TO DO THE HOROSCOPES, I EXPECTED YOU TO USE MORE THAN, "LIVE LONG AND PROSPER," AND, "BE LOGICAL." WHERE'S YOUR SENSE OF HUMOR?
ARGYLE SWEATER 2009 CALENDAR
JOURNALISM AWARD
DAILY TIMES TRIBUNE
EDITOR IN CHIEF
SCOTT HILBURN

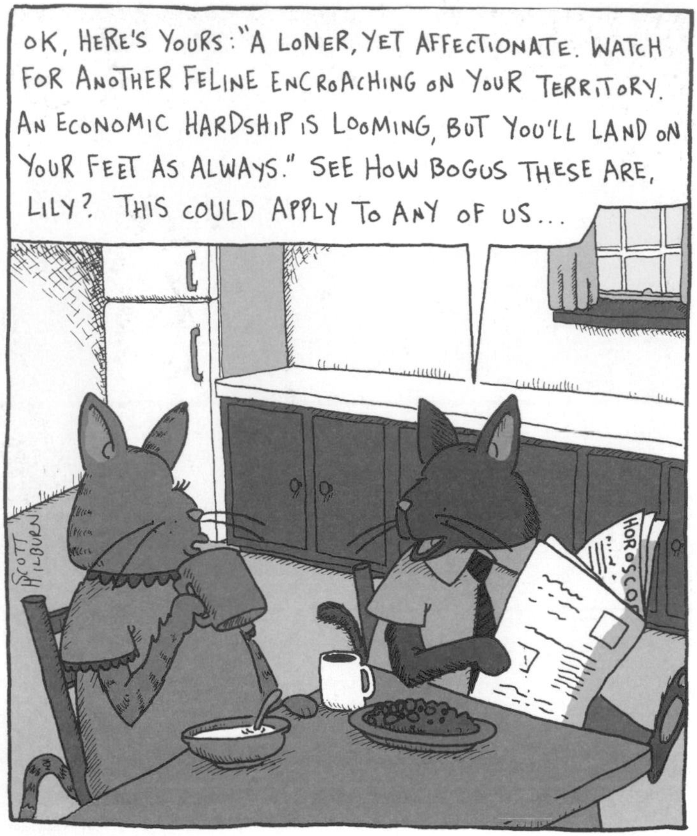
OK, HERE'S YOURS: "A LONER, YET AFFECTIONATE. WATCH FOR ANOTHER FELINE ENCROACHING ON YOUR TERRITORY. AN ECONOMIC HARDSHIP IS LOOMING, BUT YOU'LL LAND ON YOUR FEET AS ALWAYS." SEE HOW BOGUS THESE ARE, LILY? THIS COULD APPLY TO ANY OF US...
HOROSCOP
SCOTT HILBURN

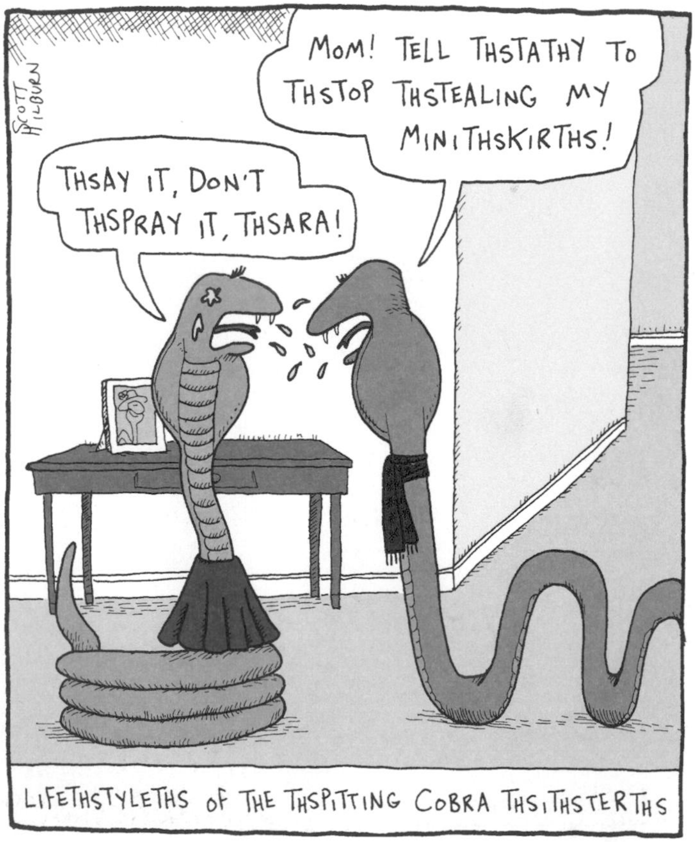
MOM! TELL THSTATHY TO THSTOP THSTEALING MY MINITHSKIRTHS!
THSAY IT, DON'T THSPRAY IT, THSARA!
SCOTT HILBURN

LIFETHSTYLETHS OF THE THSPITTING COBRA THSITHSTERTHS

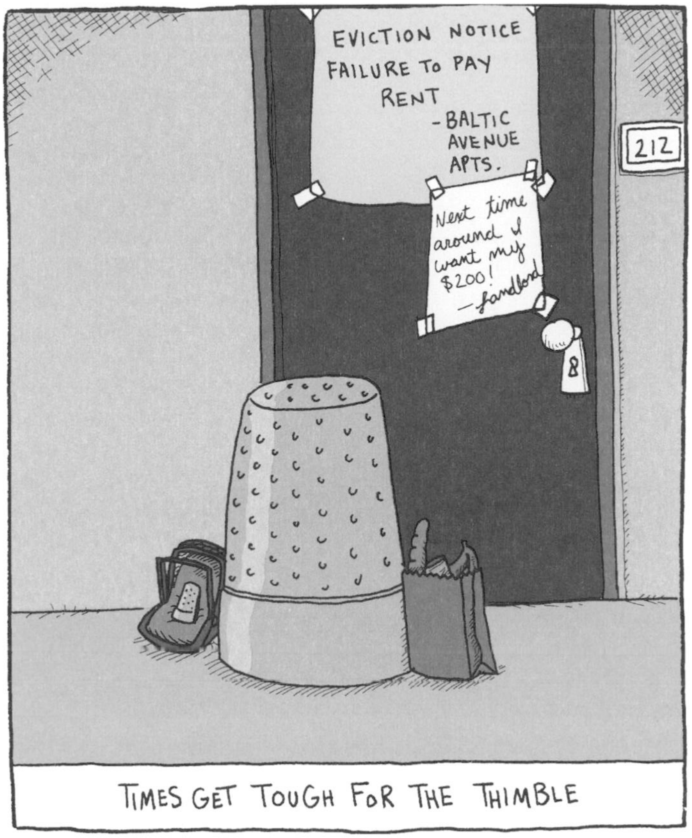
EVICTION NOTICE
FAILURE TO PAY RENT
- BALTIC AVENUE APTS.
212
Next time around I want my $200!
—Landlord
8
TIMES GET TOUGH FOR THE THIMBLE

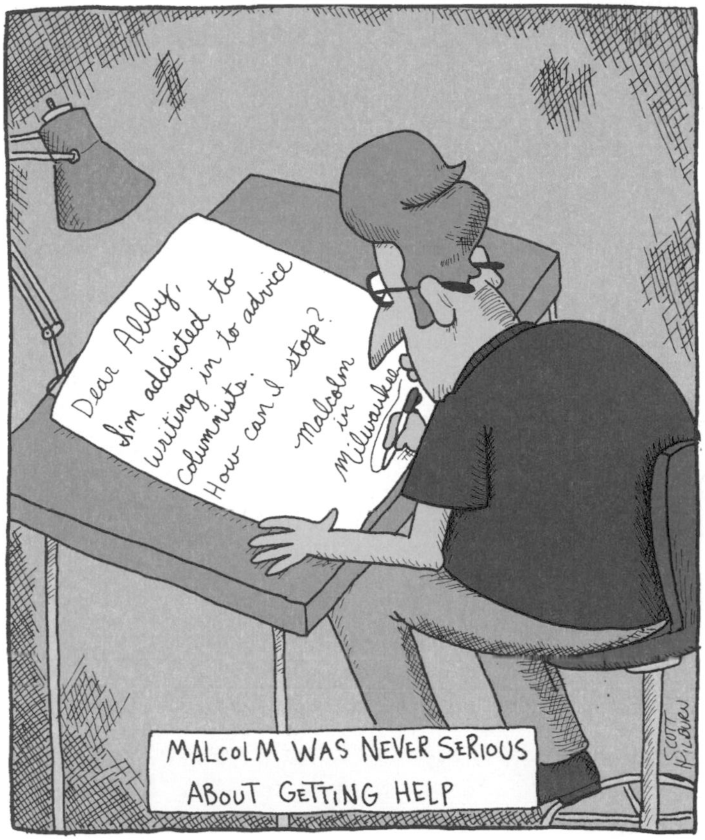
Dear Abby,
I'm addicted to writing in to advice columnists. How can I stop?
Malcolm in Milwaukee
SCOTT HILBURN
MALCOLM WAS NEVER SERIOUS ABOUT GETTING HELP

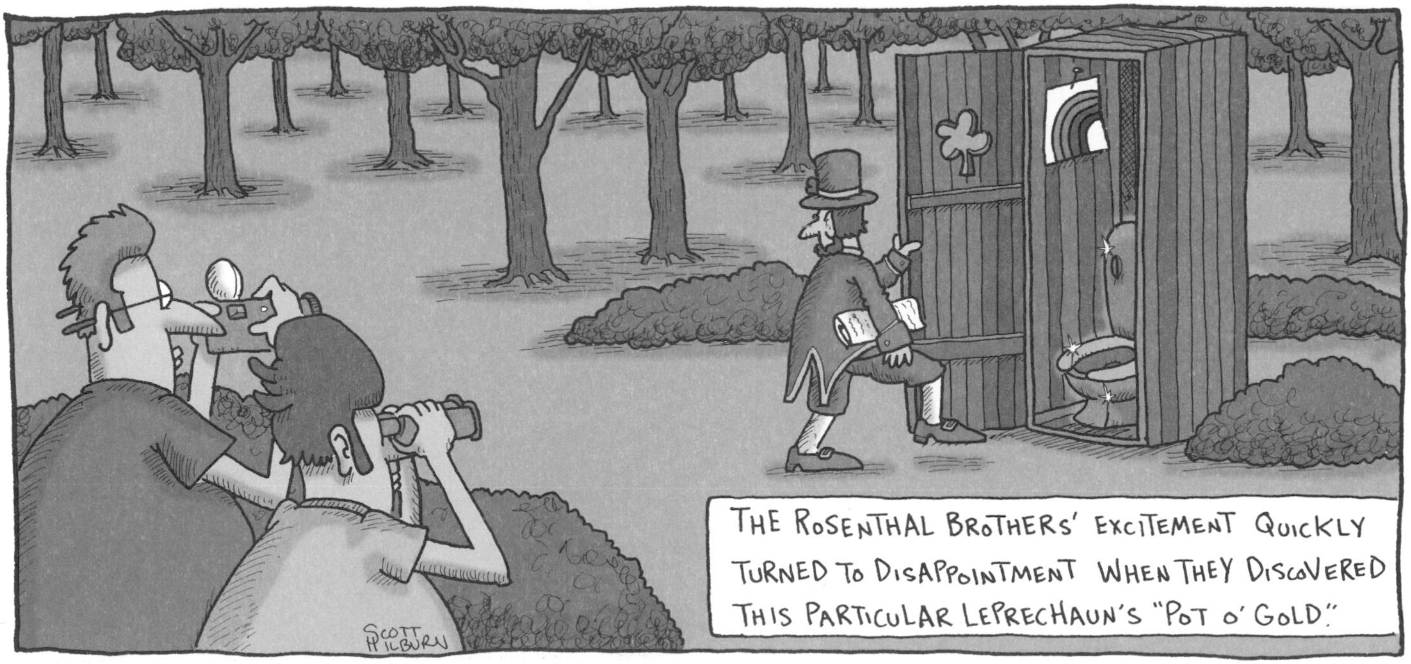
SCOTT HILBURN
THE ROSENTHAL BROTHERS' EXCITEMENT QUICKLY TURNED TO DISAPPOINTMENT WHEN THEY DISCOVERED THIS PARTICULAR LEPRECHAUN'S "POT O' GOLD."

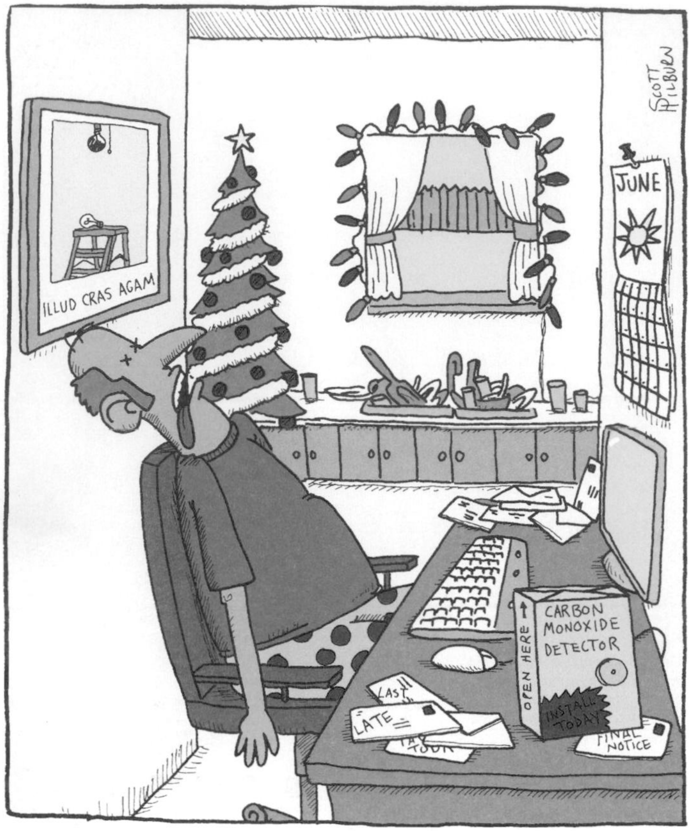
SCOTT HILBURN
ILLUD CRAS AGAM
JUNE
CARBON MONOXIDE DETECTOR
OPEN HERE
INSTALL TODAY
LAST
LATE
FINAL NOTICE

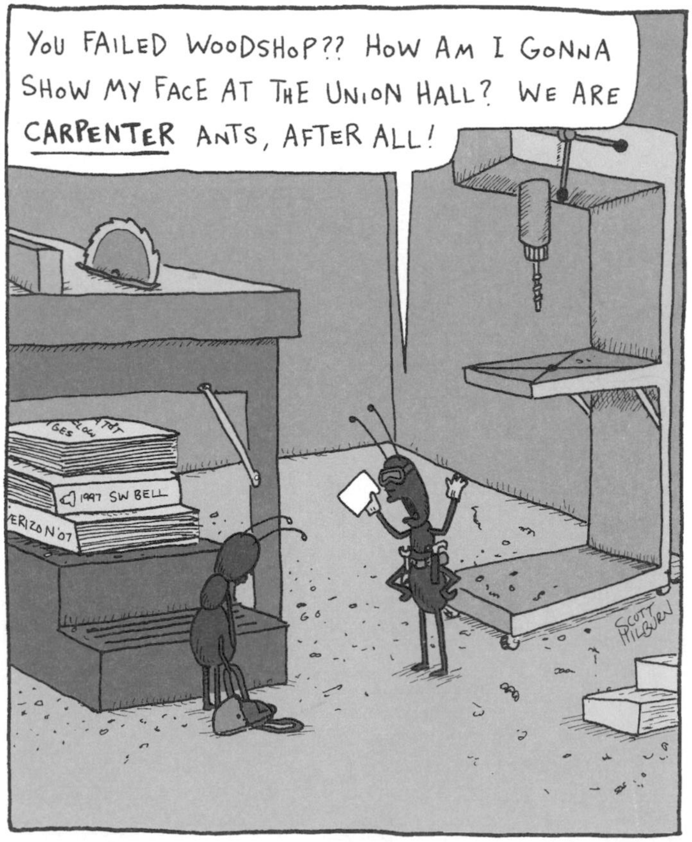
YOU FAILED WOODSHOP?? HOW AM I GONNA SHOW MY FACE AT THE UNION HALL? WE ARE CARPENTER ANTS, AFTER ALL!
1997 SW BELL
SCOTT HILBURN

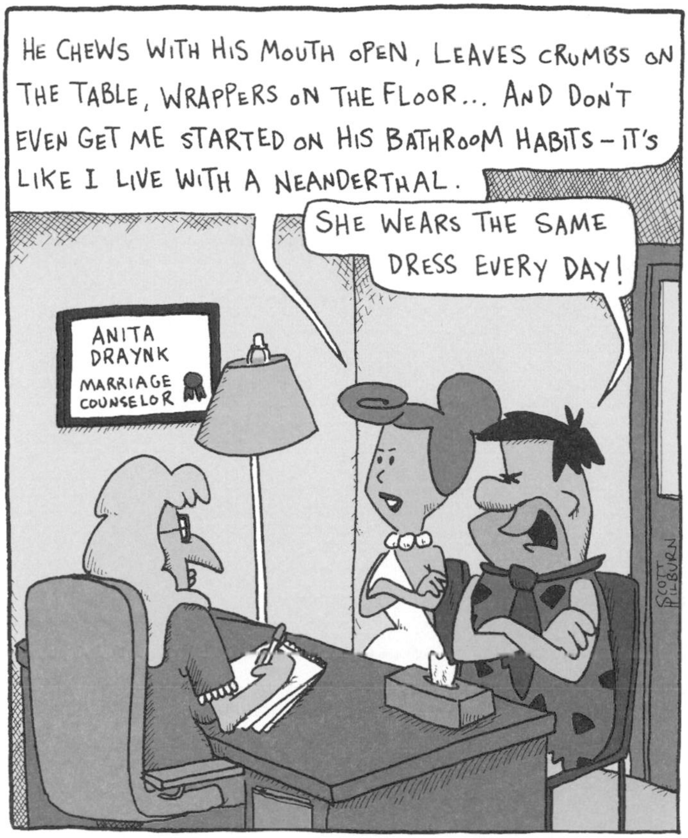
HE CHEWS WITH HIS MOUTH OPEN, LEAVES CRUMBS ON THE TABLE, WRAPPERS ON THE FLOOR... AND DON'T EVEN GET ME STARTED ON HIS BATHROOM HABITS – IT'S LIKE I LIVE WITH A NEANDERTHAL.
SHE WEARS THE SAME DRESS EVERY DAY!
ANITA DRAYNK
MARRIAGE COUNSELOR
SCOTT HILBURN

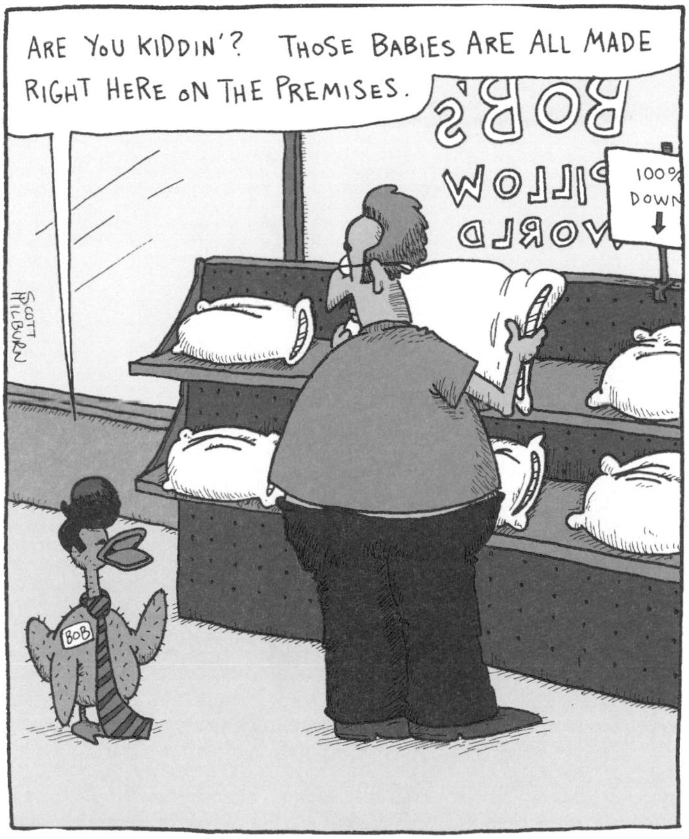
ARE YOU KIDDIN'? THOSE BABIES ARE ALL MADE RIGHT HERE ON THE PREMISES.
100% DOWN
BOB
SCOTT HILBURN

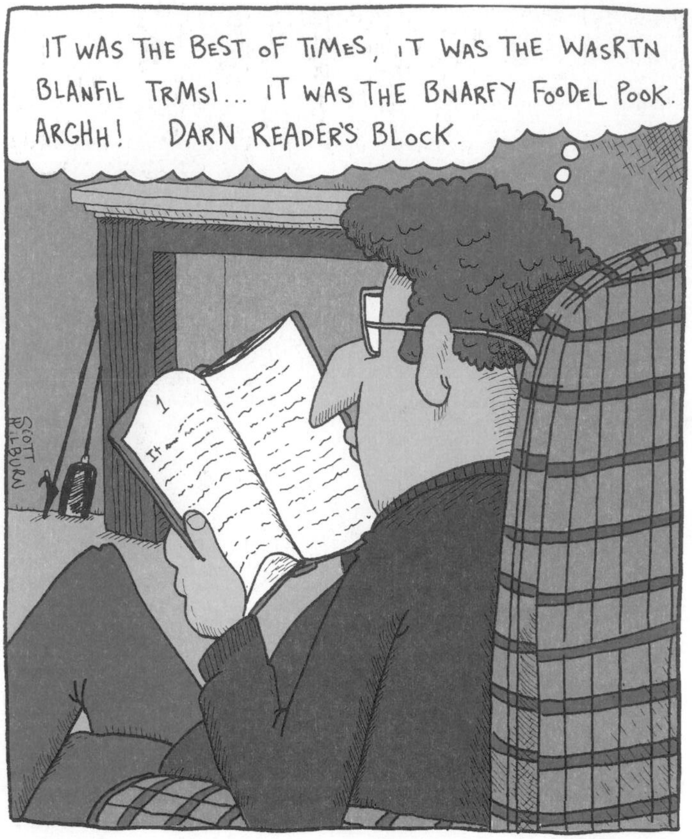
IT WAS THE BEST OF TIMES, IT WAS THE WASRTN BLANFIL TRMSI... IT WAS THE BNARFY FOODEL POOK. ARGHH! DARN READER'S BLOCK.
SCOTT HILBURN

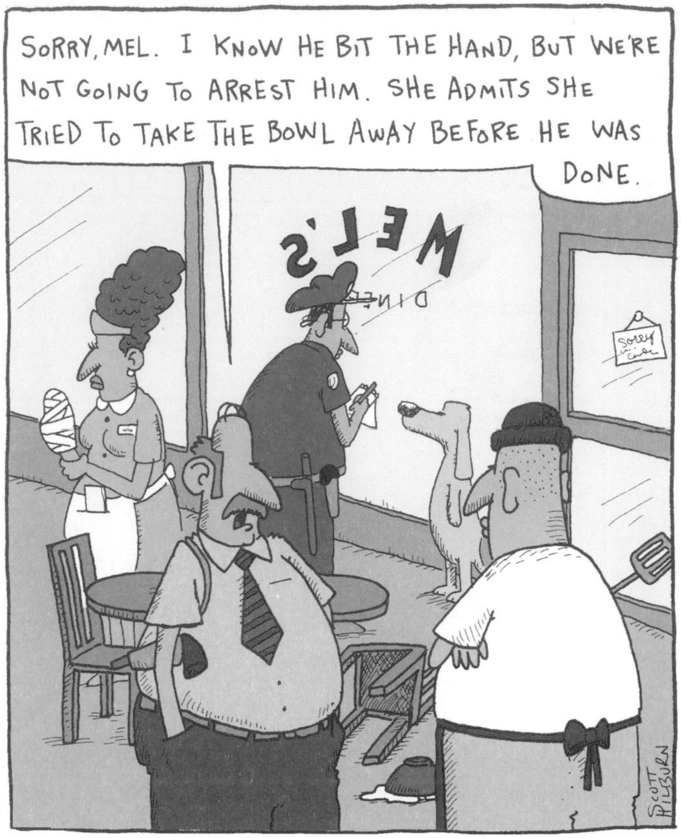
SORRY, MEL. I KNOW HE BIT THE HAND, BUT WE'RE NOT GOING TO ARREST HIM. SHE ADMITS SHE TRIED TO TAKE THE BOWL AWAY BEFORE HE WAS DONE.
SCOTT HILBURN

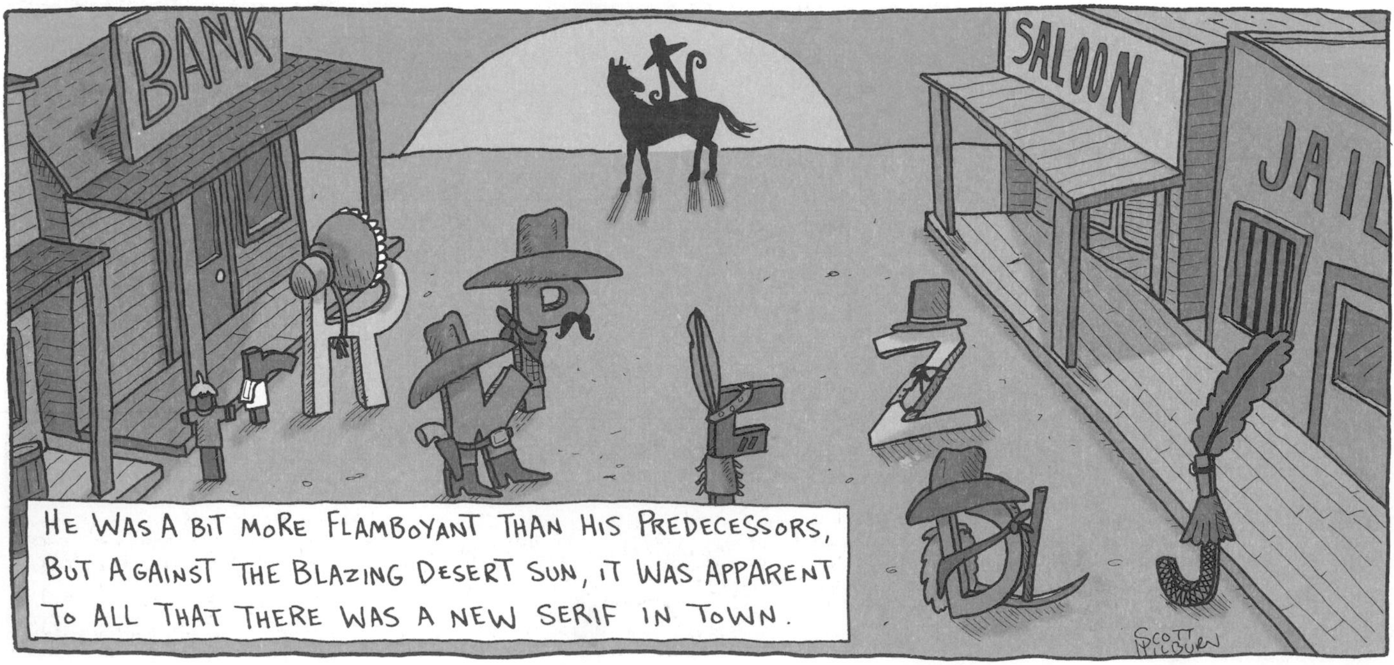
BANK
SALOON
HE WAS A BIT MORE FLAMBOYANT THAN HIS PREDECESSORS, BUT AGAINST THE BLAZING DESERT SUN, IT WAS APPARENT TO ALL THAT THERE WAS A NEW SERIF IN TOWN.
SCOTT HILBURN

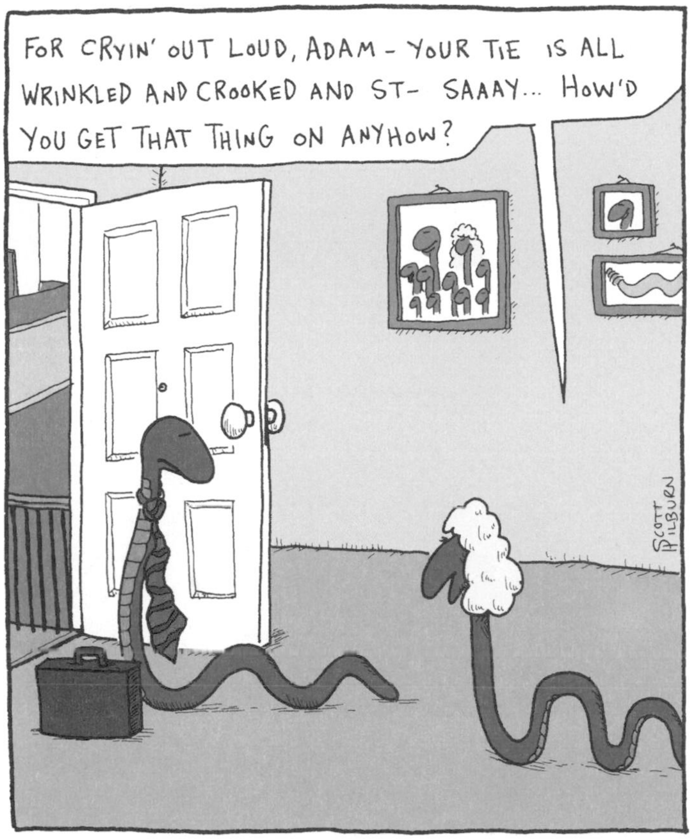
FOR CRYIN' OUT LOUD, ADAM - YOUR TIE IS ALL WRINKLED AND CROOKED AND ST- SAAAY... HOW'D YOU GET THAT THING ON ANYHOW?
SCOTT HILBURN

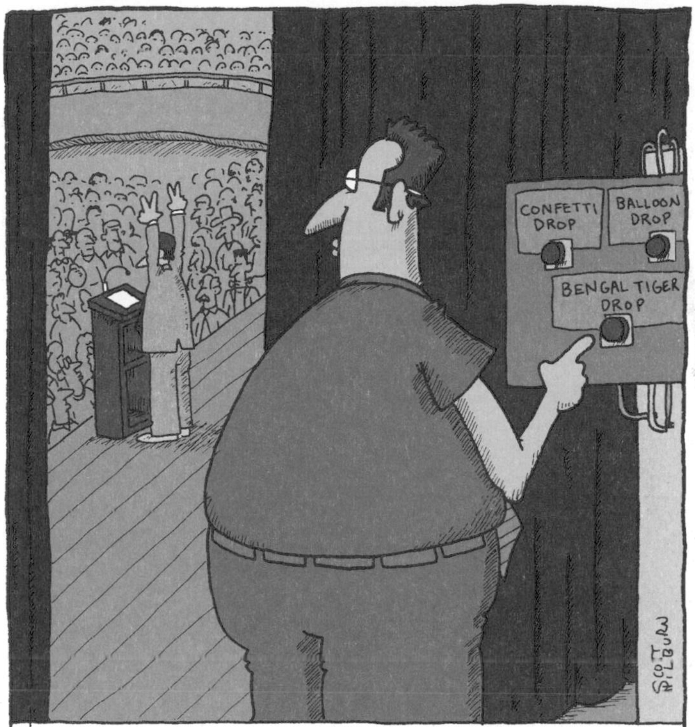
CONFETTI DROP
BALLOON DROP
BENGAL TIGER DROP
SCOTT HILBURN

DISTRACTED BY THE SENATOR'S MESMERIZING SPEECH, WILLARD INADVERTENTLY PUSHES THE WRONG BUTTON.

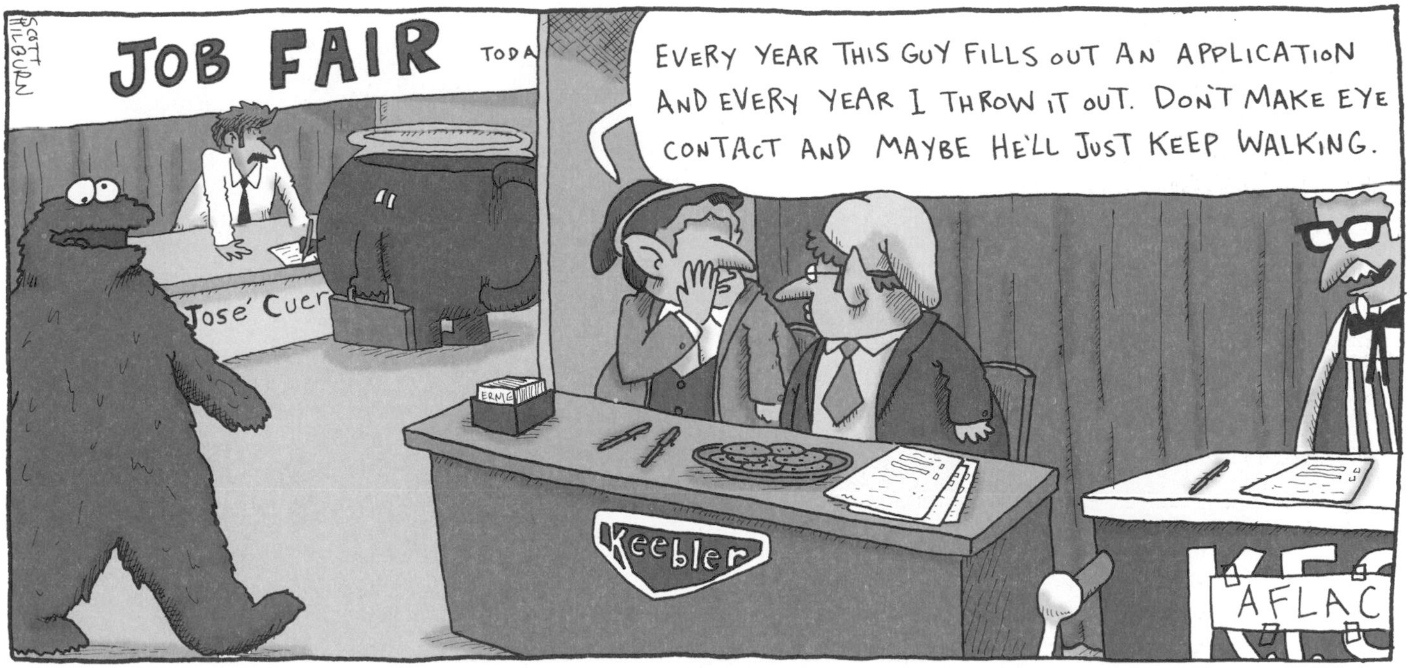
SCOTT HILBURN
JOB FAIR TODA
José Cuer
EVERY YEAR THIS GUY FILLS OUT AN APPLICATION AND EVERY YEAR I THROW IT OUT. DON'T MAKE EYE CONTACT AND MAYBE HE'LL JUST KEEP WALKING.
ERNIE
Keebler
AFLAC

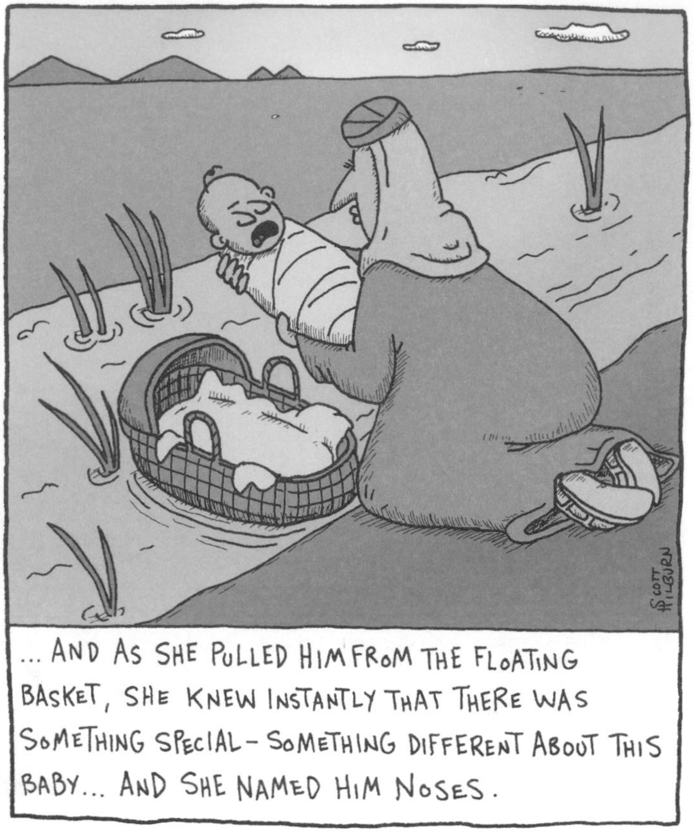
SCOTT HILBURN
... AND AS SHE PULLED HIM FROM THE FLOATING BASKET, SHE KNEW INSTANTLY THAT THERE WAS SOMETHING SPECIAL - SOMETHING DIFFERENT ABOUT THIS BABY... AND SHE NAMED HIM NOSES.

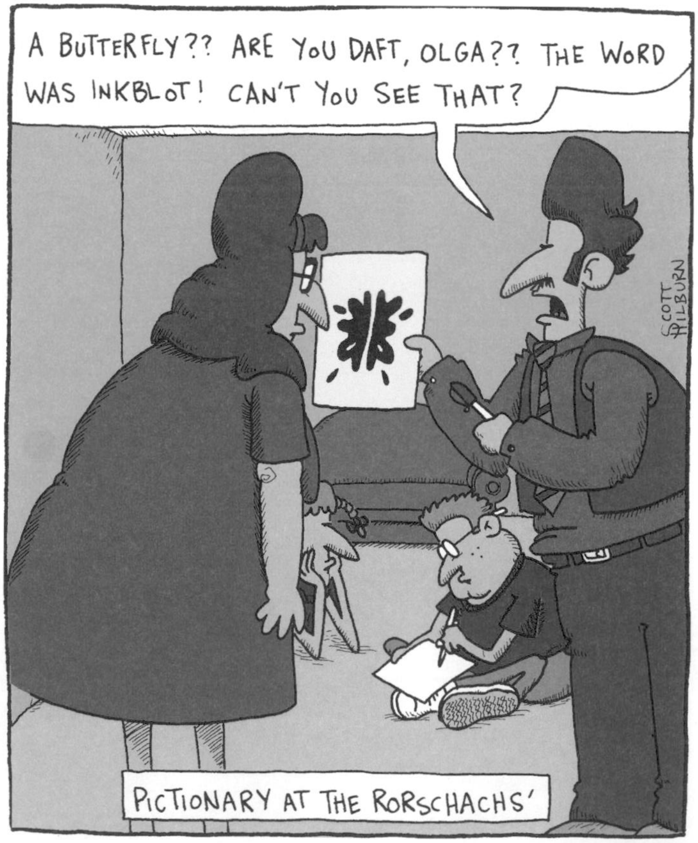
A BUTTERFLY?? ARE YOU DAFT, OLGA?? THE WORD WAS INKBLOT! CAN'T YOU SEE THAT?
SCOTT HILBURN
PICTIONARY AT THE RORSCHACHS'

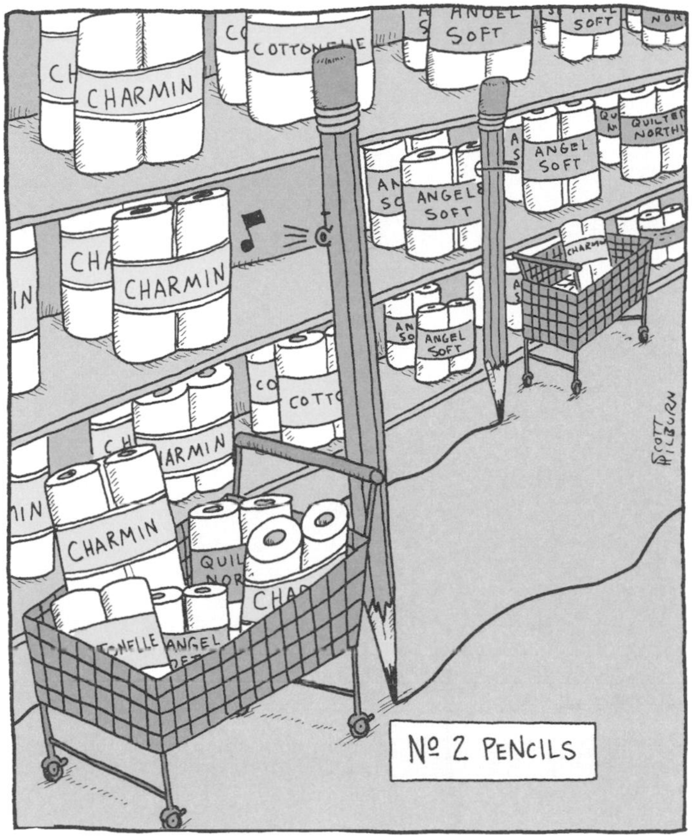

CHARMIN
COTTONELLE
ANGEL SOFT
QUILTED NORTHERN
№ 2 PENCILS
SCOTT HILBURN

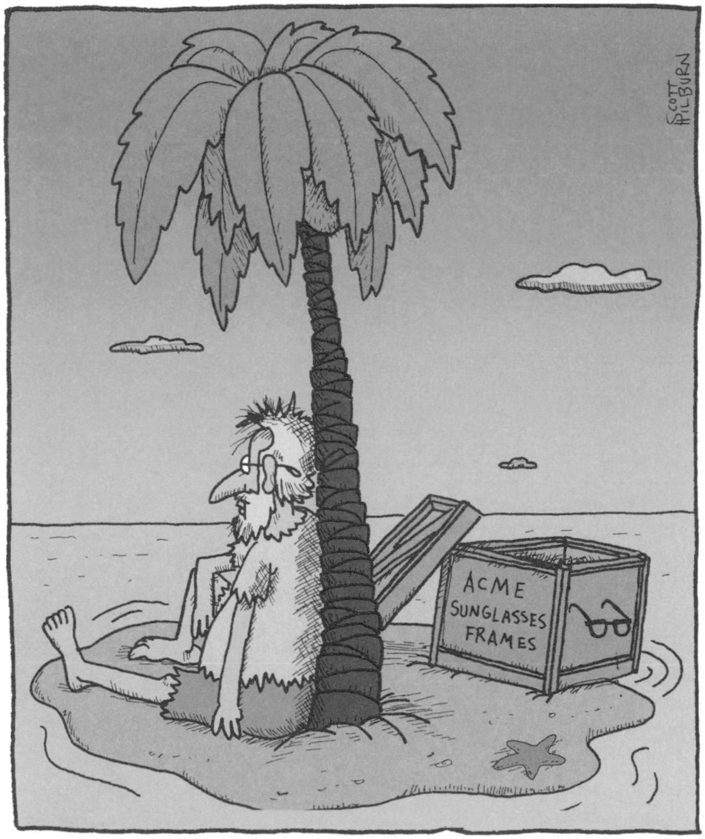

SCOTT HILBURN
ACME
SUNGLASSES
FRAMES

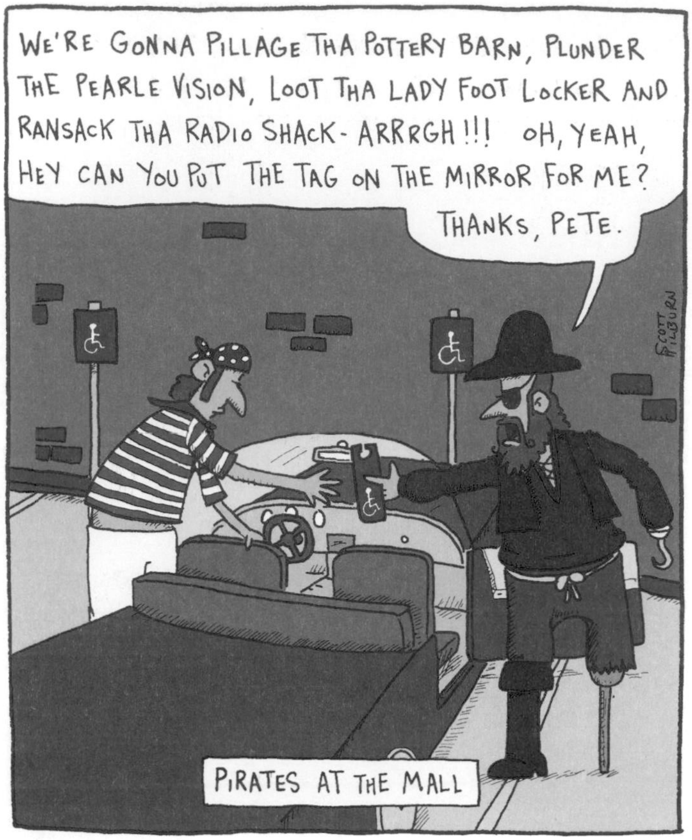
WE'RE GONNA PILLAGE THA POTTERY BARN, PLUNDER THE PEARLE VISION, LOOT THA LADY FOOT LOCKER AND RANSACK THA RADIO SHACK- ARRRGH!!! OH, YEAH, HEY CAN YOU PUT THE TAG ON THE MIRROR FOR ME? THANKS, PETE.

PIRATES AT THE MALL

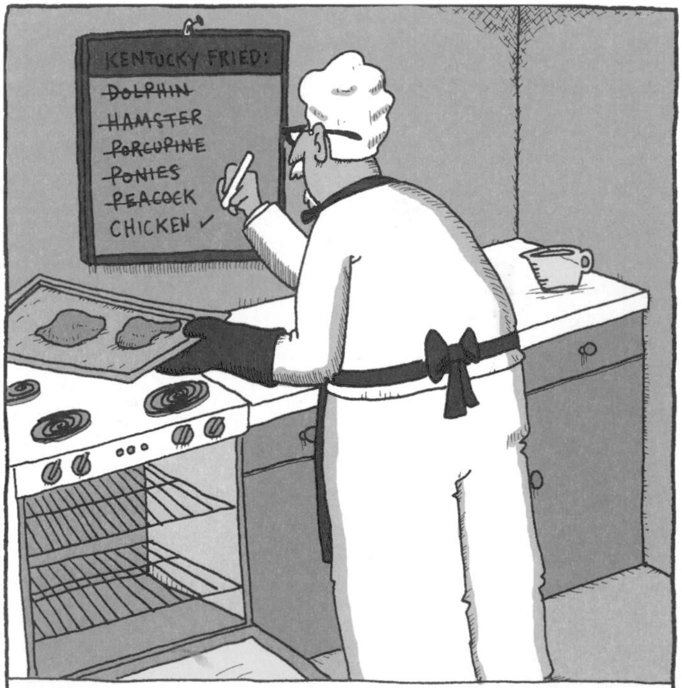
KENTUCKY FRIED:
~~DOLPHIN~~
~~HAMSTER~~
~~PORCUPINE~~
~~PONIES~~
~~PEACOCK~~
CHICKEN ✓

THROUGH TRIAL AND ERROR, THE COLONEL SUCCESSFULLY CONCOCTS THE FINAL ITERATION OF HIS FAMOUS, "ORIGINAL SECRET RECIPE."

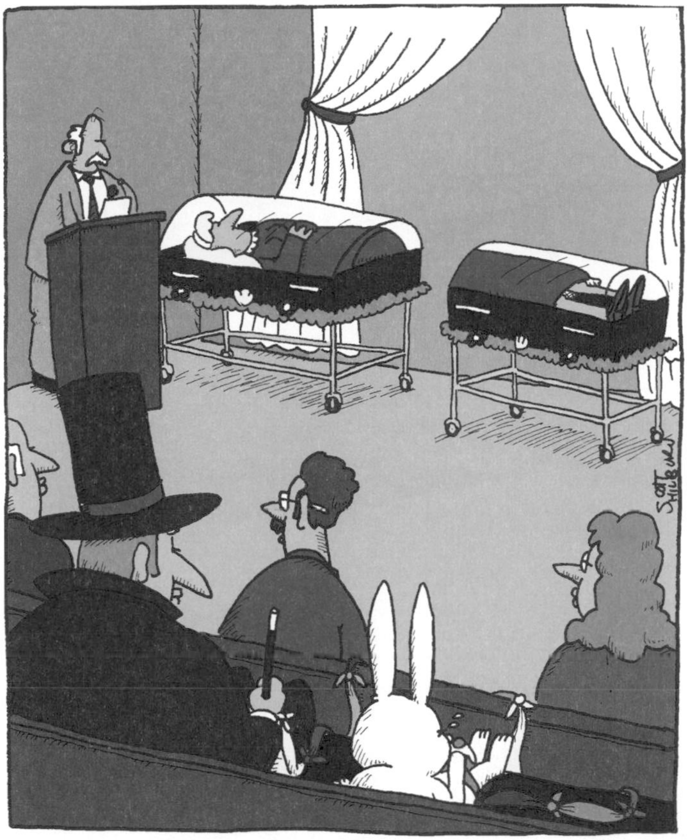

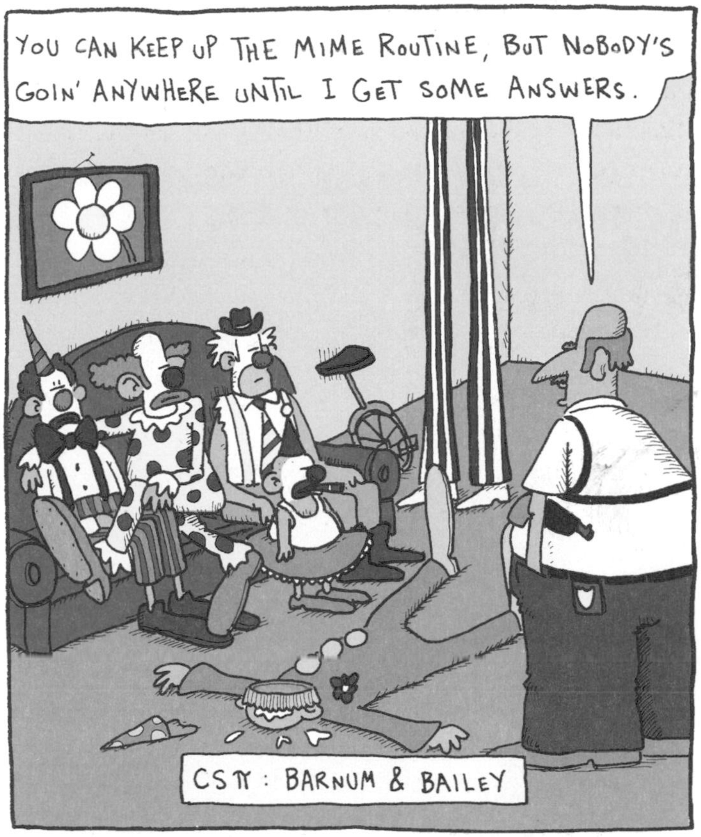
YOU CAN KEEP UP THE MIME ROUTINE, BUT NOBODY'S GOIN' ANYWHERE UNTIL I GET SOME ANSWERS.
CSI : BARNUM & BAILEY

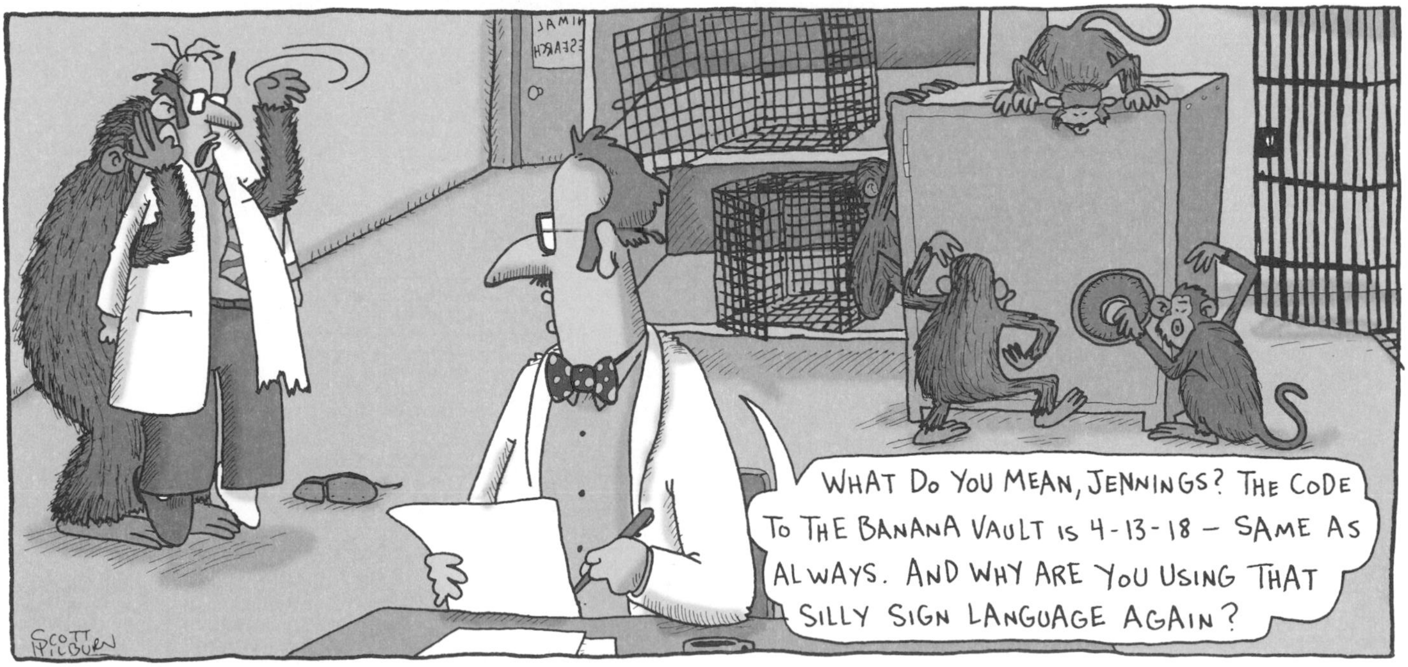
WHAT DO YOU MEAN, JENNINGS? THE CODE TO THE BANANA VAULT IS 4-13-18 – SAME AS ALWAYS. AND WHY ARE YOU USING THAT SILLY SIGN LANGUAGE AGAIN?

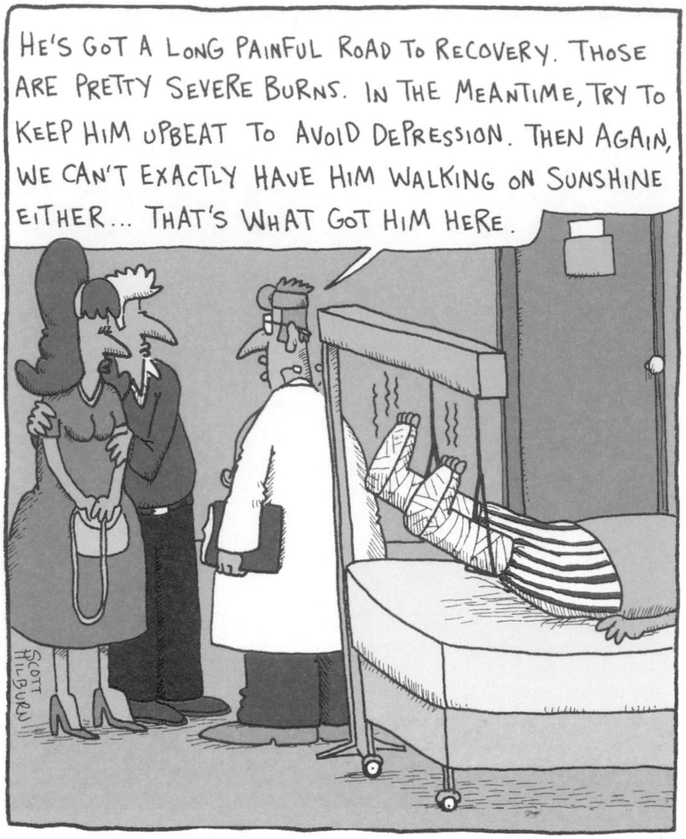
HE'S GOT A LONG PAINFUL ROAD TO RECOVERY. THOSE ARE PRETTY SEVERE BURNS. IN THE MEANTIME, TRY TO KEEP HIM UPBEAT TO AVOID DEPRESSION. THEN AGAIN, WE CAN'T EXACTLY HAVE HIM WALKING ON SUNSHINE EITHER... THAT'S WHAT GOT HIM HERE.
SCOTT HILBURN

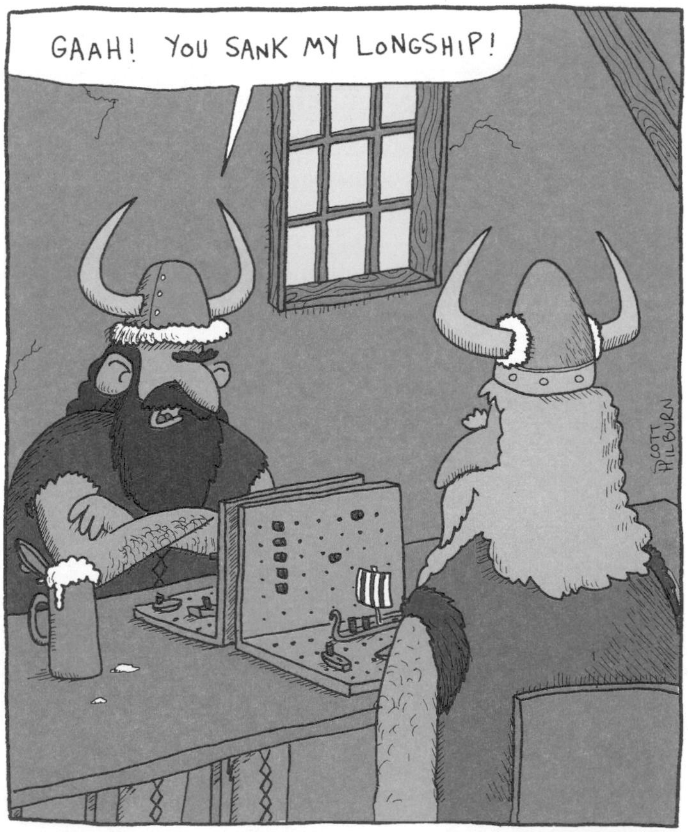
GAAH! YOU SANK MY LONGSHIP!
SCOTT HILBURN

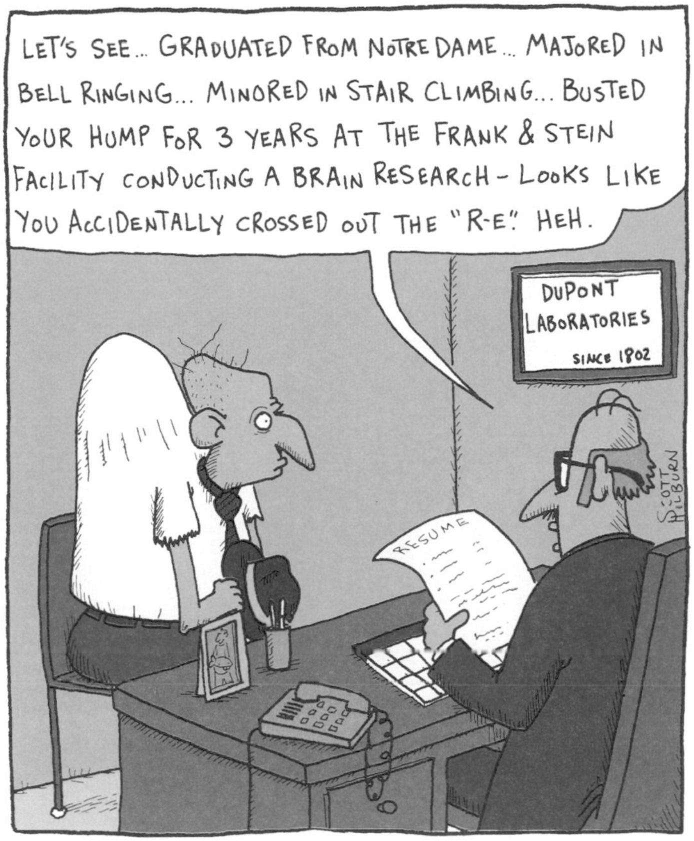
LET'S SEE... GRADUATED FROM NOTRE DAME... MAJORED IN BELL RINGING... MINORED IN STAIR CLIMBING... BUSTED YOUR HUMP FOR 3 YEARS AT THE FRANK & STEIN FACILITY CONDUCTING A BRAIN RESEARCH – LOOKS LIKE YOU ACCIDENTALLY CROSSED OUT THE "R-E." HEH.
DUPONT LABORATORIES SINCE 1802
RESUME
SCOTT HILBURN

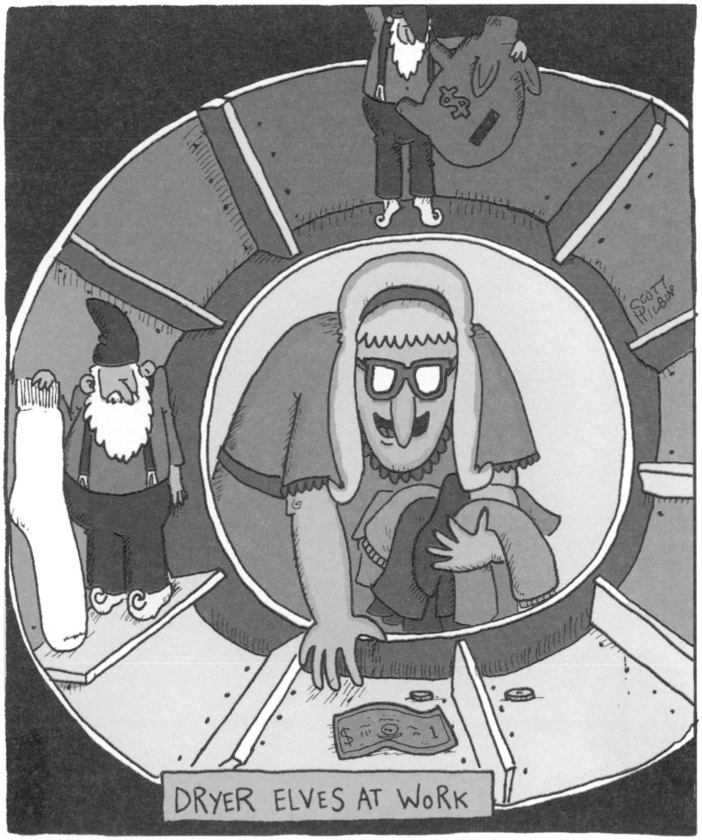
DRYER ELVES AT WORK
SCOTT HILBURN

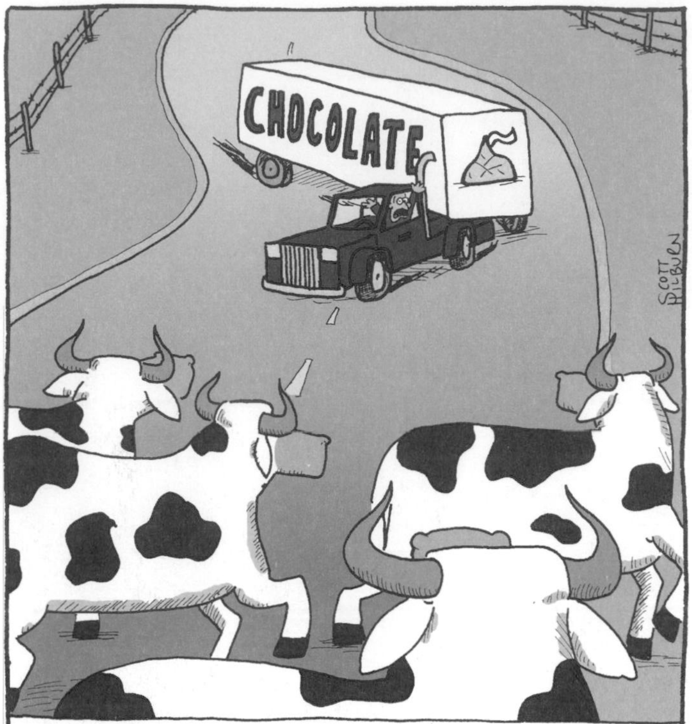
CHOCOLATE
SCOTT HILBURN

AS IS OFTEN THE CASE, MANY OF THE WORLD'S GREAT DISCOVERIES ARE ACCIDENTAL.

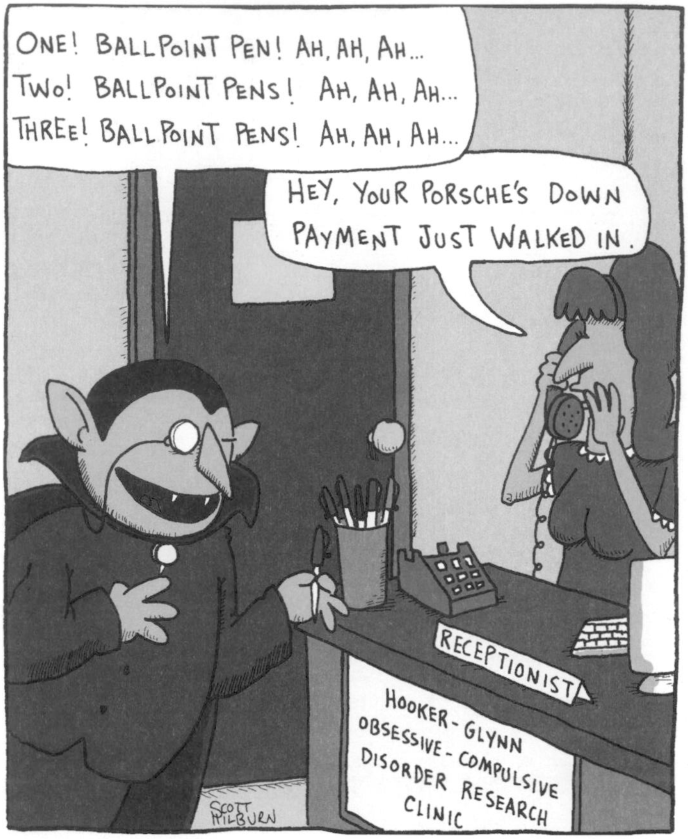
ONE! BALLPOINT PEN! AH, AH, AH...
TWO! BALLPOINT PENS! AH, AH, AH...
THREE! BALLPOINT PENS! AH, AH, AH...
HEY, YOUR PORSCHE'S DOWN PAYMENT JUST WALKED IN.
RECEPTIONIST
HOOKER-GLYNN OBSESSIVE-COMPULSIVE DISORDER RESEARCH CLINIC
SCOTT HILBURN

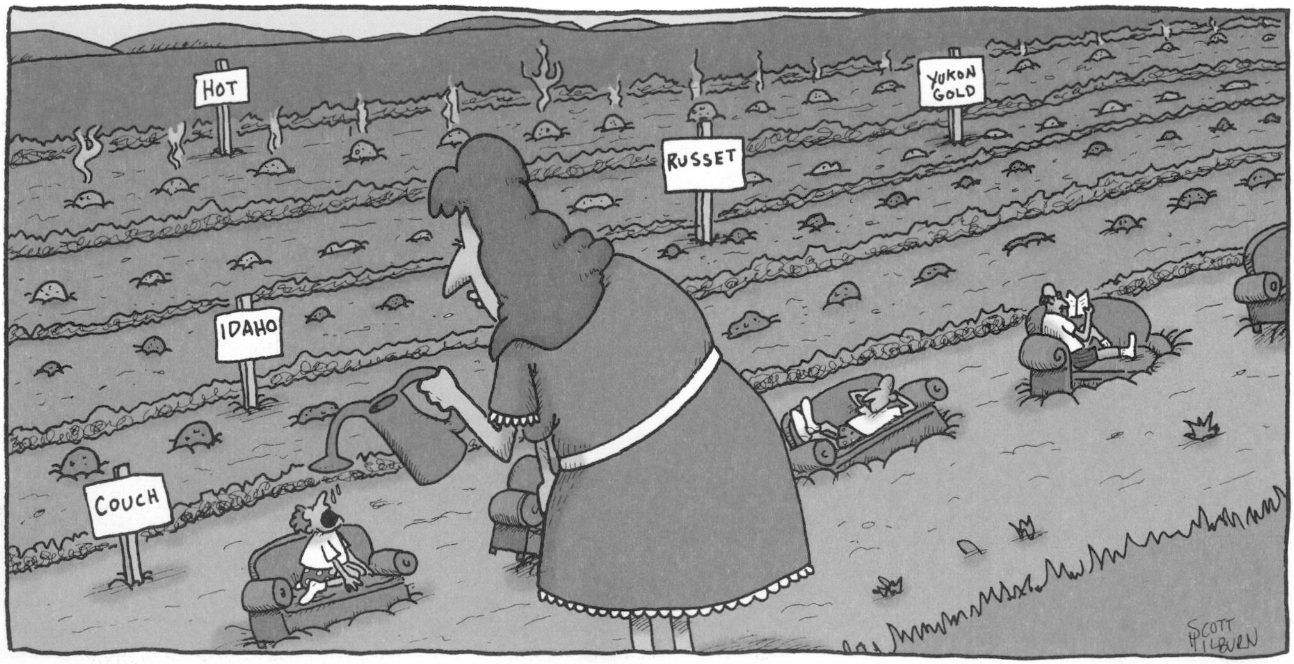
HOT
YUKON GOLD
RUSSET
IDAHO
COUCH
SCOTT HILBURN

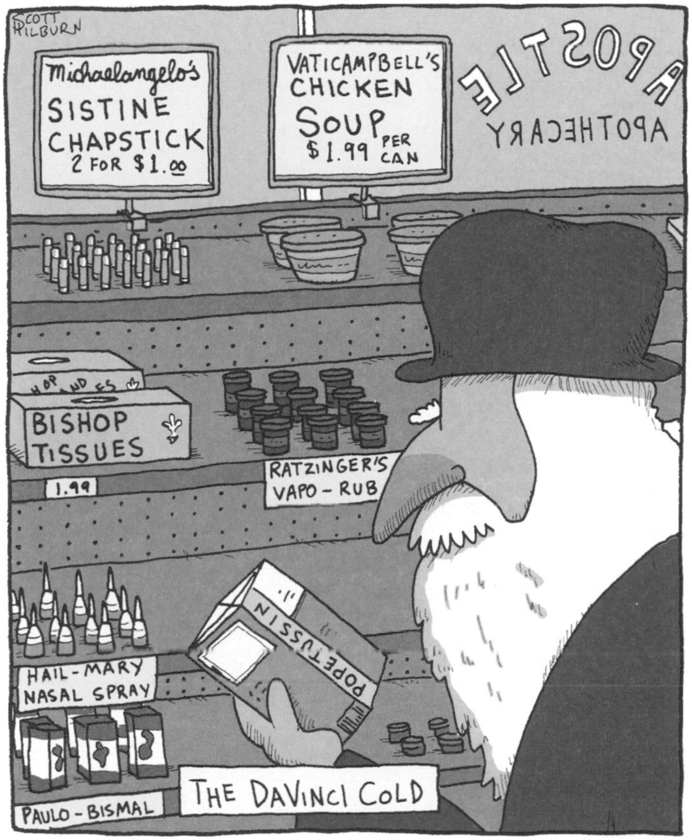
Michaelangelo's SISTINE CHAPSTICK 2 FOR $1.00
VATICAMPBELL'S CHICKEN SOUP $1.99 PER CAN
APOSTLE APOTHECARY
BISHOP TISSUES
1.99
RATZINGER'S VAPO-RUB
POPETUSSIN
HAIL-MARY NASAL SPRAY
PAULO-BISMAL
SCOTT HILBURN

THE DAVINCI COLD

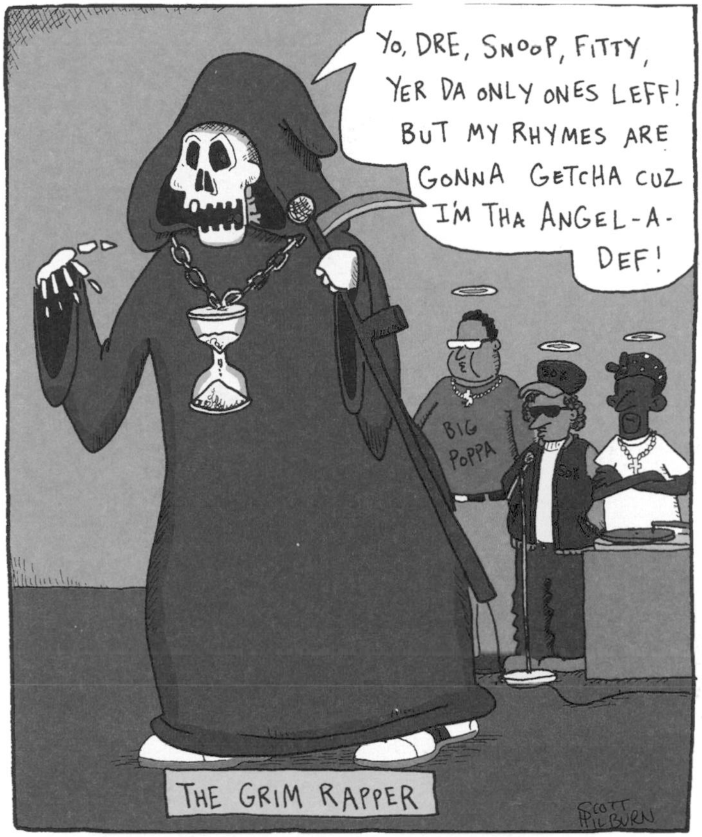
YO, DRE, SNOOP, FITTY, YER DA ONLY ONES LEFF! BUT MY RHYMES ARE GONNA GETCHA CUZ I'M THA ANGEL-A-DEF!
BIG POPPA
SCOTT HILBURN

THE GRIM RAPPER

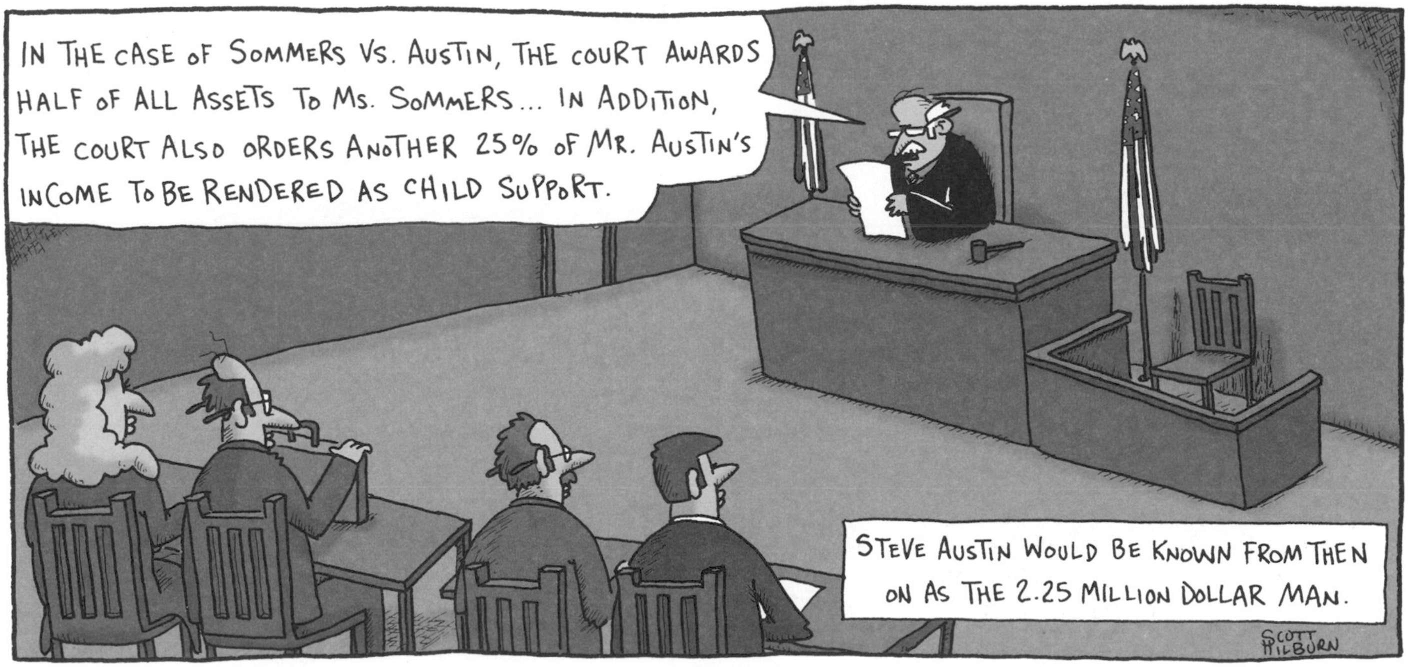
IN THE CASE OF SOMMERS VS. AUSTIN, THE COURT AWARDS HALF OF ALL ASSETS TO MS. SOMMERS... IN ADDITION, THE COURT ALSO ORDERS ANOTHER 25% OF MR. AUSTIN'S INCOME TO BE RENDERED AS CHILD SUPPORT.
SCOTT HILBURN

STEVE AUSTIN WOULD BE KNOWN FROM THEN ON AS THE 2.25 MILLION DOLLAR MAN.

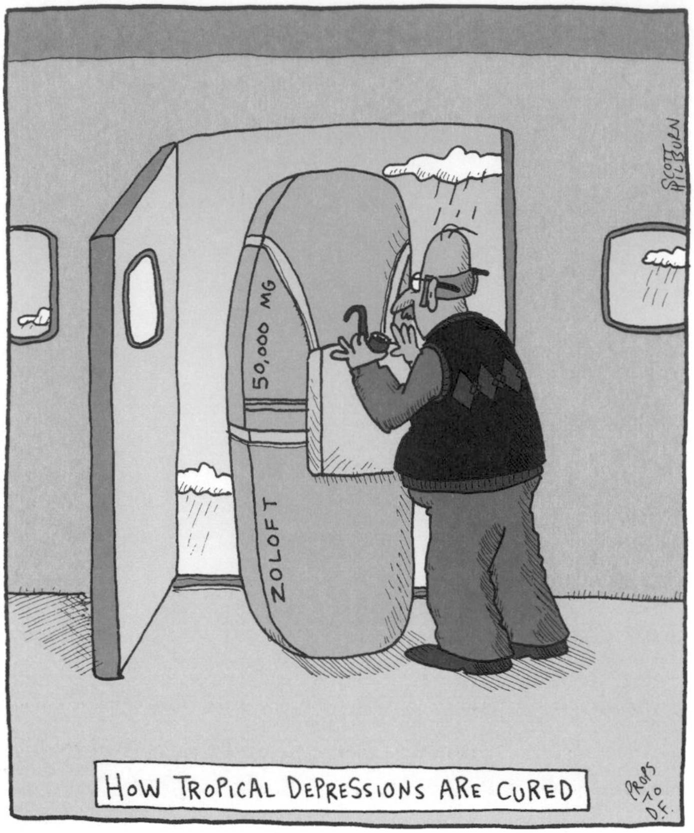
50,000 MG
ZOLOFT
SCOTT HILBURN
PROPS TO D.F.

HOW TROPICAL DEPRESSIONS ARE CURED

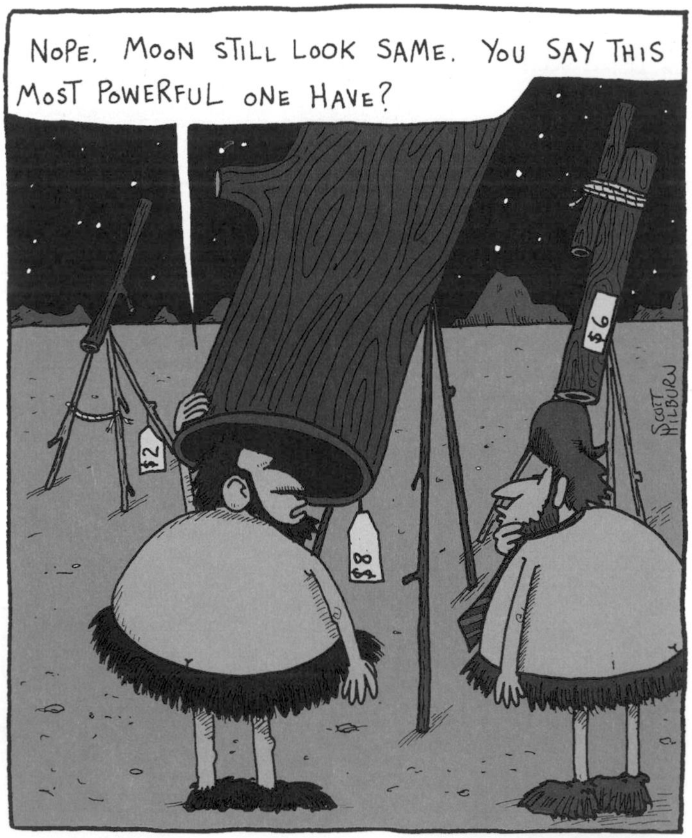
NOPE. MOON STILL LOOK SAME. YOU SAY THIS MOST POWERFUL ONE HAVE?
$2
$8
$6
SCOTT HILBURN

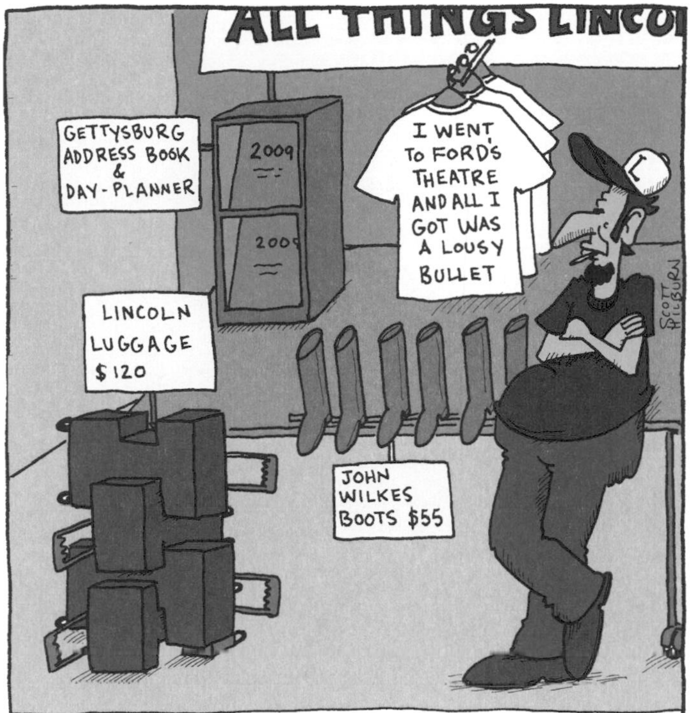
ALL THINGS LINCO
GETTYSBURG ADDRESS BOOK & DAY-PLANNER
2009
2009
I WENT TO FORD'S THEATRE AND ALL I GOT WAS A LOUSY BULLET
LINCOLN LUGGAGE $120
JOHN WILKES BOOTS $55
SCOTT HILBURN

LINCOLN'S LAST HEIR, LIKE MANY DESCENDANTS OF GREAT MEN, WASN'T ABOVE CASHING IN ON HIS GREAT-GRANDFATHER'S FAME.

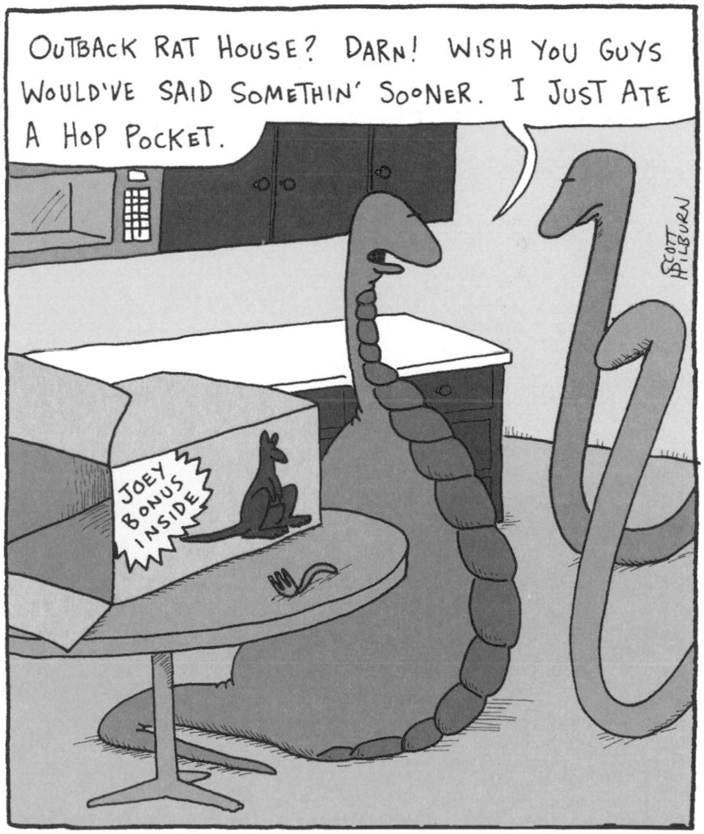
OUTBACK RAT HOUSE? DARN! WISH YOU GUYS WOULD'VE SAID SOMETHIN' SOONER. I JUST ATE A HOP POCKET.
JOEY BONUS INSIDE
SCOTT HILBURN

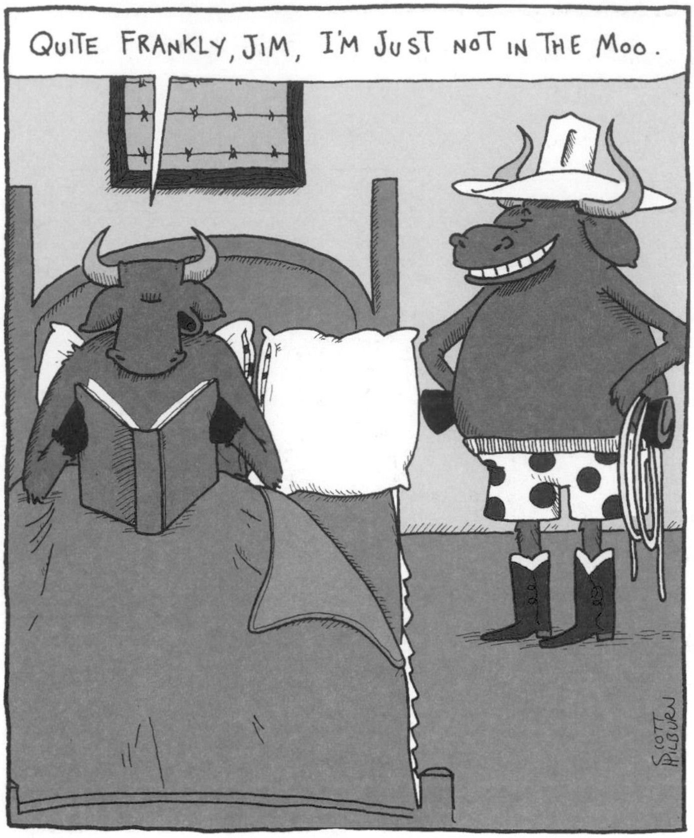
QUITE FRANKLY, JIM, I'M JUST NOT IN THE MOO.
SCOTT HILBURN

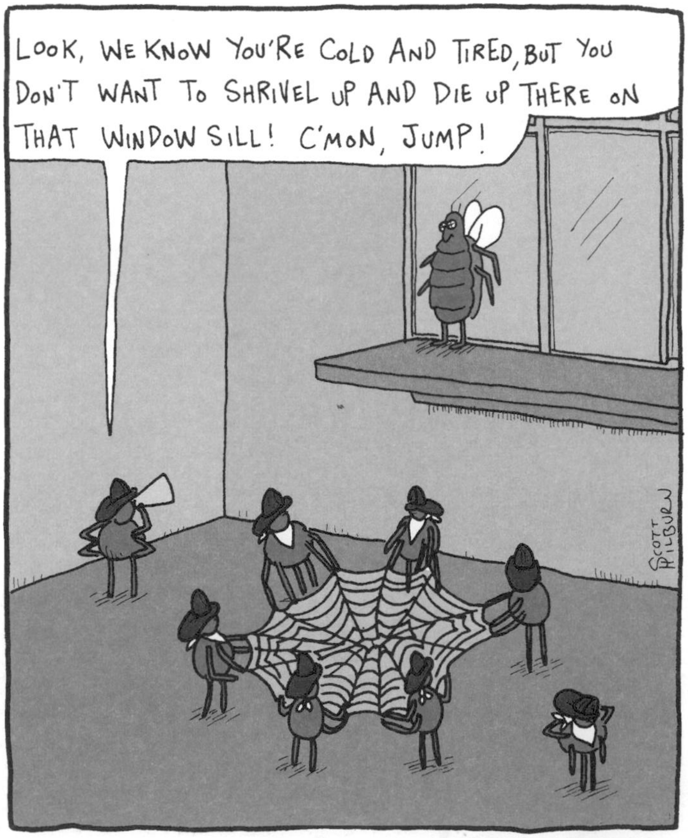
LOOK, WE KNOW YOU'RE COLD AND TIRED, BUT YOU DON'T WANT TO SHRIVEL UP AND DIE UP THERE ON THAT WINDOW SILL! C'MON, JUMP!
SCOTT HILBURN

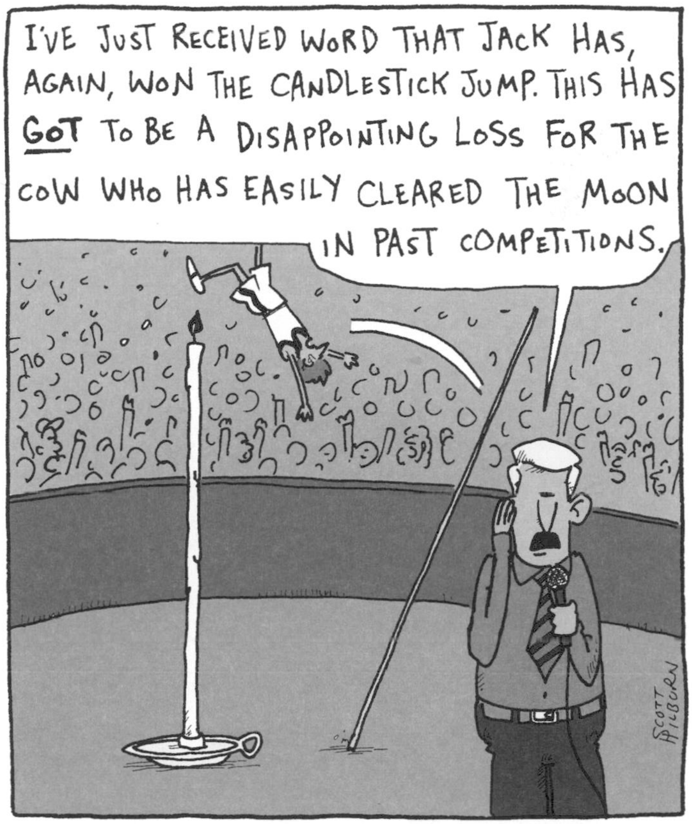
I'VE JUST RECEIVED WORD THAT JACK HAS, AGAIN, WON THE CANDLESTICK JUMP. THIS HAS GOT TO BE A DISAPPOINTING LOSS FOR THE COW WHO HAS EASILY CLEARED THE MOON IN PAST COMPETITIONS.
SCOTT HILBURN

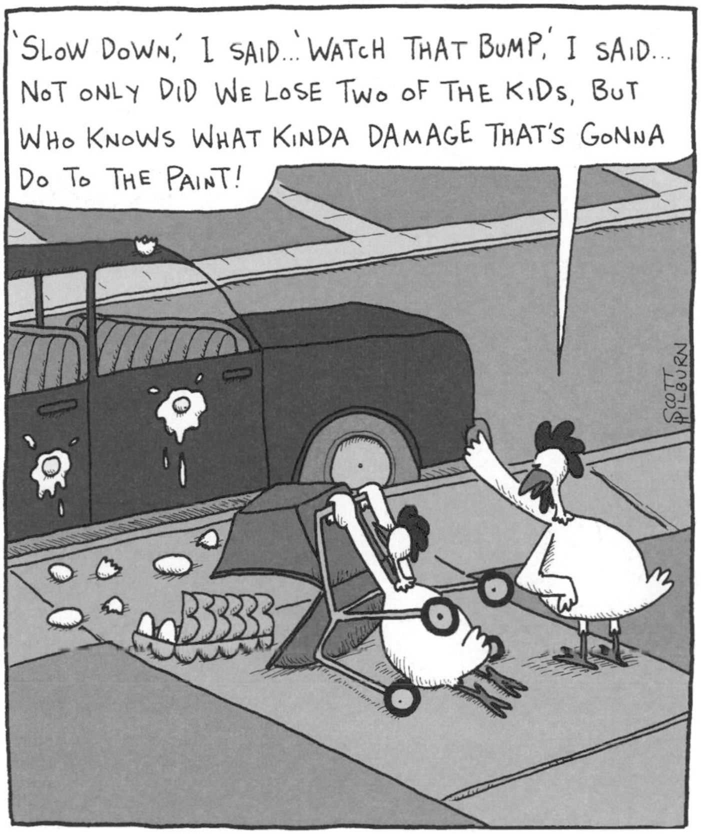
'SLOW DOWN,' I SAID... 'WATCH THAT BUMP,' I SAID... NOT ONLY DID WE LOSE TWO OF THE KIDS, BUT WHO KNOWS WHAT KINDA DAMAGE THAT'S GONNA DO TO THE PAINT!
SCOTT HILBURN

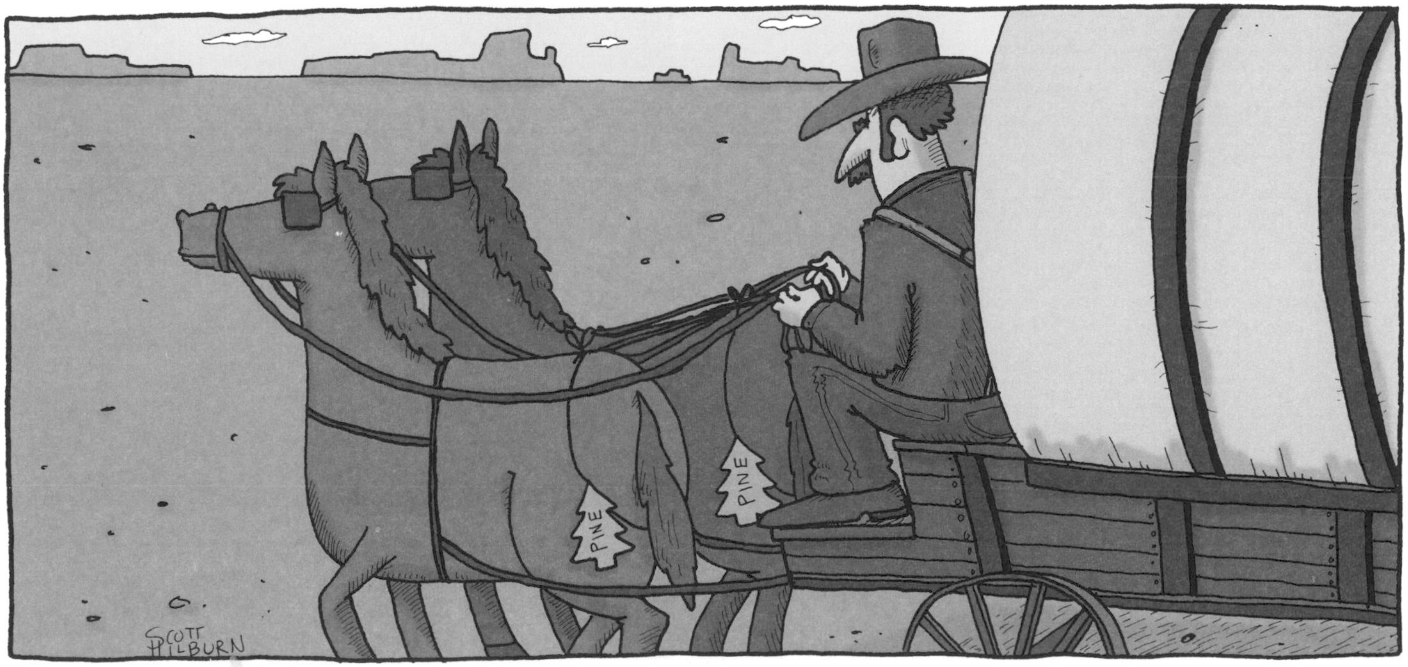
PINE
PINE
SCOTT HILBURN

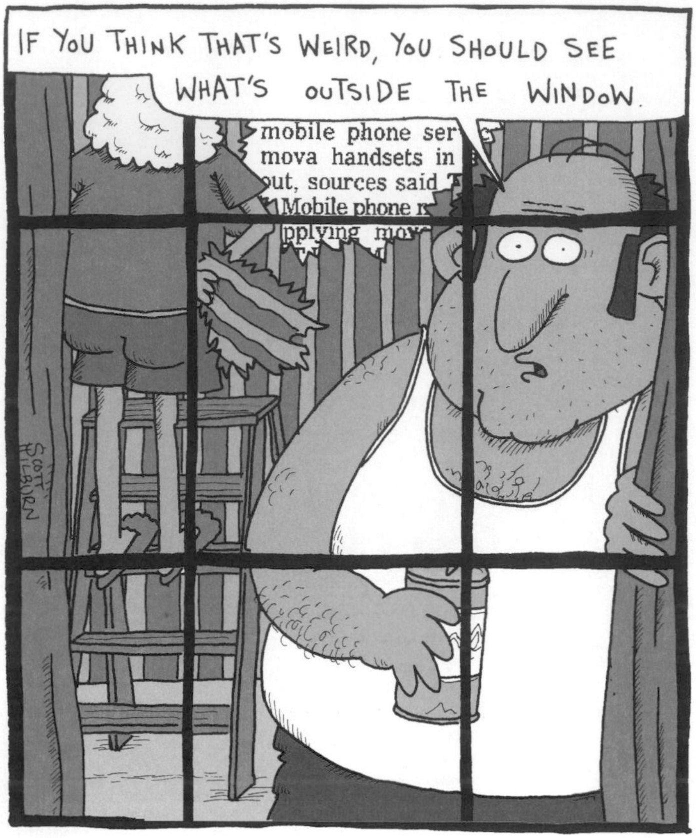
IF YOU THINK THAT'S WEIRD, YOU SHOULD SEE WHAT'S OUTSIDE THE WINDOW.
SCOTT HILBURN

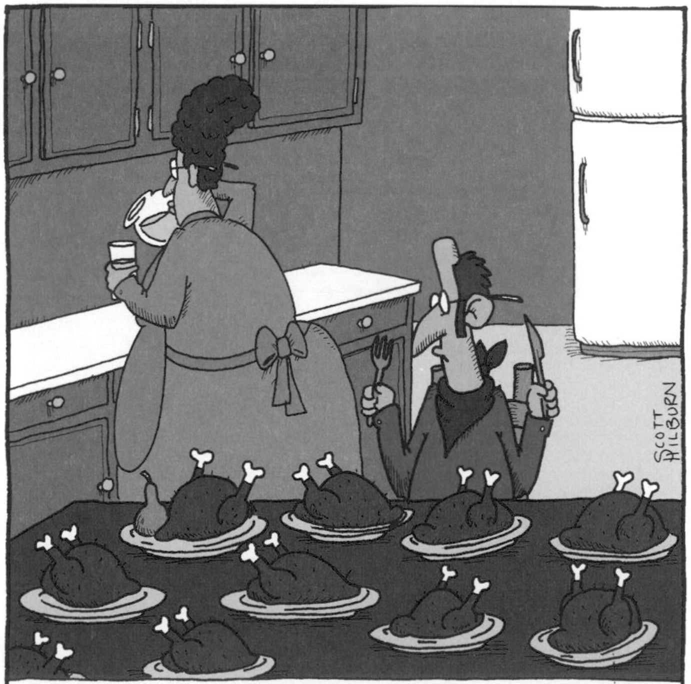
SCOTT HILBURN

GRATEFUL FOR THE PREVIOUS FOUR DAYS OF GIFTS, ON THE FIFTH DAY OF CHRISTMAS, WESLEY'S TRUE LOVE COOKED FOR HIM.

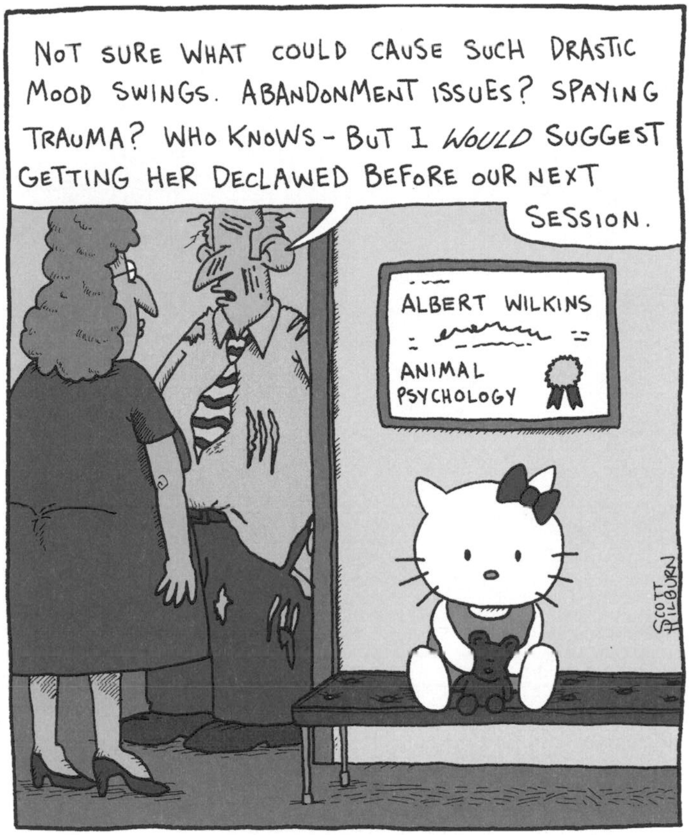
NOT SURE WHAT COULD CAUSE SUCH DRASTIC MOOD SWINGS. ABANDONMENT ISSUES? SPAYING TRAUMA? WHO KNOWS - BUT I *WOULD* SUGGEST GETTING HER DECLAWED BEFORE OUR NEXT SESSION.
ALBERT WILKINS
ANIMAL PSYCHOLOGY
SCOTT HILBURN

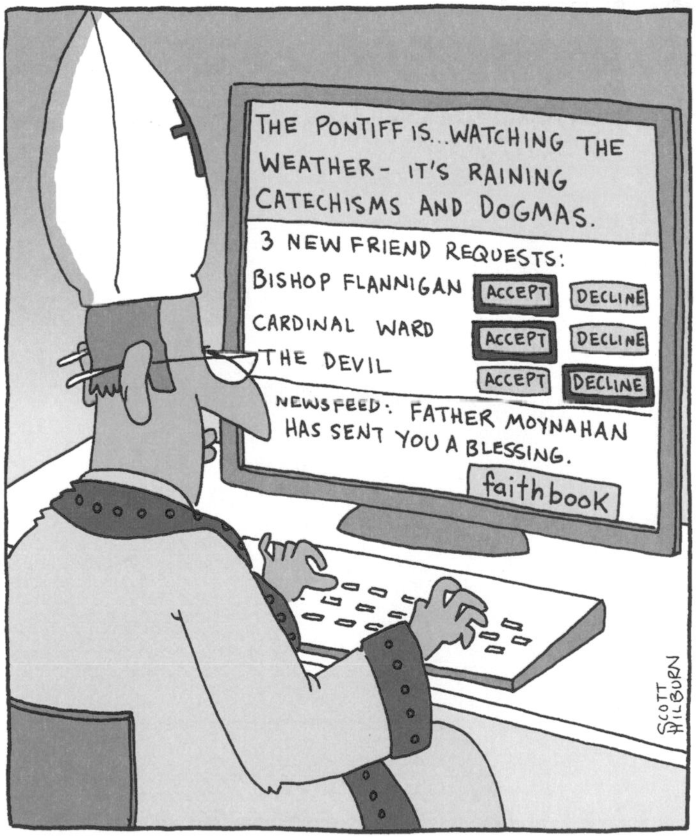
THE PONTIFF IS...WATCHING THE WEATHER - IT'S RAINING CATECHISMS AND DOGMAS.
3 NEW FRIEND REQUESTS:
BISHOP FLANNIGAN ACCEPT DECLINE
CARDINAL WARD ACCEPT DECLINE
THE DEVIL ACCEPT DECLINE
NEWSFEED: FATHER MOYNAHAN HAS SENT YOU A BLESSING.
faithbook
SCOTT HILBURN

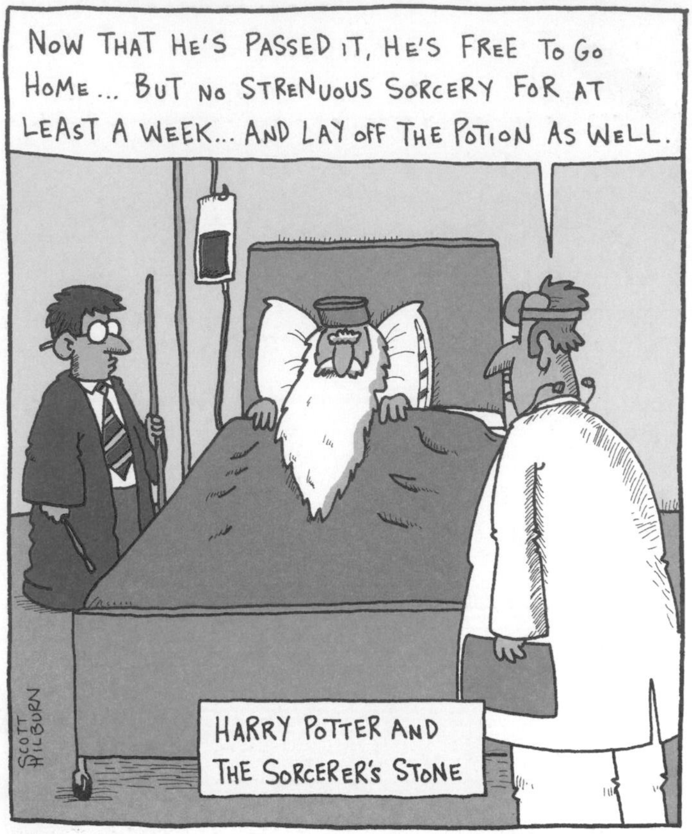
NOW THAT HE'S PASSED iT, HE'S FREE TO GO HOME... BUT NO STRENUOUS SORCERY FOR AT LEAST A WEEK... AND LAY OFF THE POTION AS WELL.
HARRY POTTER AND THE SORCERER'S STONE
SCOTT HILBURN

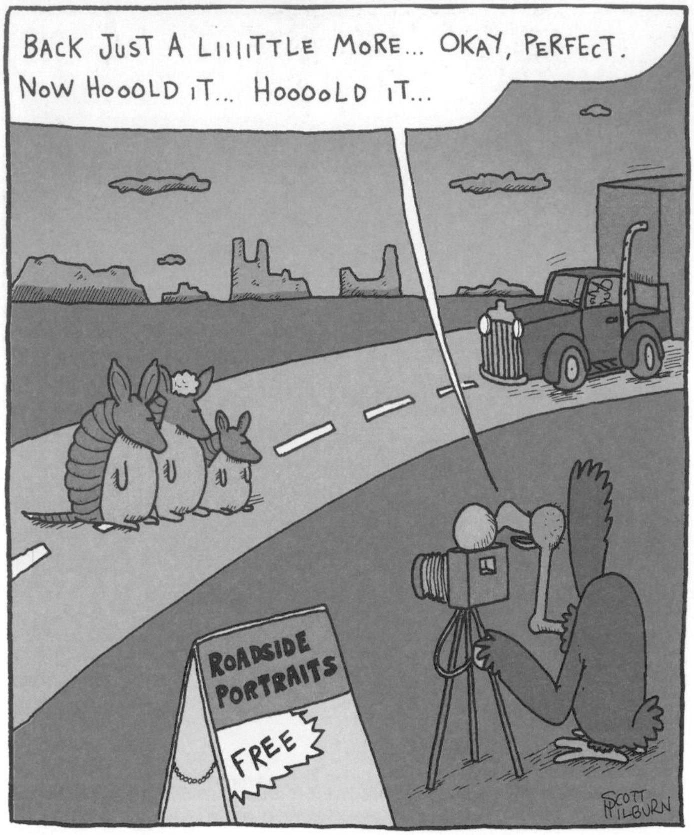
BACK JUST A LIiiiTTLE MORE... OKAY, PERFECT. NOW HOOOLD iT... HOOOOLD iT...
ROADSIDE PORTRAITS
FREE
SCOTT HILBURN

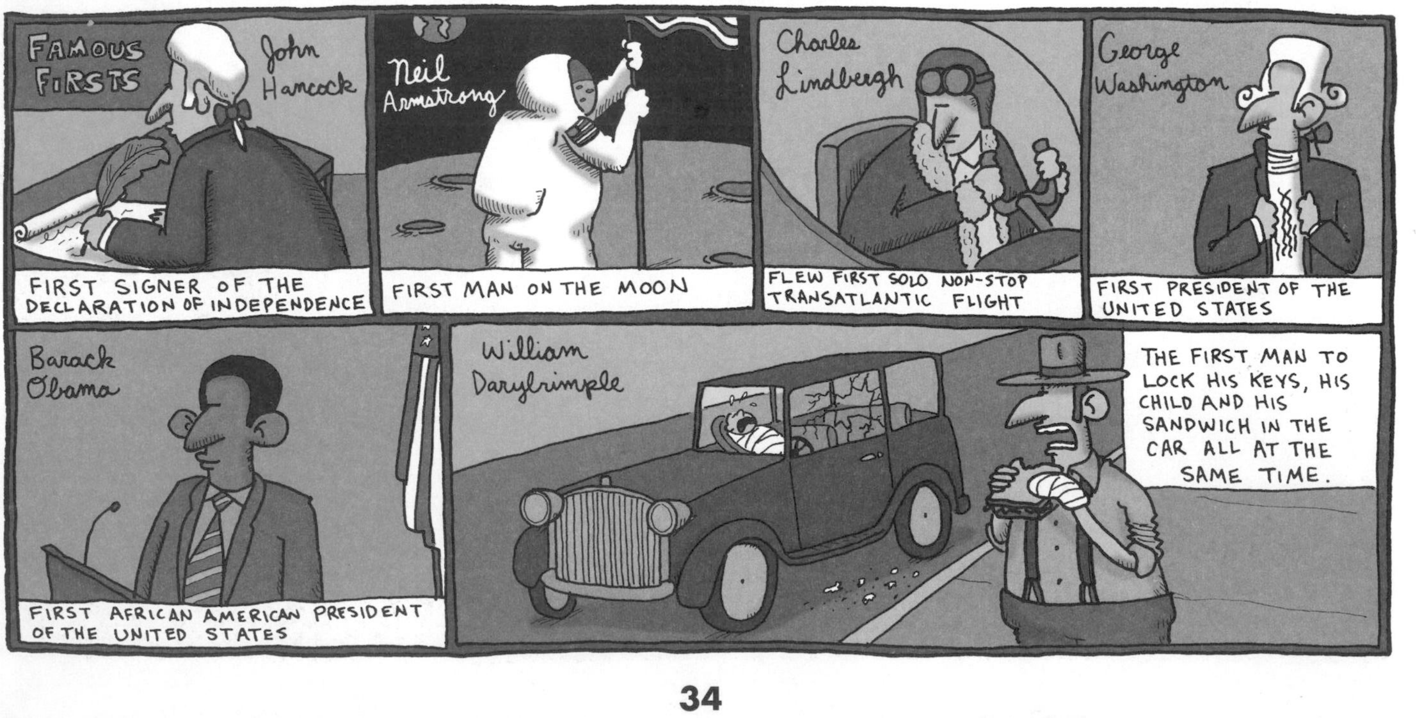
FAMOUS FIRSTS
John Hancock
FIRST SIGNER OF THE DECLARATION OF INDEPENDENCE
Neil Armstrong
FIRST MAN ON THE MOON
Charles Lindbergh
FLEW FIRST SOLO NON-STOP TRANSATLANTIC FLIGHT
George Washington
FIRST PRESIDENT OF THE UNITED STATES
Barack Obama
FIRST AFRICAN AMERICAN PRESIDENT OF THE UNITED STATES
William Darylrimple
THE FIRST MAN TO LOCK HIS KEYS, HIS CHILD AND HIS SANDWICH IN THE CAR ALL AT THE SAME TIME.

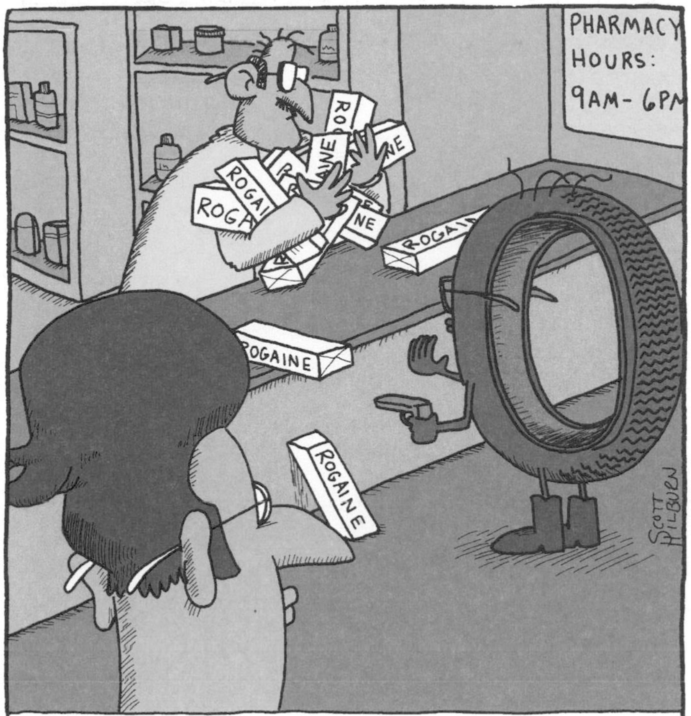
PHARMACY
HOURS:
9AM-6P
ROGAINE
ROGAINE
ROGAINE
SCOTT HILBURN

PERRY BECAME PAINFULLY AWARE OF JUST HOW DANGEROUS BALD TIRES CAN BE.

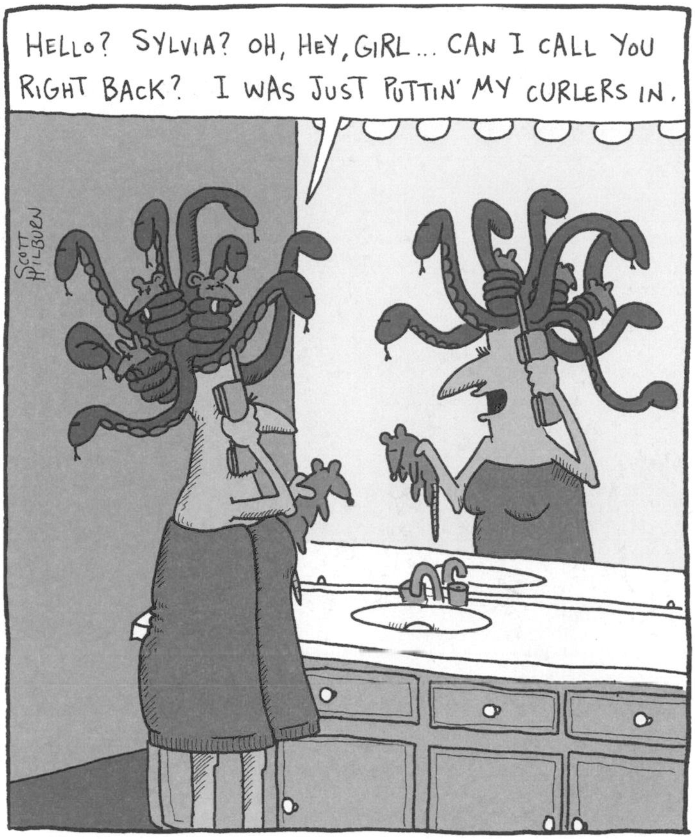
HELLO? SYLVIA? OH, HEY, GIRL... CAN I CALL YOU RIGHT BACK? I WAS JUST PUTTIN' MY CURLERS IN.
SCOTT HILBURN

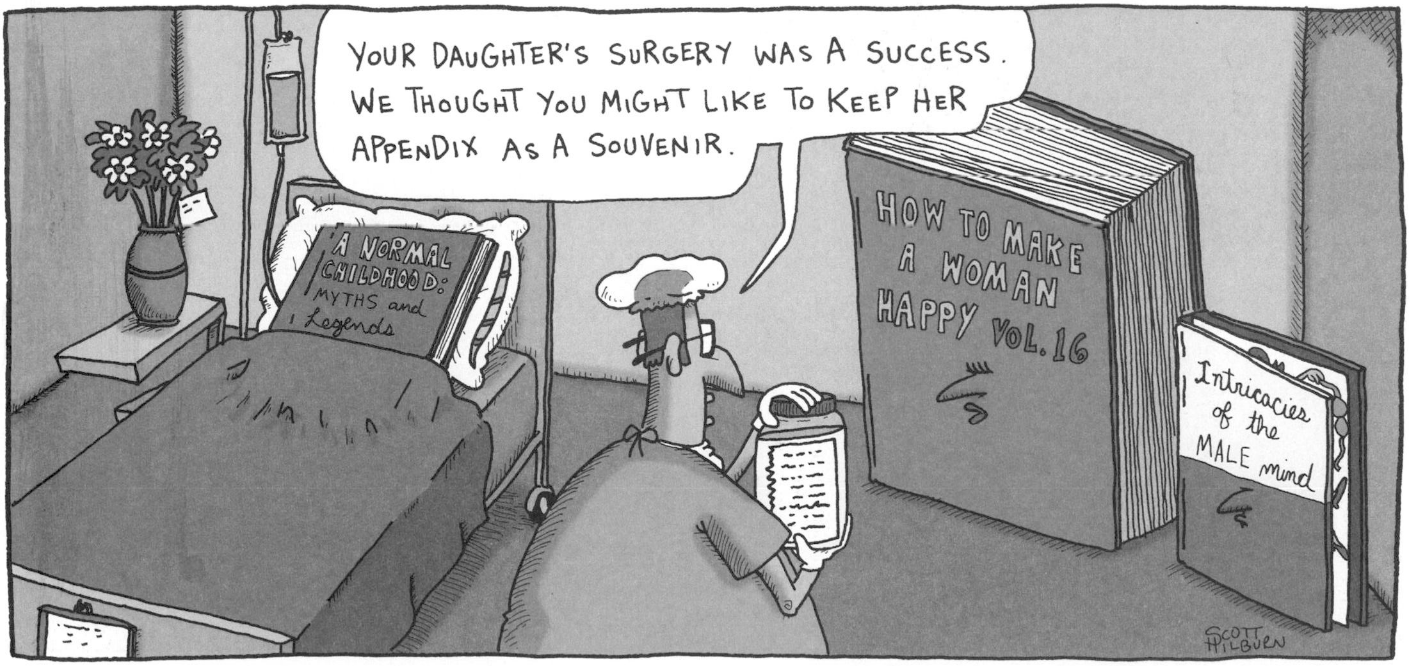
YOUR DAUGHTER'S SURGERY WAS A SUCCESS. WE THOUGHT YOU MIGHT LIKE TO KEEP HER APPENDIX AS A SOUVENIR.
A NORMAL CHILDHOOD: MYTHS and Legends
HOW TO MAKE A WOMAN HAPPY VOL. 16
Intricacies of the MALE mind
SCOTT HILBURN

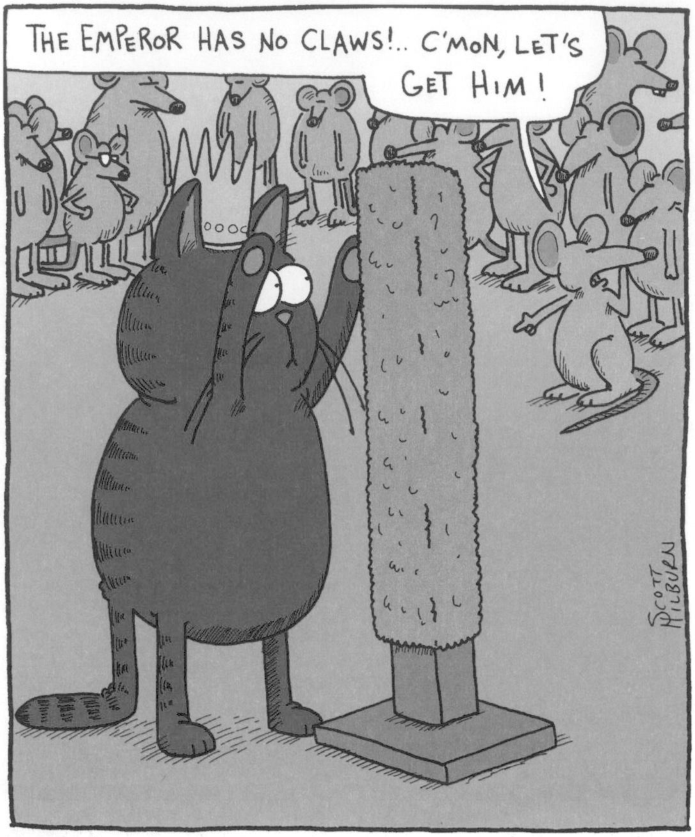
THE EMPEROR HAS NO CLAWS!.. C'MON, LET'S GET HIM!
SCOTT HILBURN

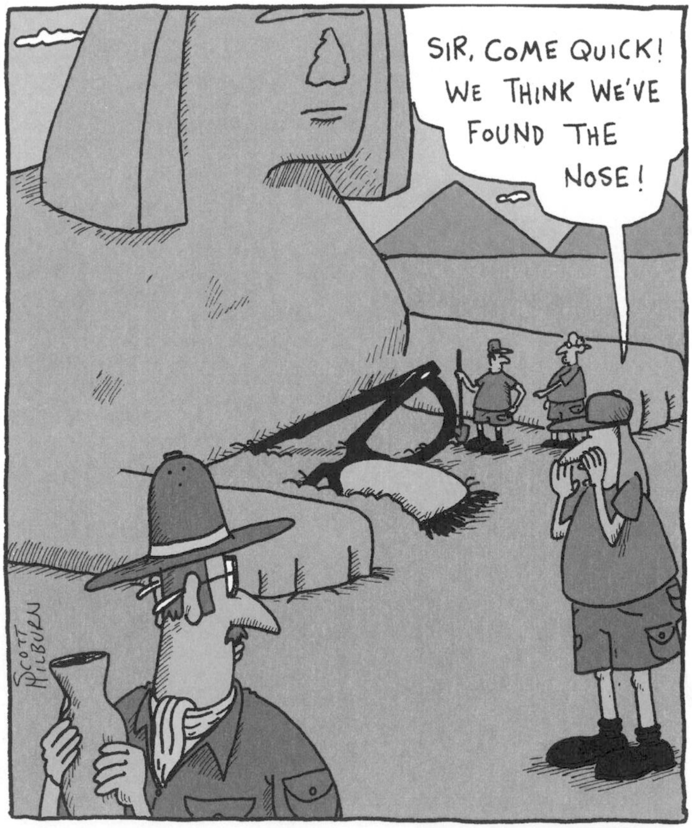
SIR, COME QUICK! WE THINK WE'VE FOUND THE NOSE!
SCOTT HILBURN

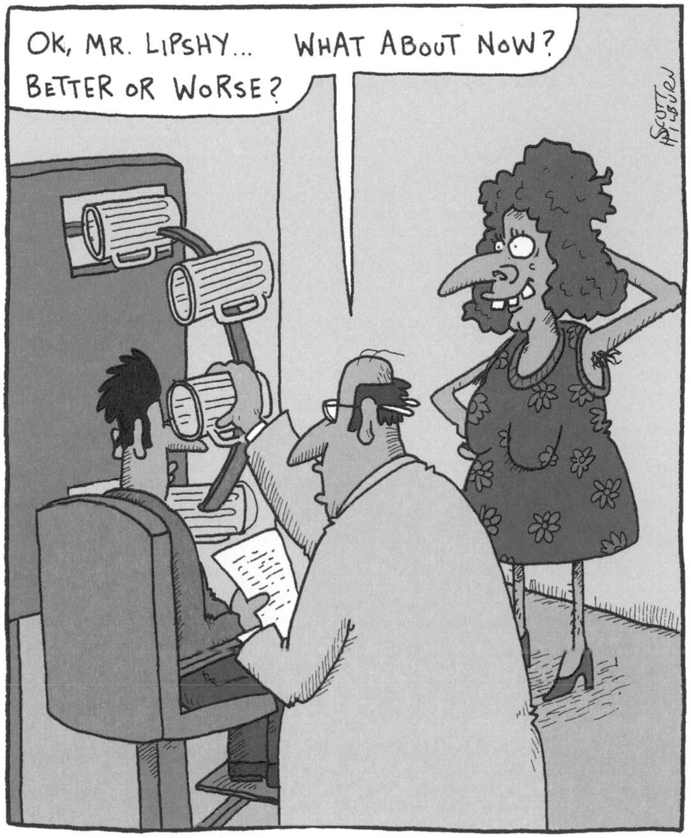
OK, MR. LIPSHY... BETTER OR WORSE?
WHAT ABOUT NOW?

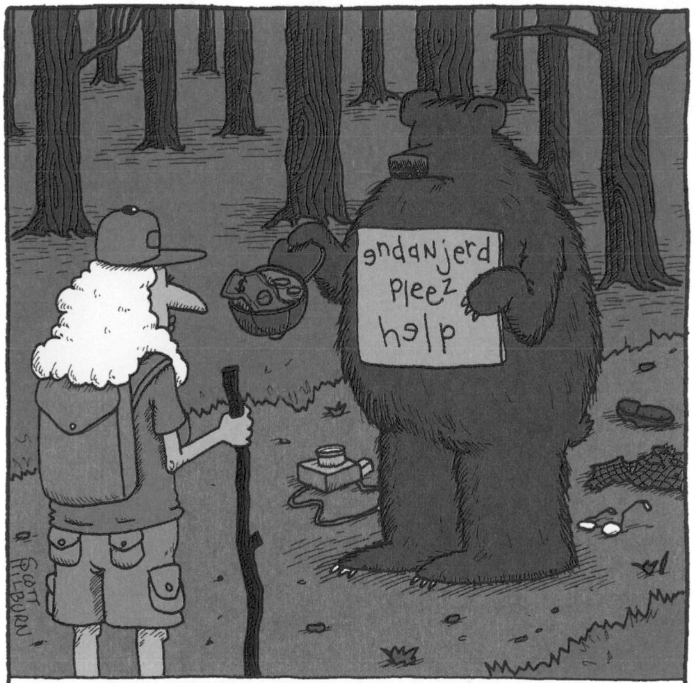
endanjerd
pleez
help

TORN BETWEEN TAKING THE ADVICE IN HER HIKING MANUAL AND HER IMPULSE TO HELP, MORGAN HIRSCHI IS FROZEN WITH INDECISION.

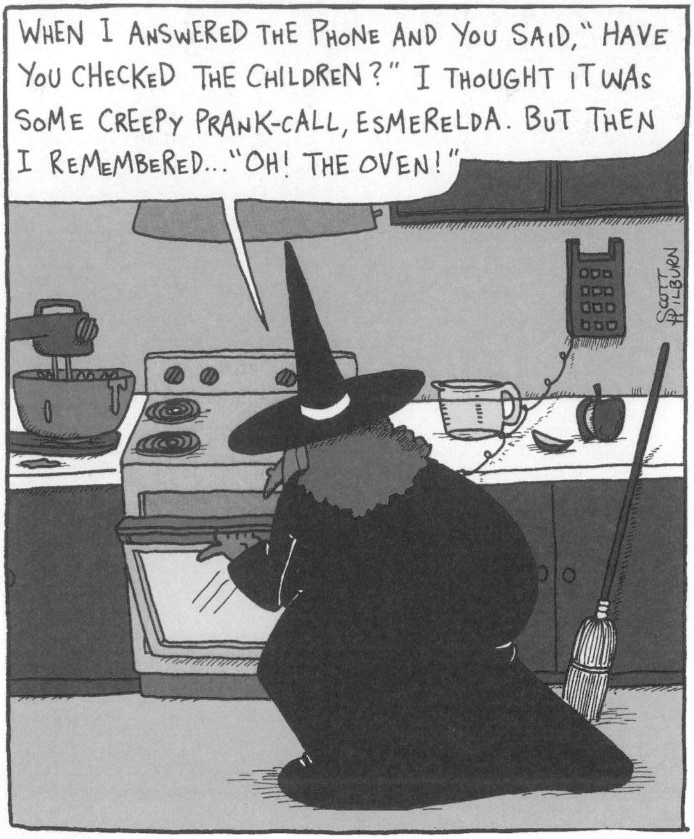
WHEN I ANSWERED THE PHONE AND YOU SAID, "HAVE YOU CHECKED THE CHILDREN?" I THOUGHT IT WAS SOME CREEPY PRANK-CALL, ESMERELDA. BUT THEN I REMEMBERED..."OH! THE OVEN!"
SCOTT HILBURN

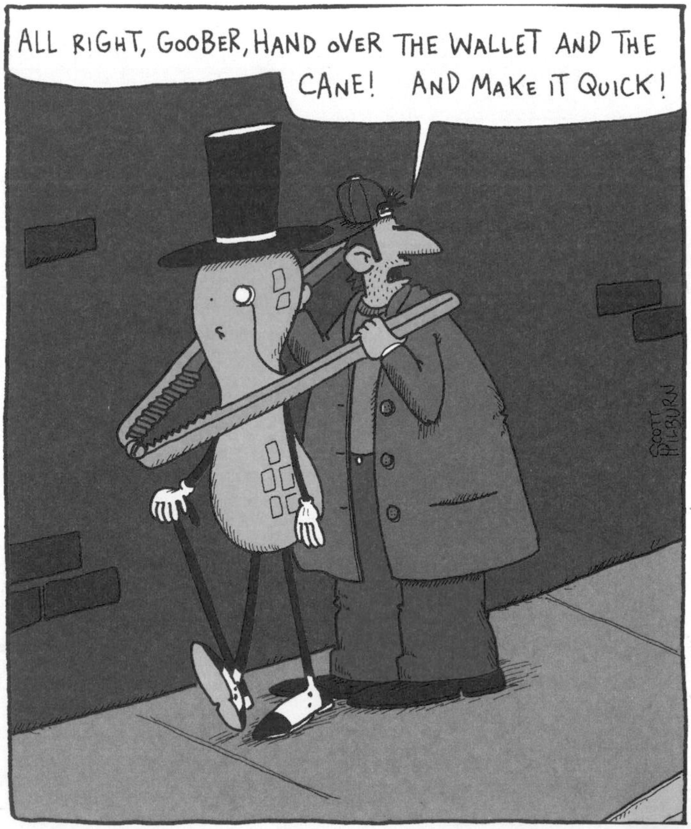
ALL RIGHT, GOOBER, HAND OVER THE WALLET AND THE CANE! AND MAKE IT QUICK!
SCOTT HILBURN

GREAT. ANOTHER CUP WITH A HOLE IN IT - AND MORE SPILLED KOOL-AID. THERE'S GOTTA BE A BETTER WAY TO DO THIS, EARL.
SCOTT HILBURN
LEMMING CULTS

STARBUCKS COFFEE
OOD/YEAR
WHITE WALL SALE
THE FUTURE WAS A FRIGHTENING PLACE FOR AHAB.

SCOTT HILBURN
HARIBO
THOUGH ENCOUNTERS WITH THIS SPECIES WERE RARELY FATAL, WARREN AND REGGIE HAD GOTTEN BETWEEN THE MOTHER AND HER CUBS AND FOUND THEMSELVES IN A STICKY SITUATION.

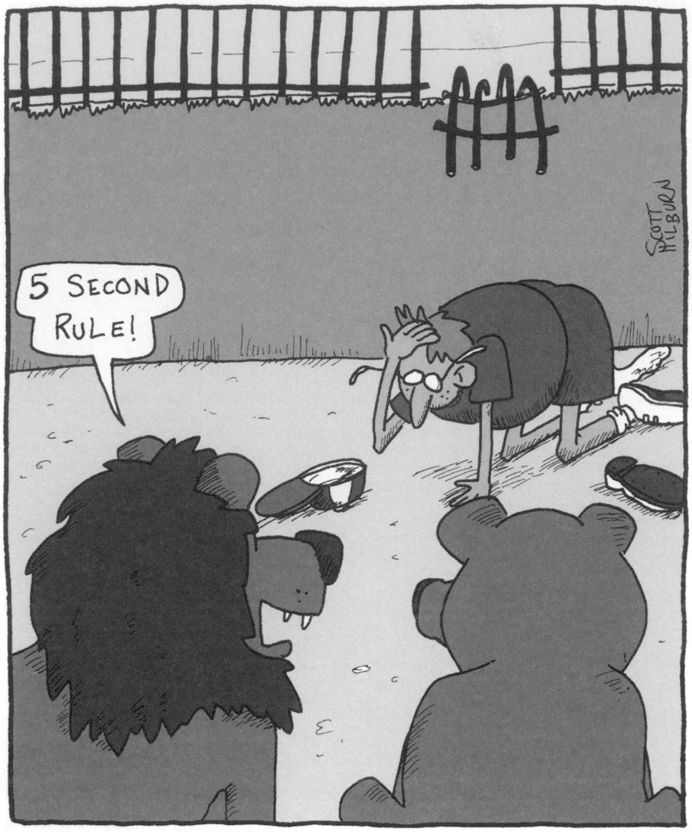
5 SECOND RULE!
SCOTT HILBURN

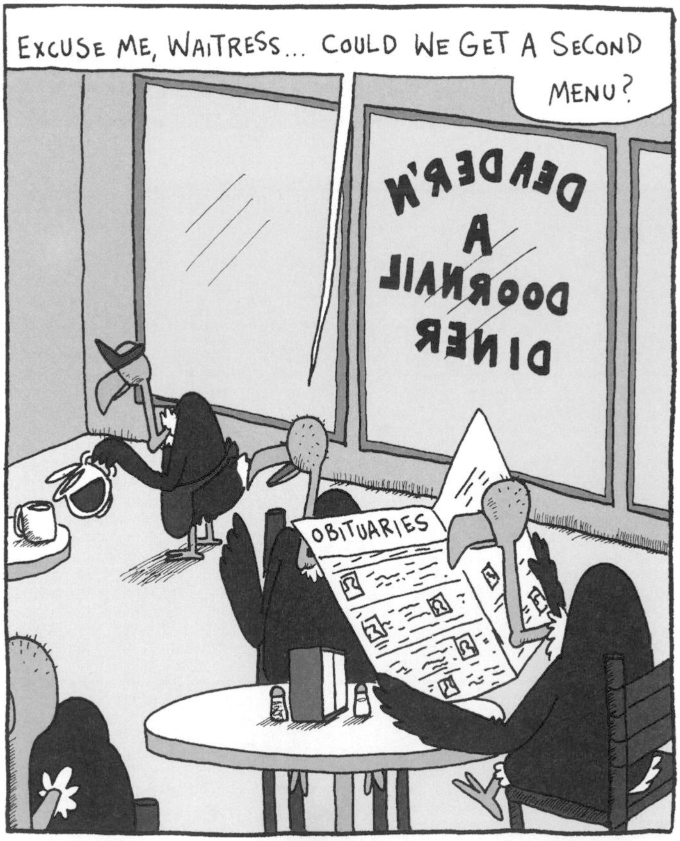
EXCUSE ME, WAITRESS... COULD WE GET A SECOND MENU?
DEADER'N A DOORNAIL DINER
OBITUARIES

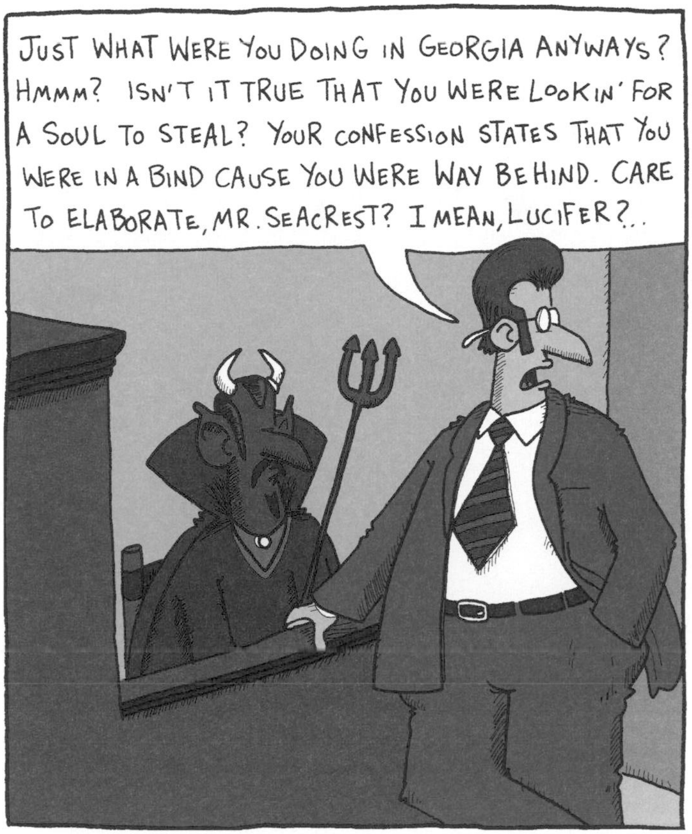
JUST WHAT WERE YOU DOING IN GEORGIA ANYWAYS? HMMM? ISN'T IT TRUE THAT YOU WERE LOOKIN' FOR A SOUL TO STEAL? YOUR CONFESSION STATES THAT YOU WERE IN A BIND CAUSE YOU WERE WAY BEHIND. CARE TO ELABORATE, MR. SEACREST? I MEAN, LUCIFER?..

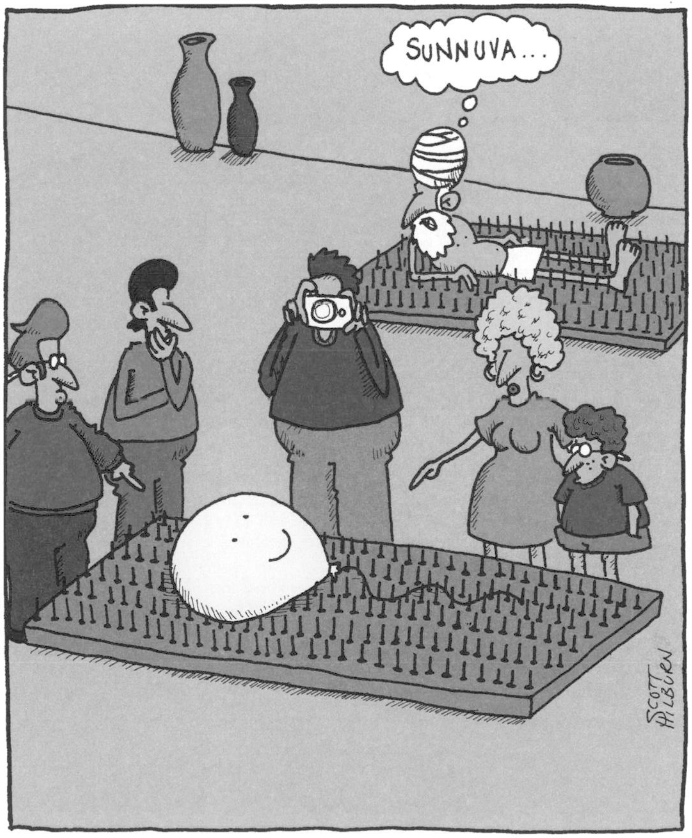
SUNNUVA...
SCOTT HILBURN

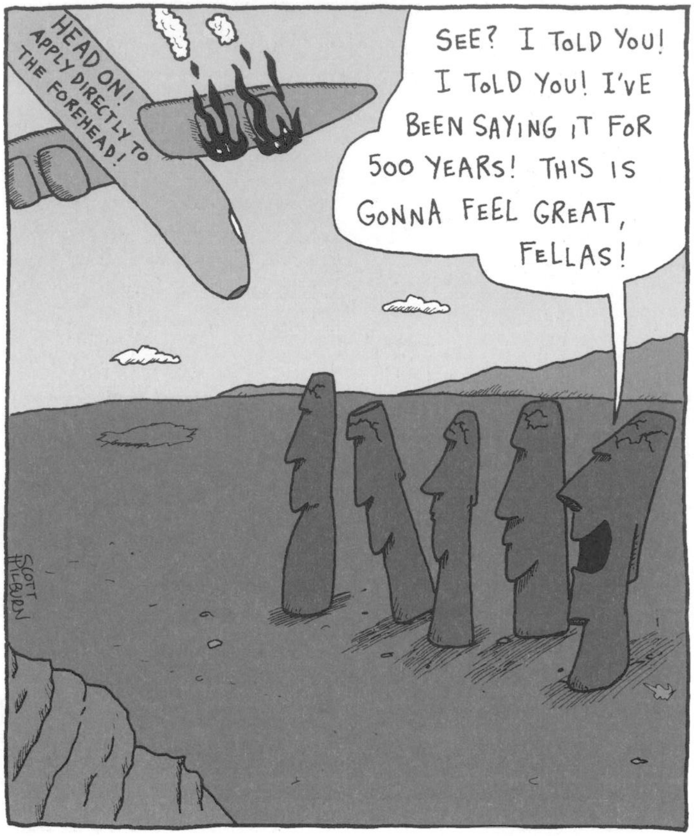
HEAD ON! APPLY DIRECTLY TO THE FOREHEAD!
SEE? I TOLD YOU! I TOLD YOU! I'VE BEEN SAYING IT FOR 500 YEARS! THIS IS GONNA FEEL GREAT, FELLAS!
SCOTT HILBURN

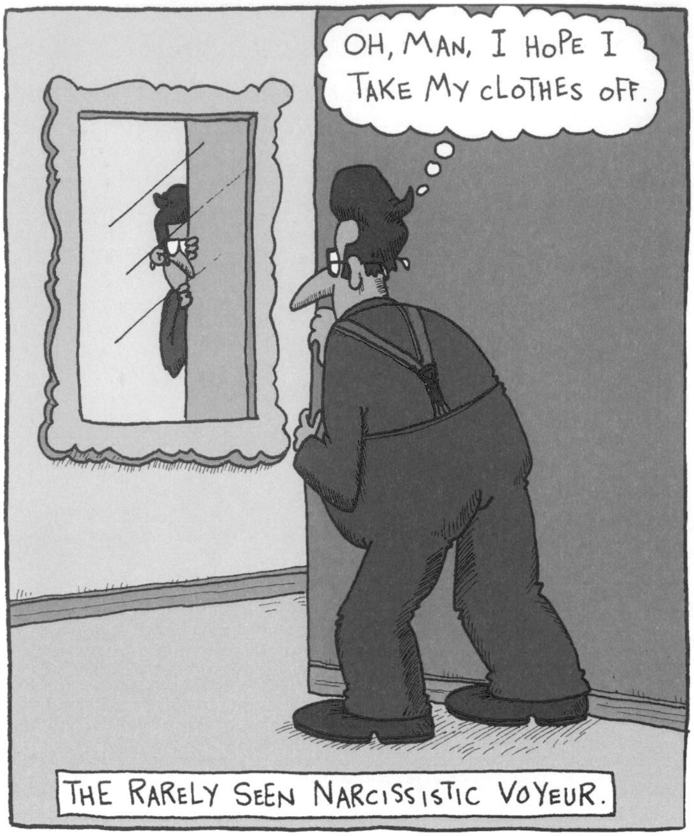
OH, MAN, I HOPE I TAKE MY CLOTHES OFF.
THE RARELY SEEN NARCISSISTIC VOYEUR.

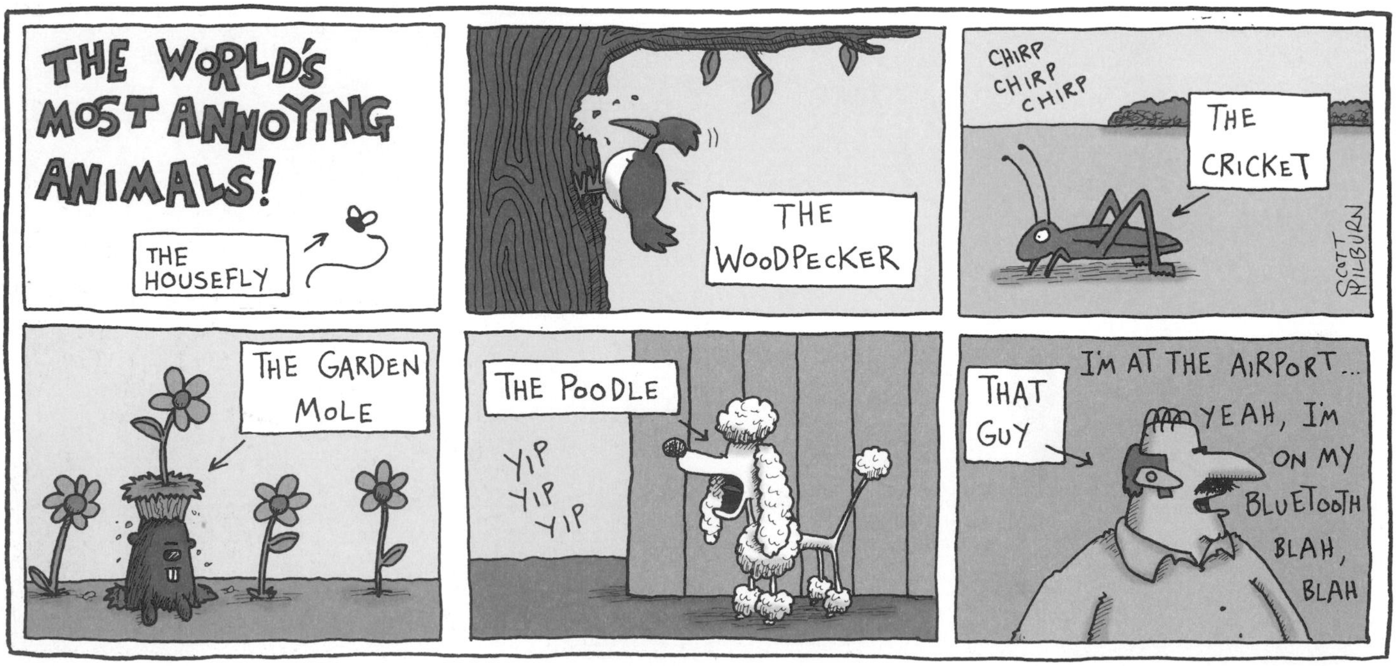
THE WORLD'S MOST ANNOYING ANIMALS!
THE HOUSEFLY
THE WOODPECKER
CHIRP CHIRP CHIRP
THE CRICKET
SCOTT HILBURN
THE GARDEN MOLE
THE POODLE
YIP YIP YIP
THAT GUY
I'M AT THE AIRPORT... YEAH, I'M ON MY BLUETOOTH BLAH, BLAH

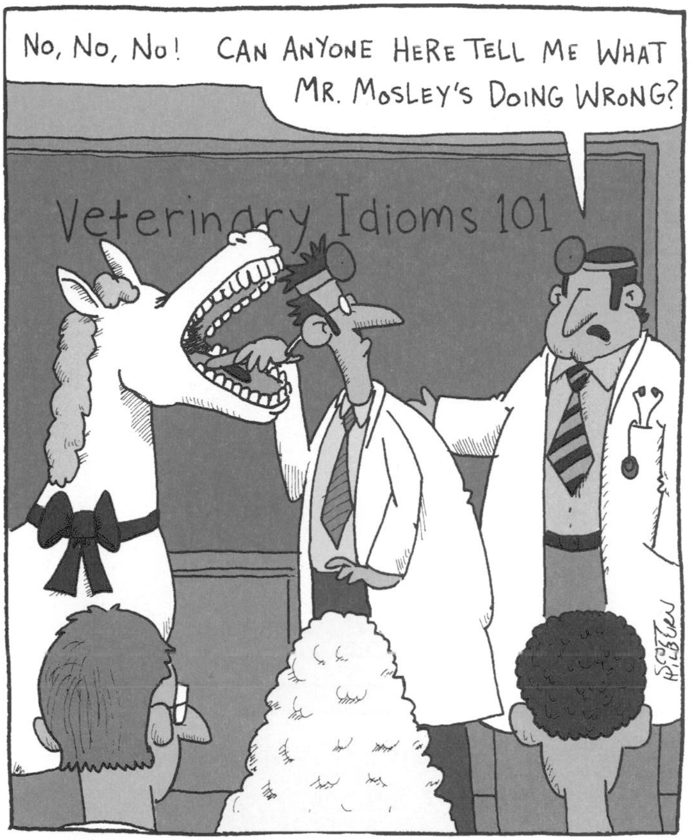
No, No, No! Can anyone here tell me what Mr. Mosley's doing wrong?
Veterinary Idioms 101

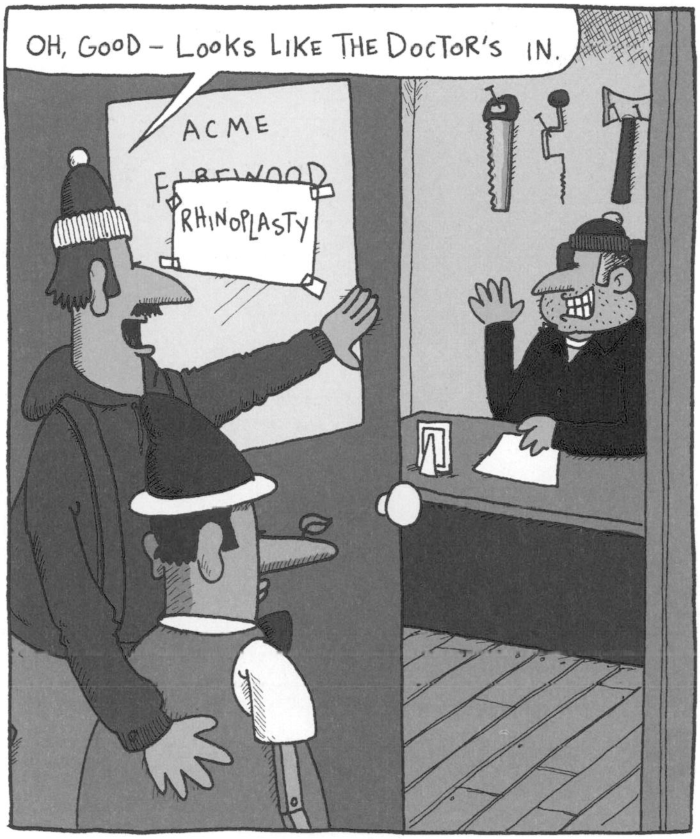
Oh, good – looks like the Doctor's in.
ACME
RHINOPLASTY

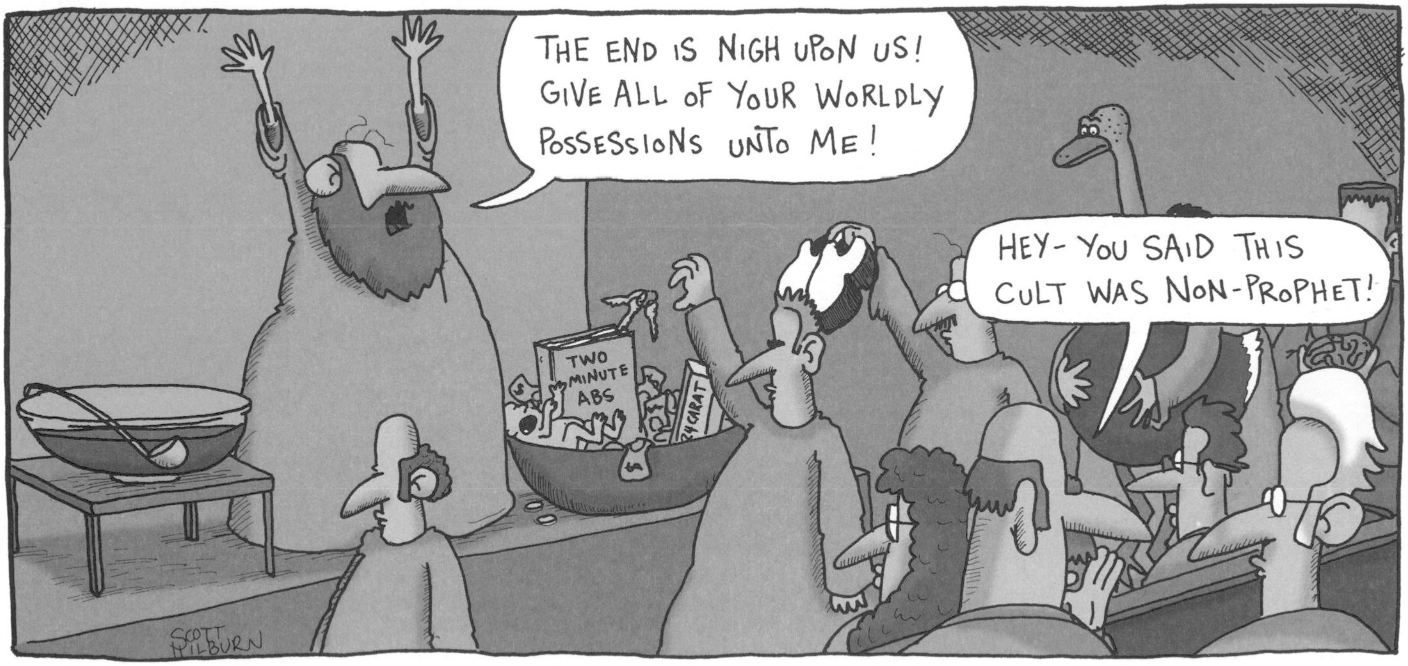
The end is nigh upon us! Give all of your worldly possessions unto me!
Hey- you said this cult was non-prophet!
TWO MINUTE ABS
SCOTT HILBURN

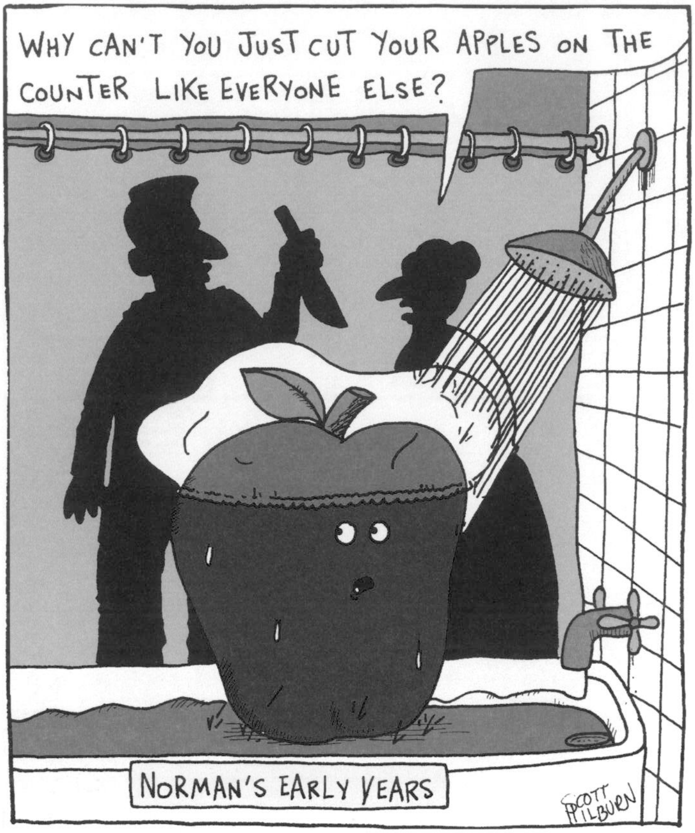
WHY CAN'T YOU JUST CUT YOUR APPLES ON THE COUNTER LIKE EVERYONE ELSE?
NORMAN'S EARLY YEARS
SCOTT HILBURN

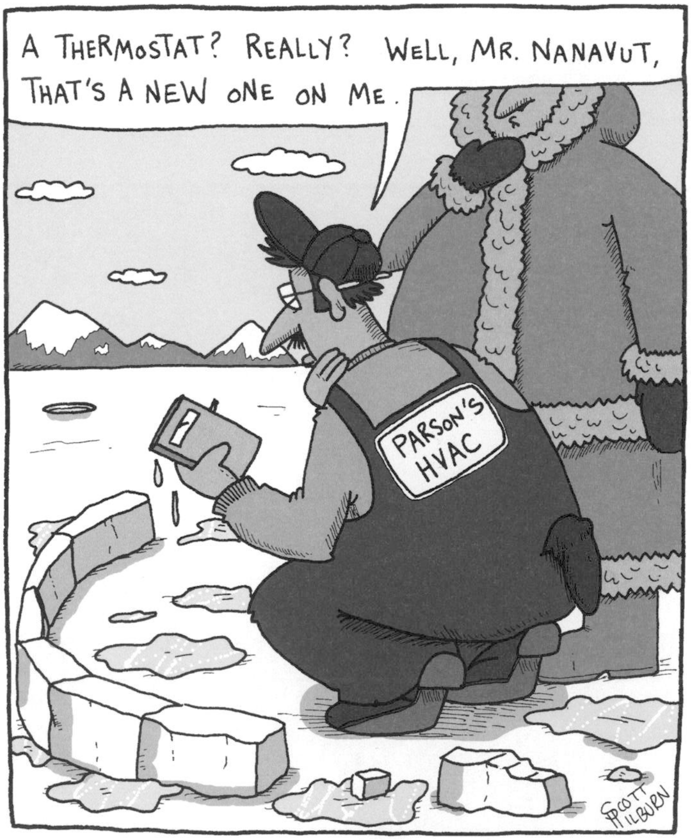
A THERMOSTAT? REALLY? WELL, MR. NANAVUT, THAT'S A NEW ONE ON ME.
PARSON'S HVAC
SCOTT HILBURN

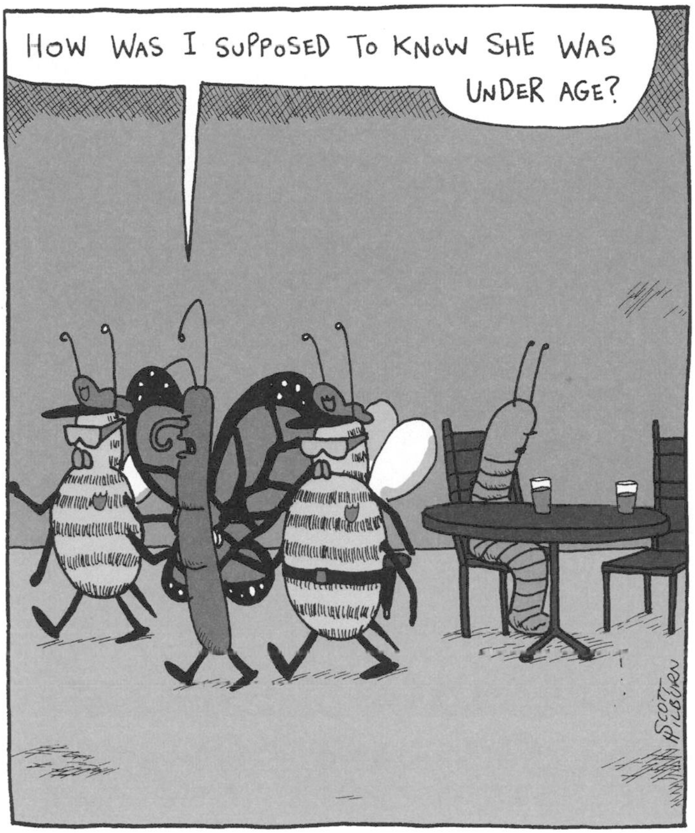
HOW WAS I SUPPOSED TO KNOW SHE WAS UNDER AGE?

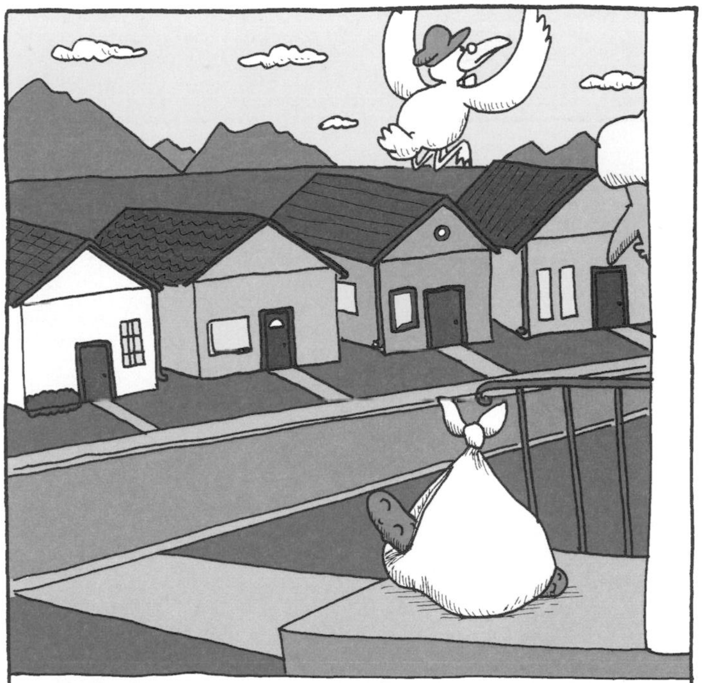

ALREADY OVERWORKED AT THE VLASIC PLANT, AN EXHAUSTED STORK SHATTERS A YOUNG COUPLE'S DREAMS.

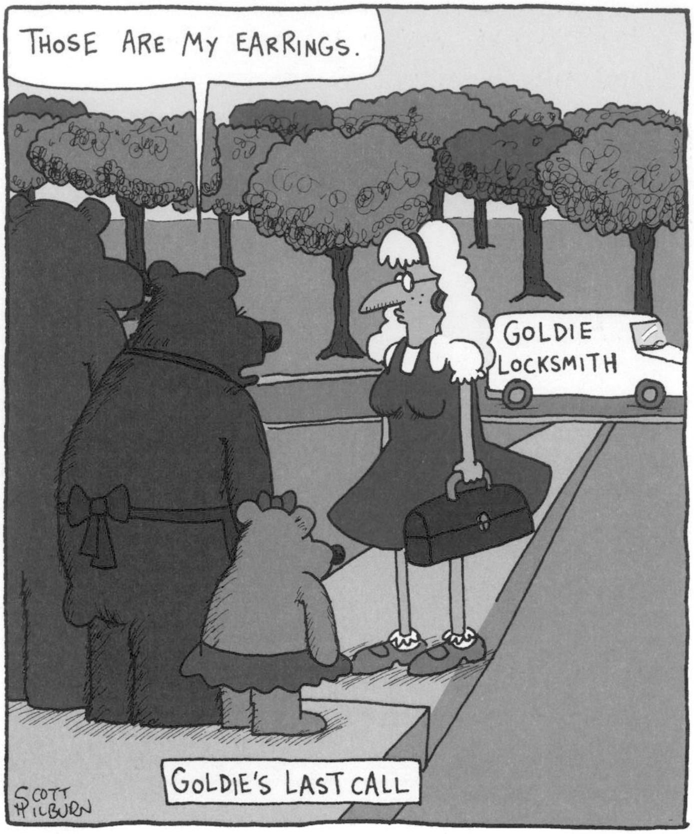
THOSE ARE MY EARRINGS.
GOLDIE LOCKSMITH
GOLDIE'S LAST CALL
SCOTT HILBURN

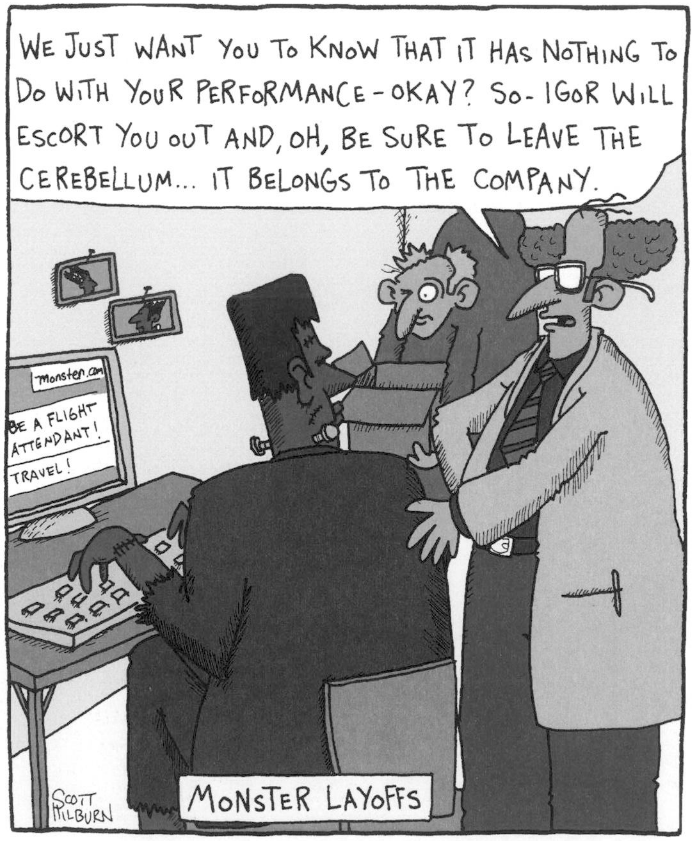
WE JUST WANT YOU TO KNOW THAT IT HAS NOTHING TO DO WITH YOUR PERFORMANCE - OKAY? SO- IGOR WILL ESCORT YOU OUT AND, OH, BE SURE TO LEAVE THE CEREBELLUM... IT BELONGS TO THE COMPANY.
monster.com
BE A FLIGHT ATTENDANT!
TRAVEL!
MONSTER LAYOFFS
SCOTT HILBURN

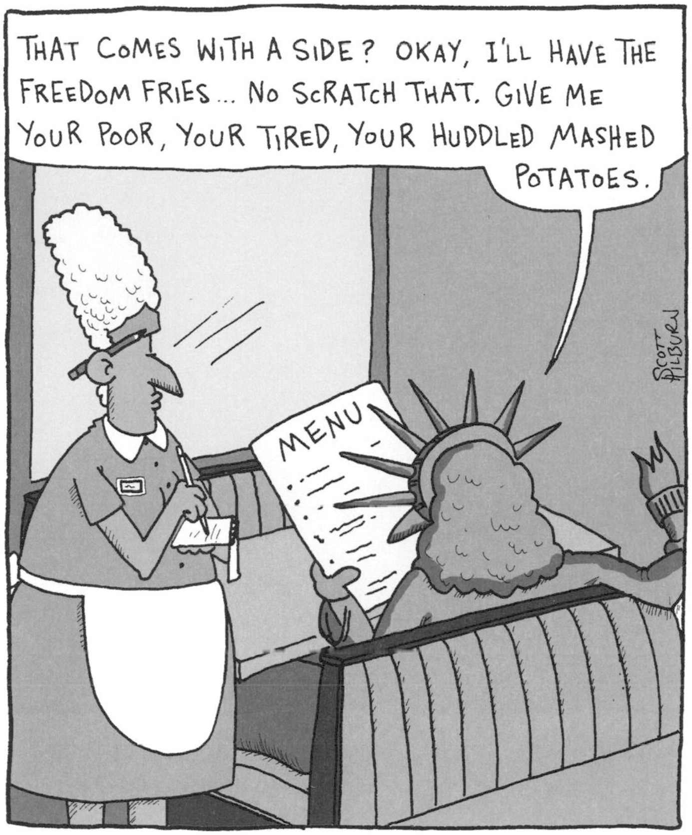
THAT COMES WITH A SIDE? OKAY, I'LL HAVE THE FREEDOM FRIES... NO SCRATCH THAT. GIVE ME YOUR POOR, YOUR TIRED, YOUR HUDDLED MASHED POTATOES.
MENU
SCOTT HILBURN

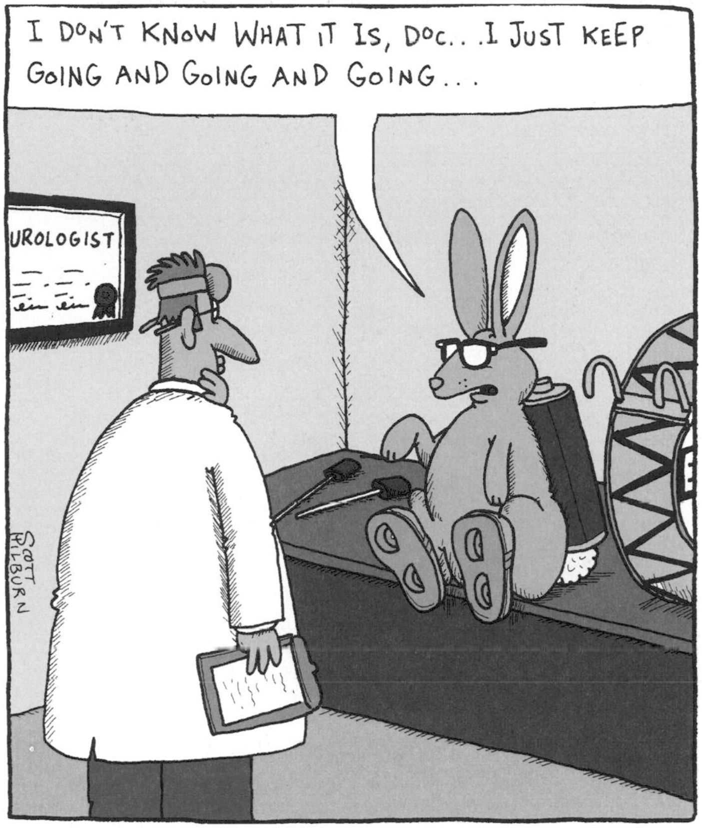
I DON'T KNOW WHAT IT IS, DOC... I JUST KEEP GOING AND GOING AND GOING...
UROLOGIST
SCOTT HILBURN

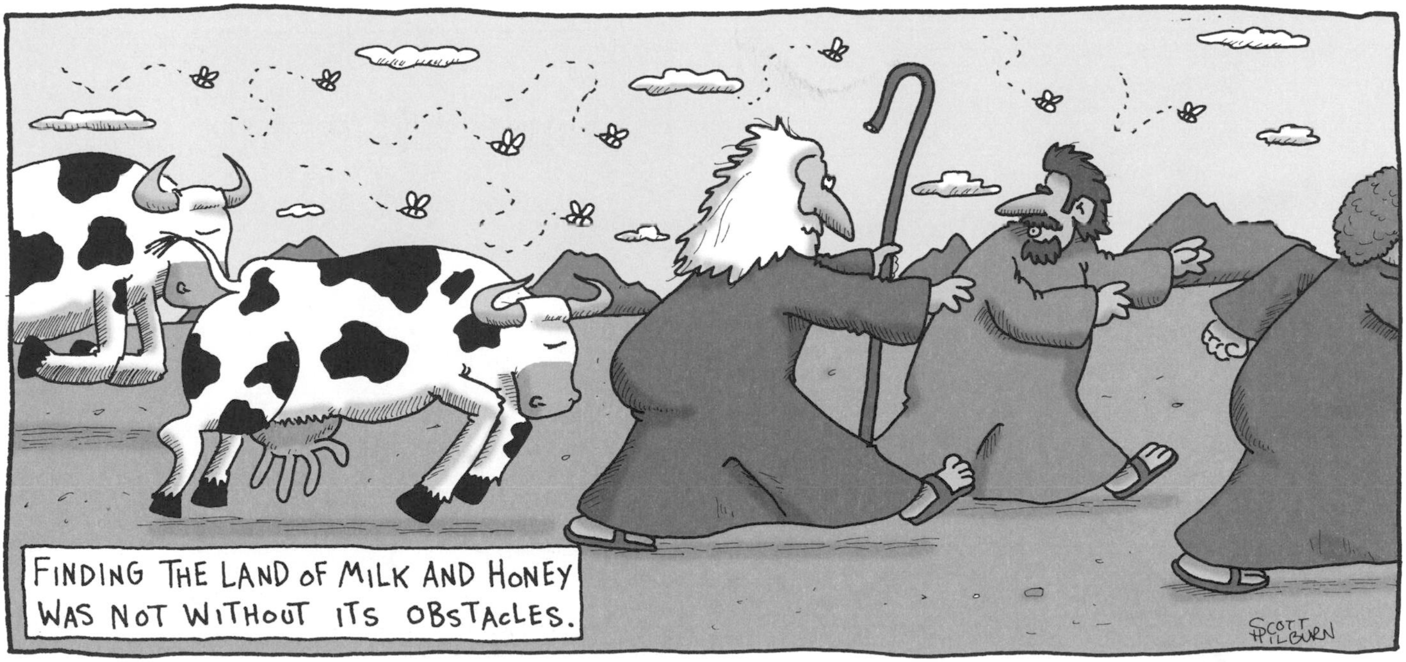
FINDING THE LAND OF MILK AND HONEY WAS NOT WITHOUT ITS OBSTACLES.
SCOTT HILBURN

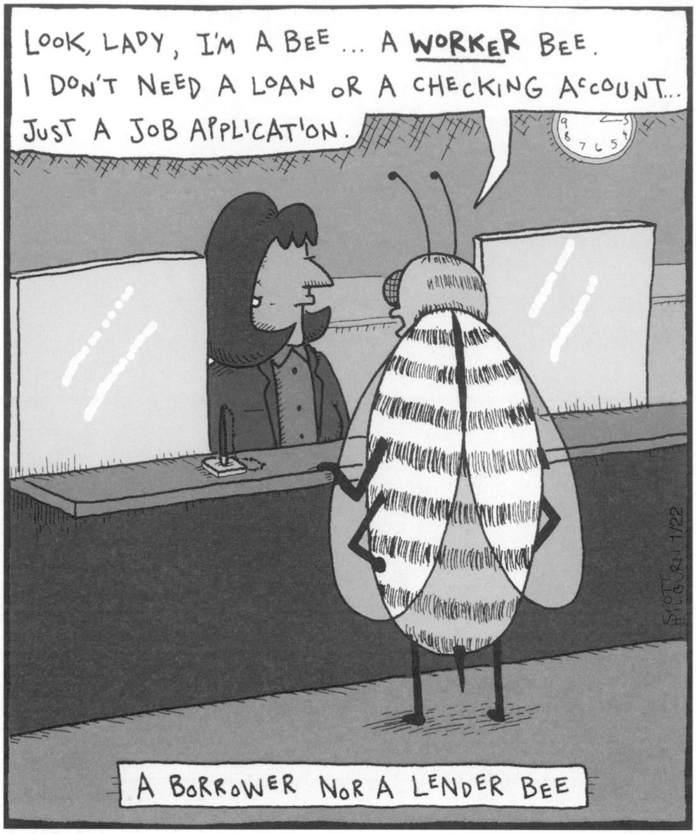
LOOK, LADY, I'M A BEE ... A WORKER BEE. I DON'T NEED A LOAN OR A CHECKING ACCOUNT... JUST A JOB APPLICATION.
SCOTT HILBURN 1/22

A BORROWER NOR A LENDER BEE

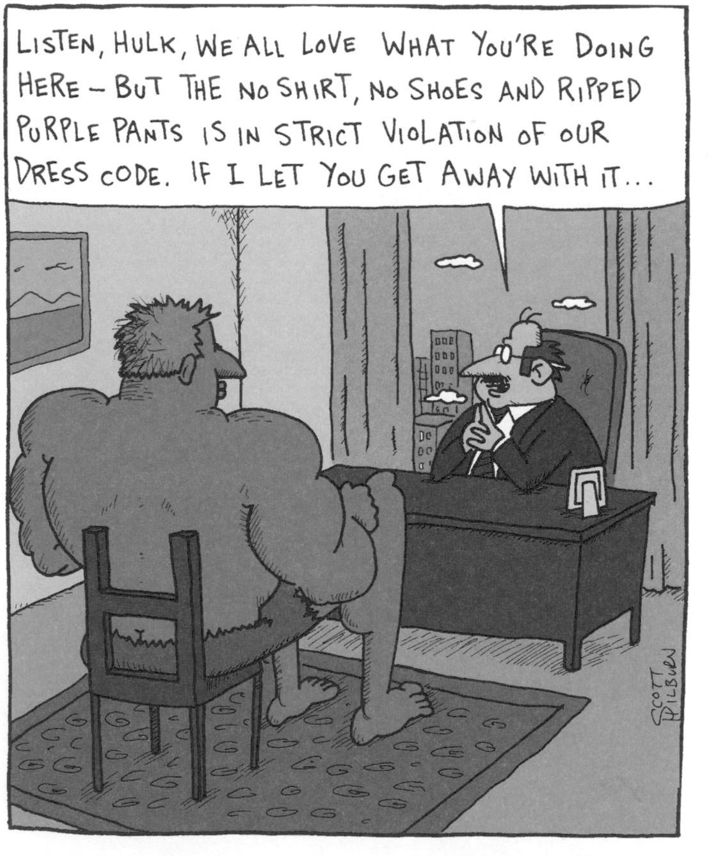
LISTEN, HULK, WE ALL LOVE WHAT YOU'RE DOING HERE – BUT THE NO SHIRT, NO SHOES AND RIPPED PURPLE PANTS IS IN STRICT VIOLATION OF OUR DRESS CODE. IF I LET YOU GET AWAY WITH IT...
SCOTT HILBURN

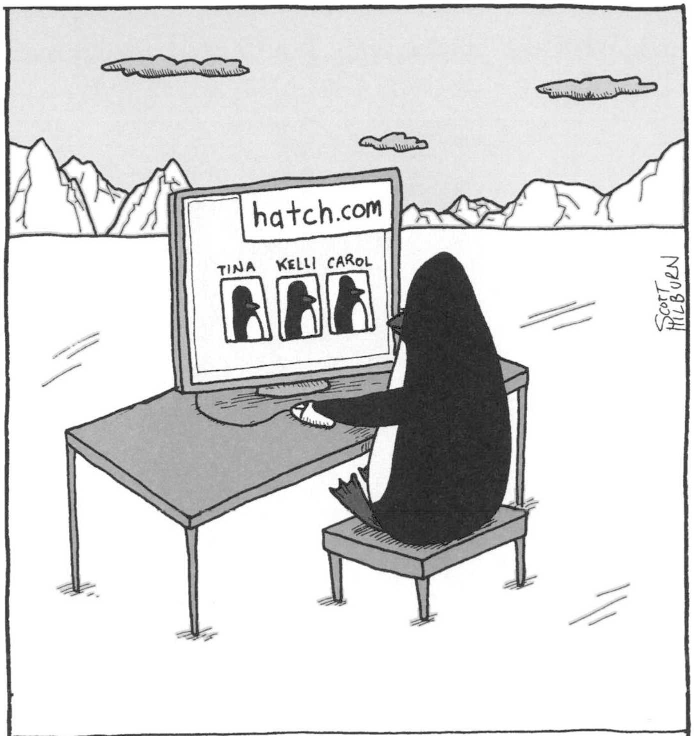
hatch.com
TINA
KELLI
CAROL
SCOTT HILBURN

IMMEDIATLEY AFTER THE BABIES ARE BORN, THE ADULTS BEGIN THE CYCLE ALL OVER AGAIN.

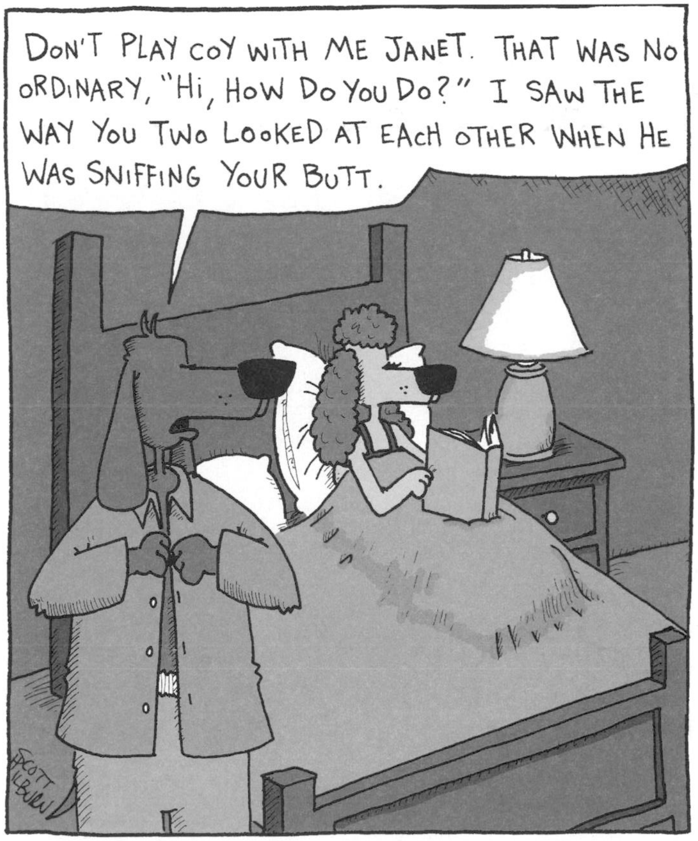
DON'T PLAY COY WITH ME JANET. THAT WAS NO ORDINARY, "HI, HOW DO YOU DO?" I SAW THE WAY YOU TWO LOOKED AT EACH OTHER WHEN HE WAS SNIFFING YOUR BUTT.

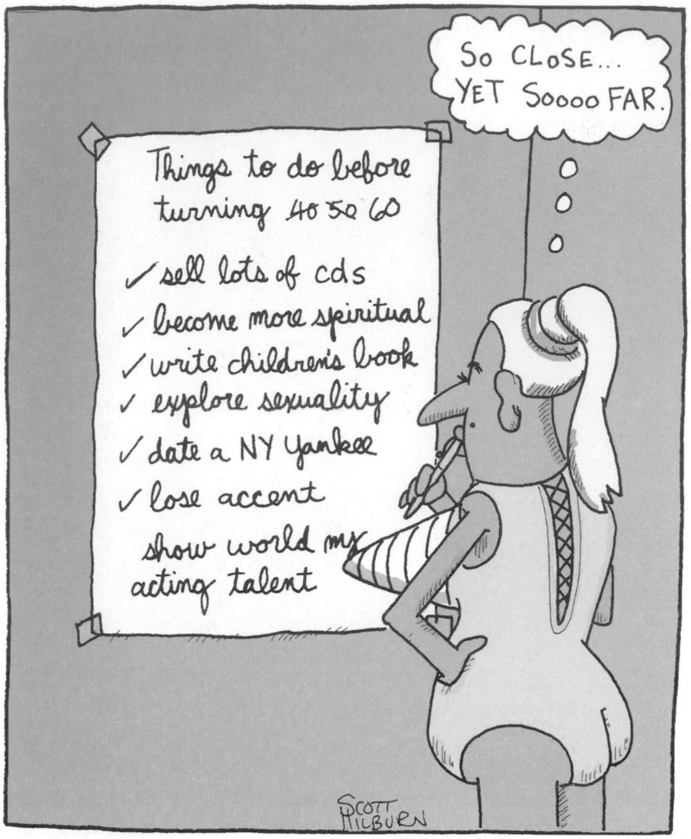
So CLOSE...
YET Soooo FAR.
Things to do before turning 40 50 60
✓ sell lots of cds
✓ become more spiritual
✓ write children's book
✓ explore sexuality
✓ date a NY Yankee
✓ lose accent
show world my acting talent
SCOTT HILBURN

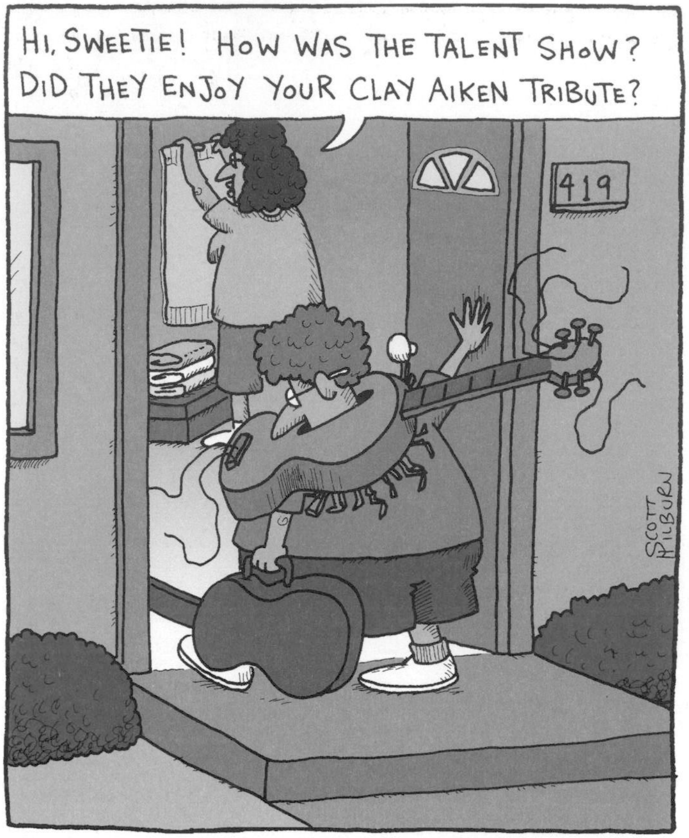
HI, SWEETIE! HOW WAS THE TALENT SHOW? DID THEY ENJOY YOUR CLAY AIKEN TRIBUTE?
419
SCOTT HILBURN

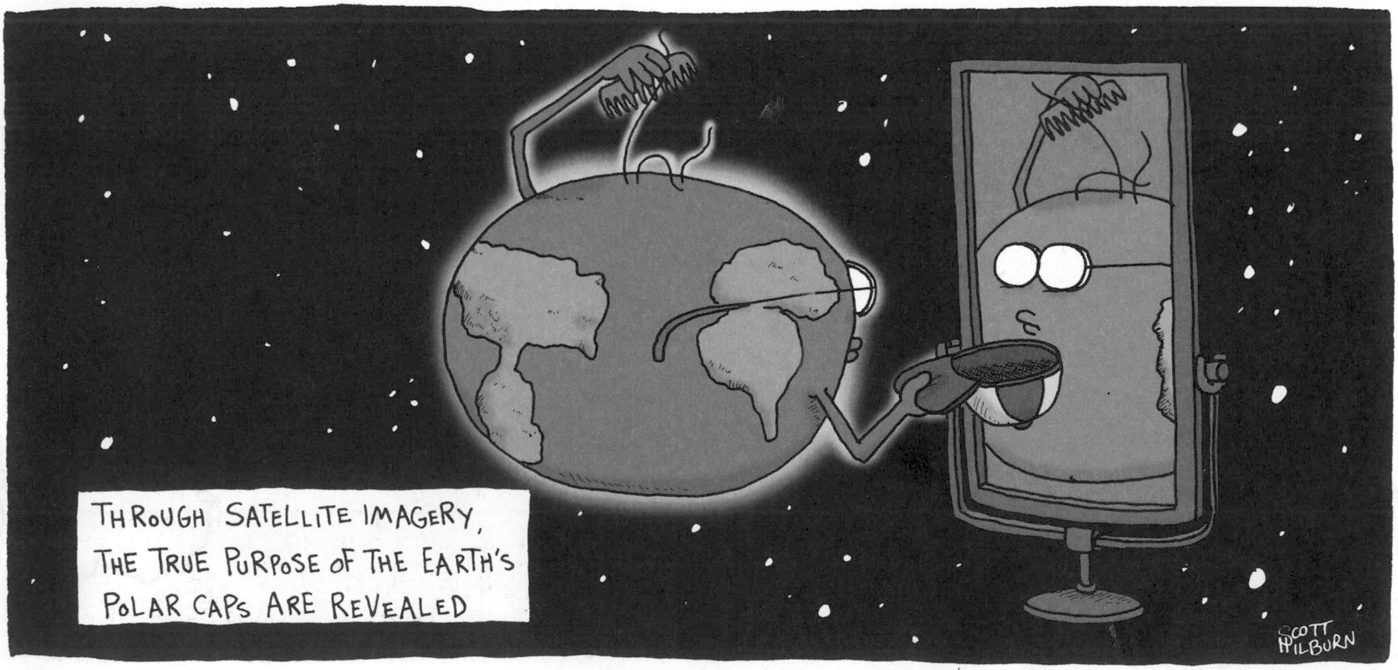
THROUGH SATELLITE IMAGERY, THE TRUE PURPOSE OF THE EARTH'S POLAR CAPS ARE REVEALED
SCOTT HILBURN

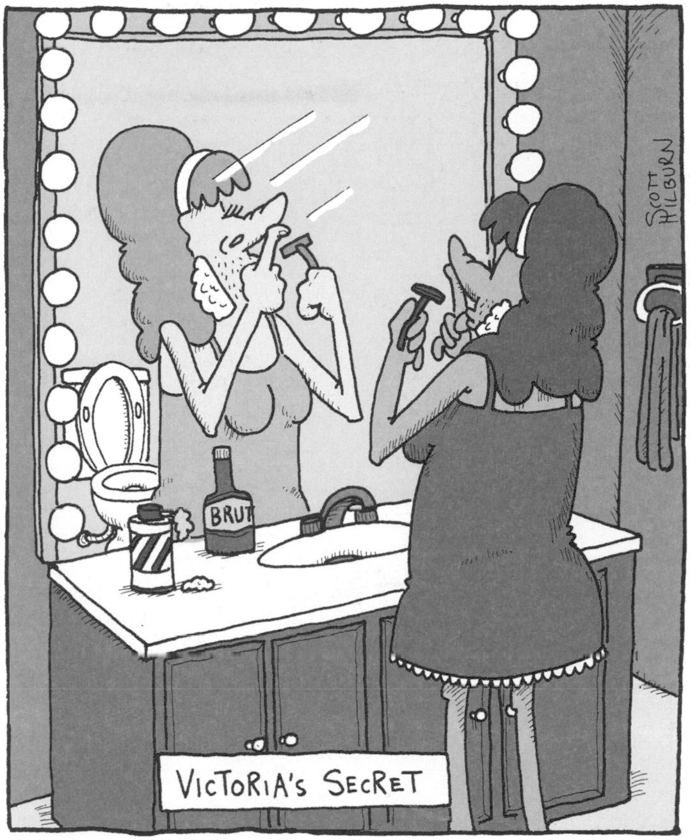
SCOTT HILBURN
BRUT
VICTORIA'S SECRET

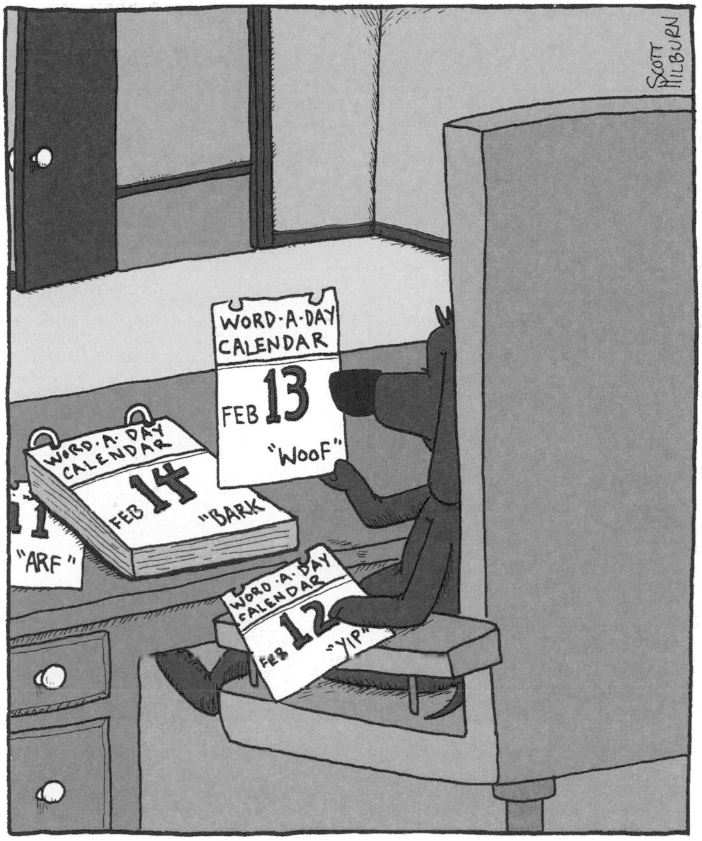
SCOTT HILBURN
WORD-A-DAY CALENDAR
FEB 13
"WOOF"
WORD-A-DAY CALENDAR
FEB 14
"BARK"
"ARF"
WORD-A-DAY CALENDAR
FEB 12
"YIP"

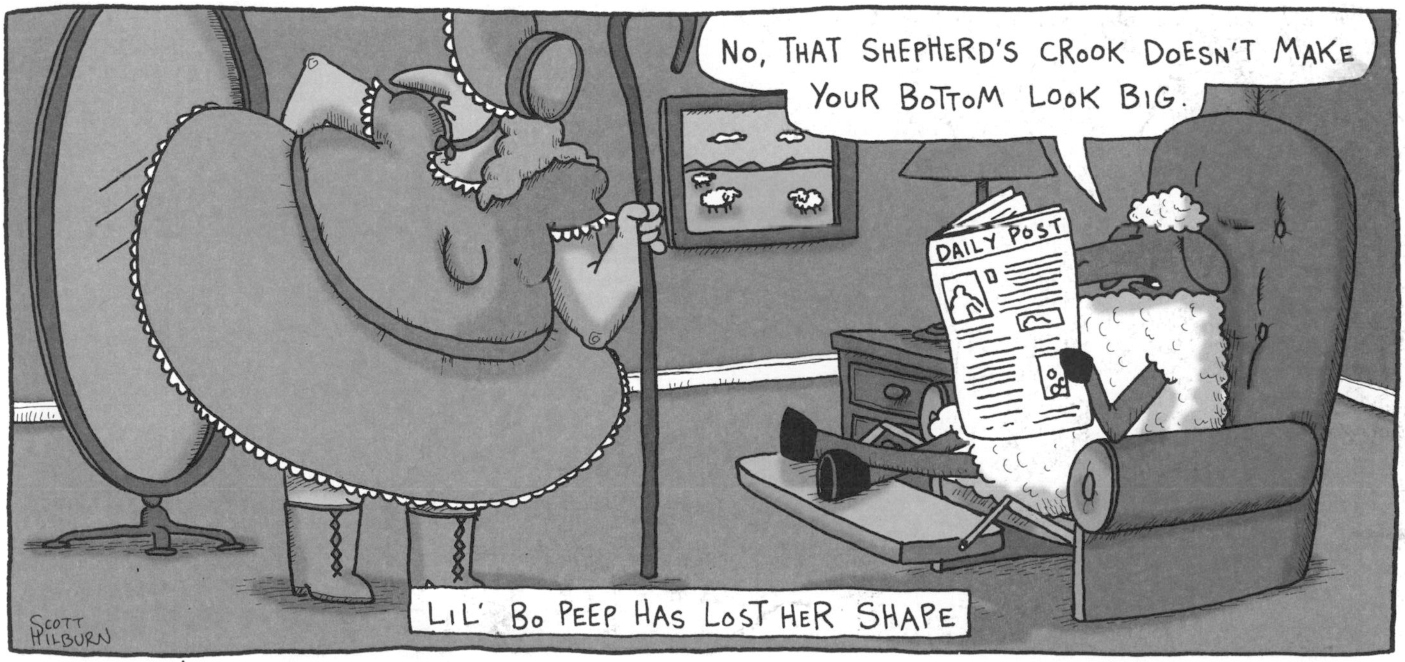
NO, THAT SHEPHERD'S CROOK DOESN'T MAKE YOUR BOTTOM LOOK BIG.
DAILY POST
LIL' BO PEEP HAS LOST HER SHAPE
SCOTT HILBURN

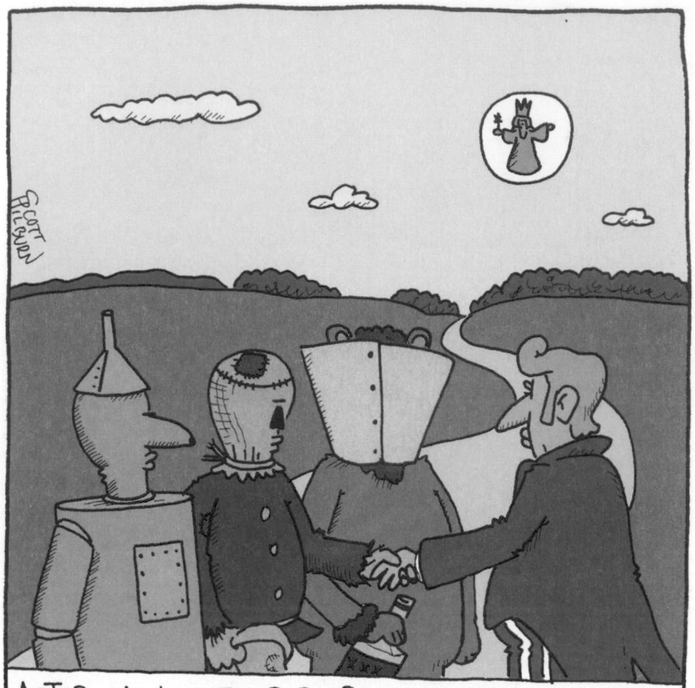
SCOTT HILBURN

AFTER EACH OF THEIR RESPECTIVE SURGERIES, THE TIN MAN, THE SCARECROW AND THE LION THANK THE WIZARD FOR THEIR HEART, BRAIN AND "COURAGE."

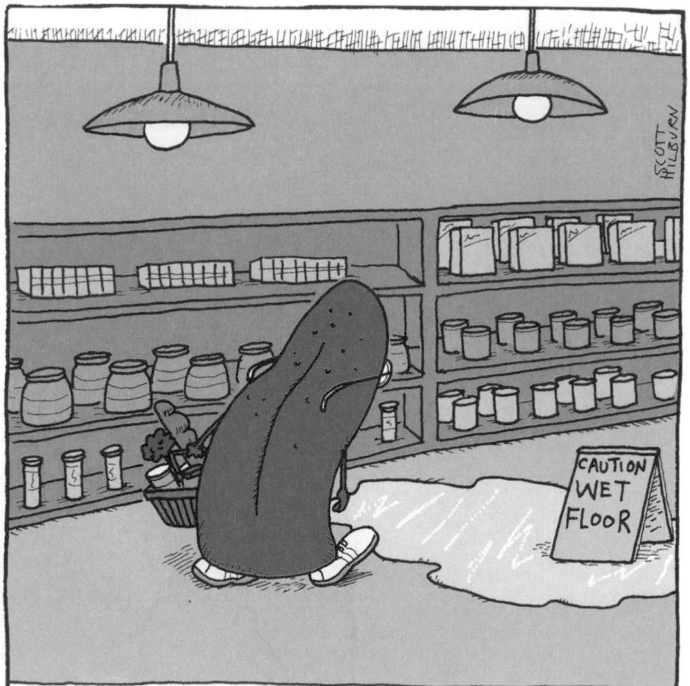
SCOTT HILBURN
CAUTION WET FLOOR

ON THAT FATEFUL VISIT TO THE SUPERMARKET, IT WAS TONGUE'S MISSTEP THAT WOULD LEAD TO A FALL, A LAWSUIT AND AN EVENTUAL CATCH-PHRASE.

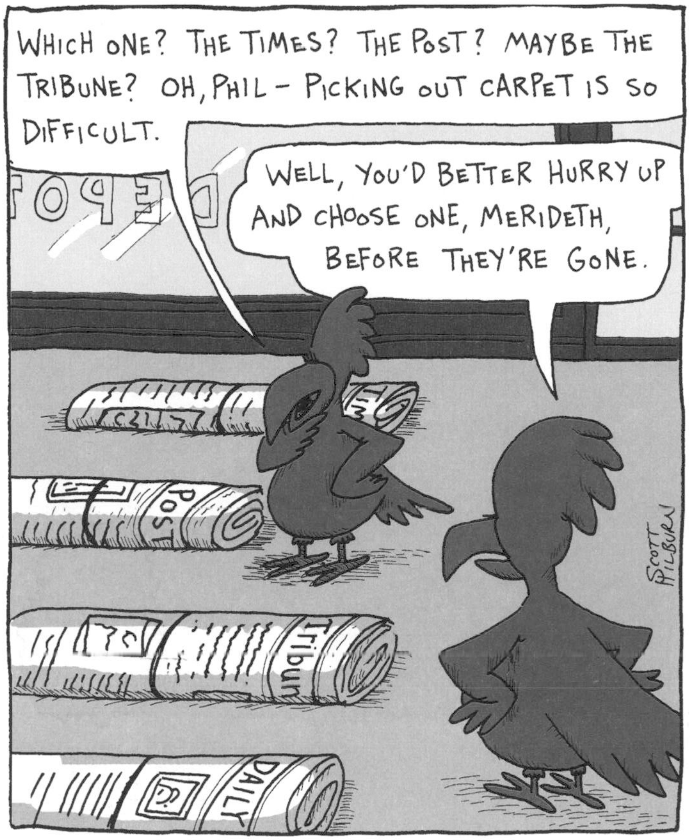
WHICH ONE? THE TIMES? THE POST? MAYBE THE TRIBUNE? OH, PHIL – PICKING OUT CARPET IS SO DIFFICULT.
WELL, YOU'D BETTER HURRY UP AND CHOOSE ONE, MERIDETH, BEFORE THEY'RE GONE.
POST
DAILY
SCOTT HILBURN

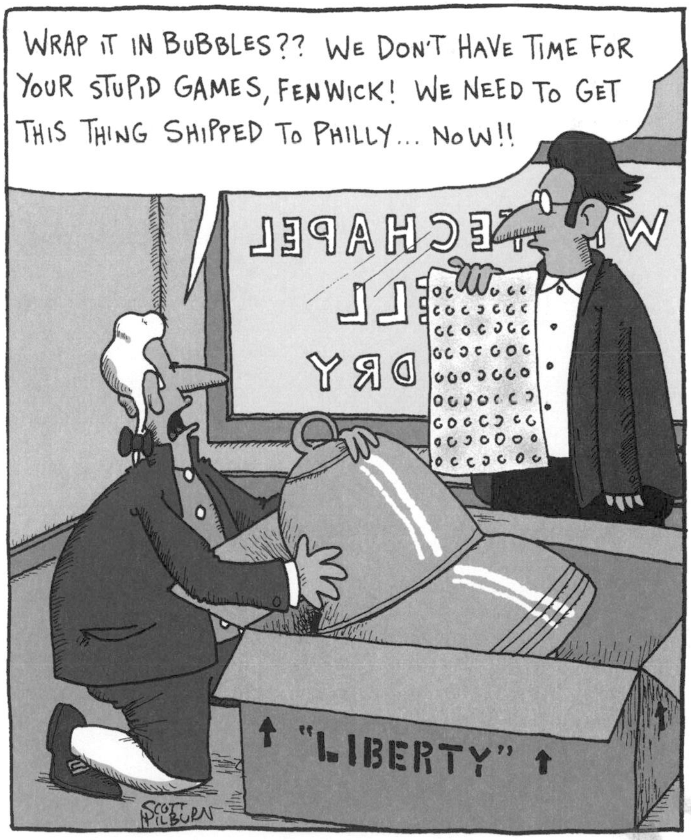
WRAP IT IN BUBBLES?? WE DON'T HAVE TIME FOR YOUR STUPID GAMES, FENWICK! WE NEED TO GET THIS THING SHIPPED TO PHILLY... NOW!!
"LIBERTY"
SCOTT HILBURN

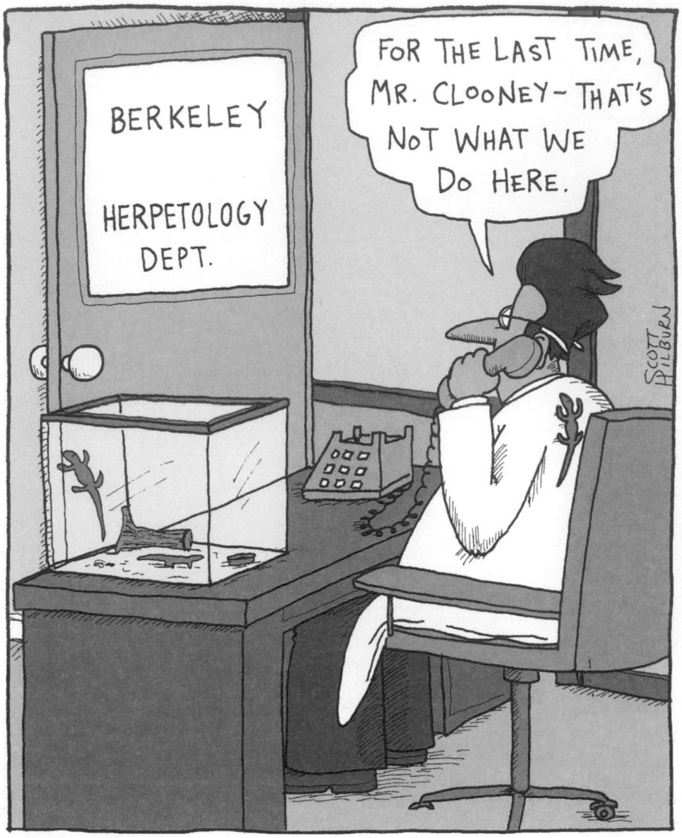
BERKELEY
HERPETOLOGY DEPT.
FOR THE LAST TIME, MR. CLOONEY - THAT'S NOT WHAT WE DO HERE.
SCOTT HILBURN

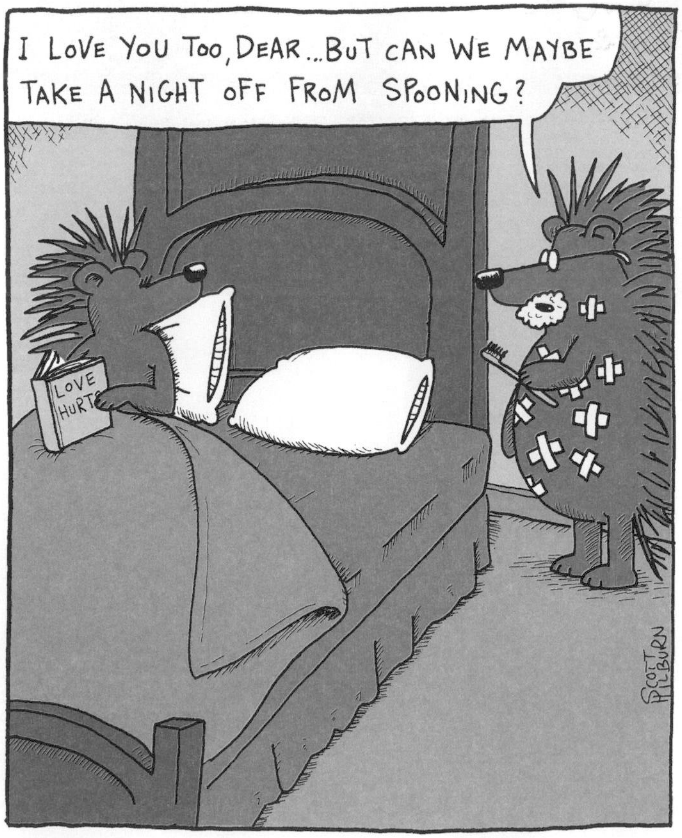
I LOVE YOU TOO, DEAR... BUT CAN WE MAYBE TAKE A NIGHT OFF FROM SPOONING?
LOVE HURTS
SCOTT HILBURN

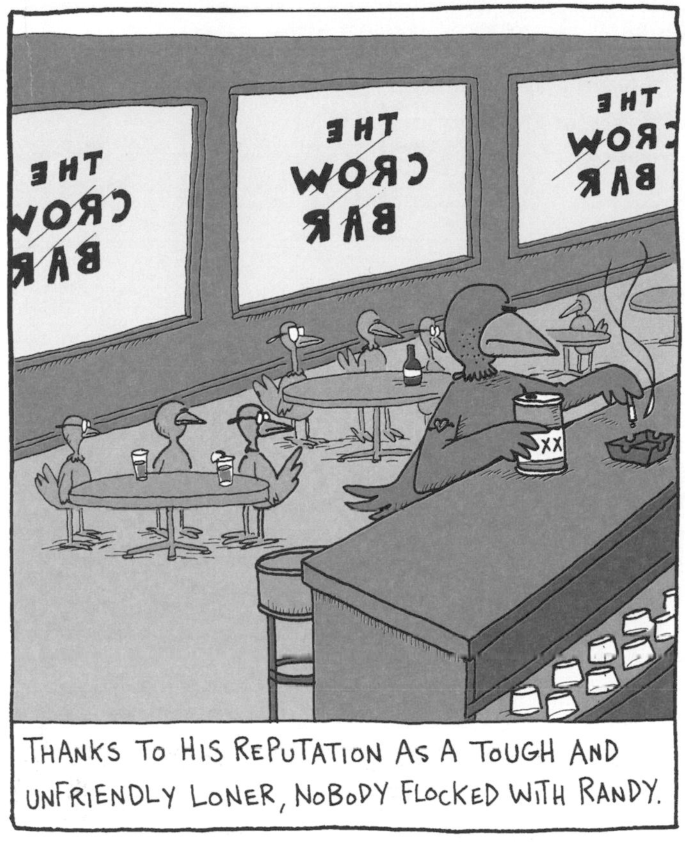

THANKS TO HIS REPUTATION AS A TOUGH AND UNFRIENDLY LONER, NOBODY FLOCKED WITH RANDY.

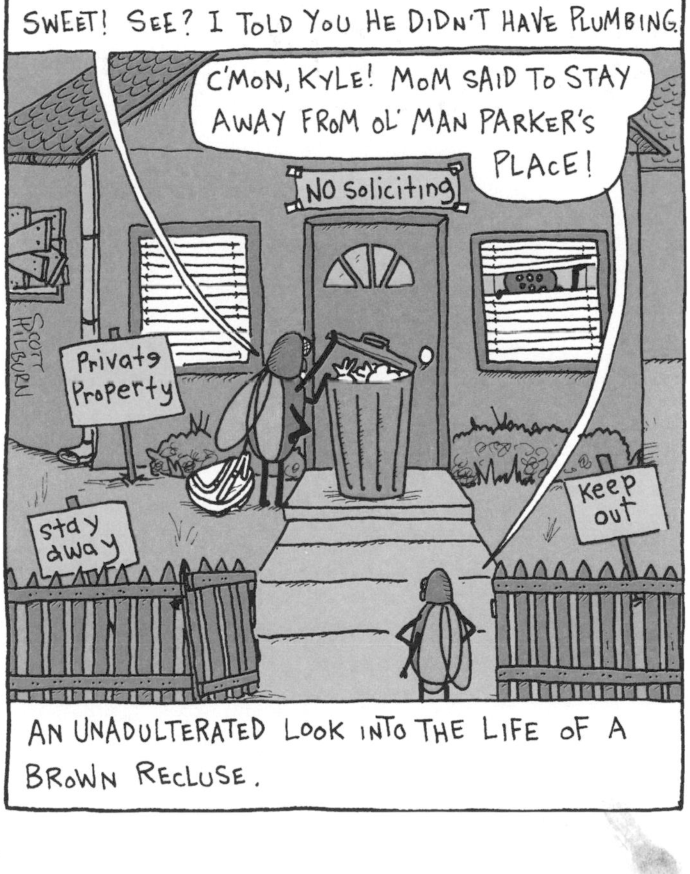
SWEET! SEE? I TOLD YOU HE DIDN'T HAVE PLUMBING.
C'MON, KYLE! MOM SAID TO STAY AWAY FROM OL' MAN PARKER'S PLACE!
NO Soliciting
Private Property
stay away
Keep out
SCOTT HILBURN

AN UNADULTERATED LOOK INTO THE LIFE OF A BROWN RECLUSE.

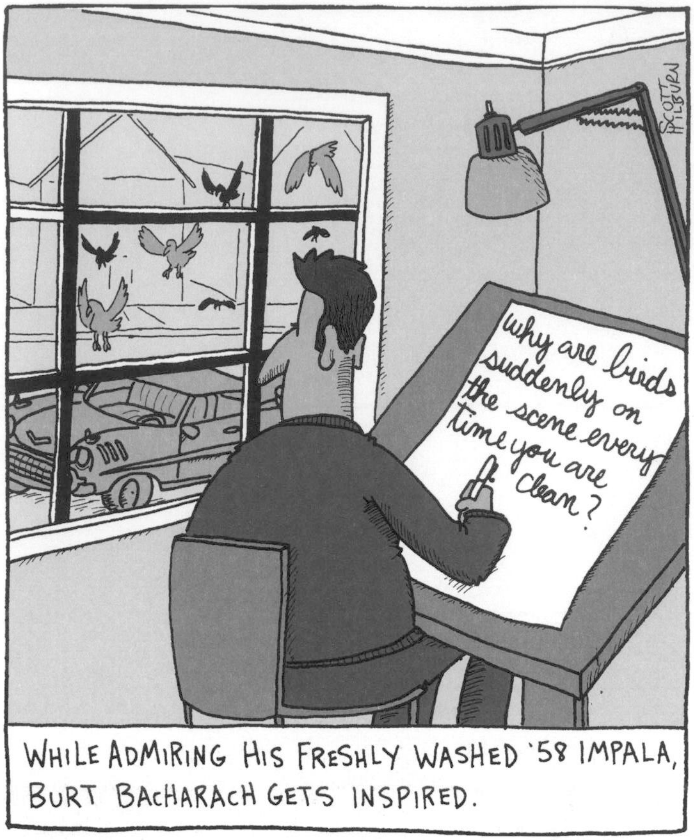
SCOTT HILBURN
why are birds suddenly on the scene every time you are clean?
WHILE ADMIRING HIS FRESHLY WASHED '58 IMPALA, BURT BACHARACH GETS INSPIRED.

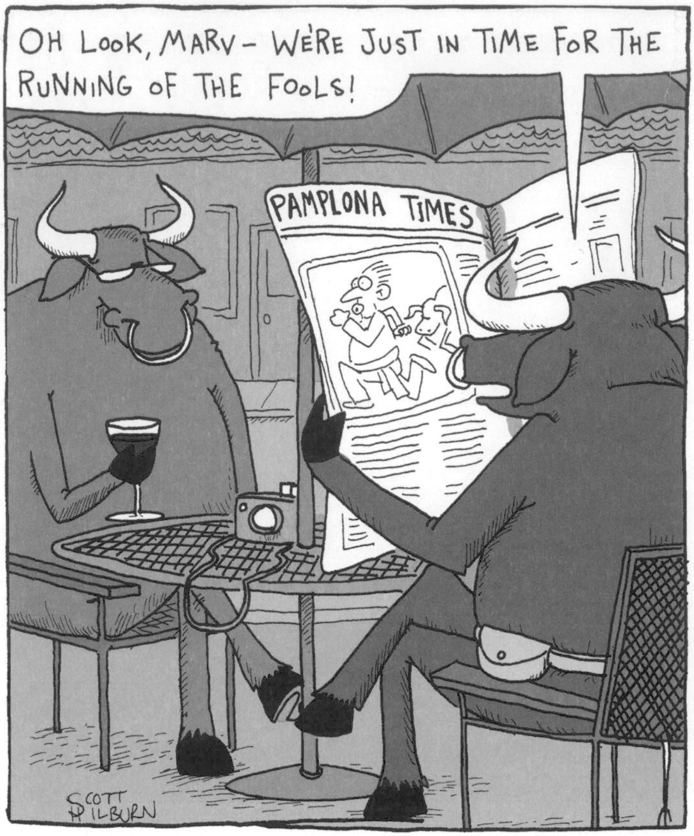
OH LOOK, MARV – WE'RE JUST IN TIME FOR THE RUNNING OF THE FOOLS!
PAMPLONA TIMES
SCOTT HILBURN

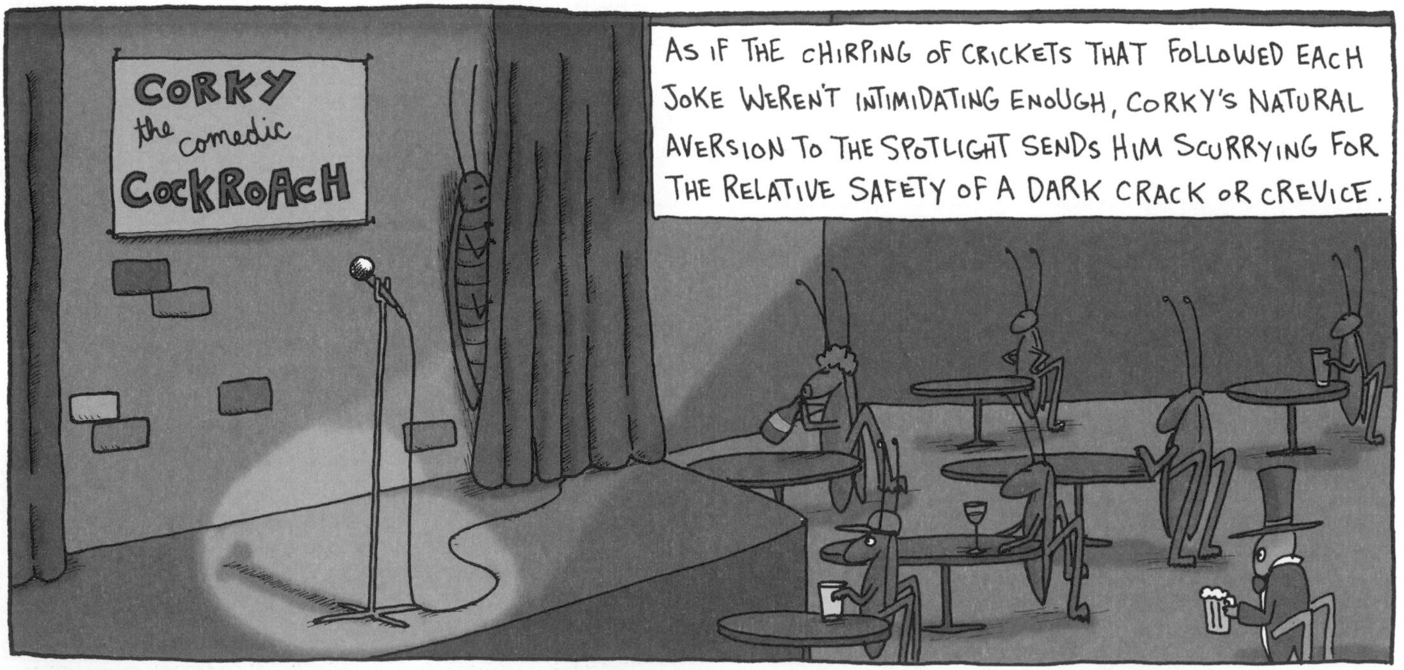
CORKY the comedic COCKROACH
AS IF THE CHIRPING OF CRICKETS THAT FOLLOWED EACH JOKE WEREN'T INTIMIDATING ENOUGH, CORKY'S NATURAL AVERSION TO THE SPOTLIGHT SENDS HIM SCURRYING FOR THE RELATIVE SAFETY OF A DARK CRACK OR CREVICE.

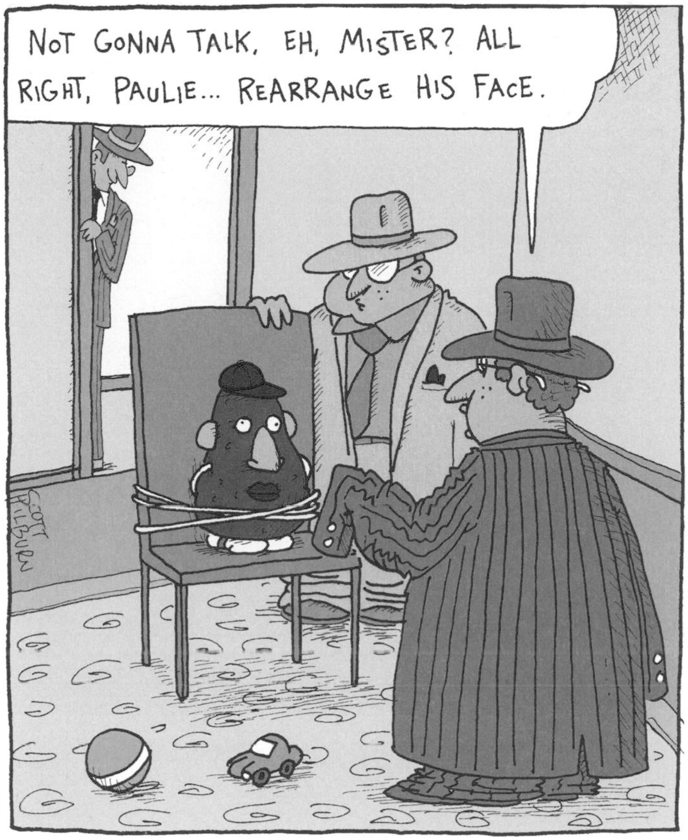
NOT GONNA TALK, EH, MISTER? ALL RIGHT, PAULIE... REARRANGE HIS FACE.
SCOTT HILBURN

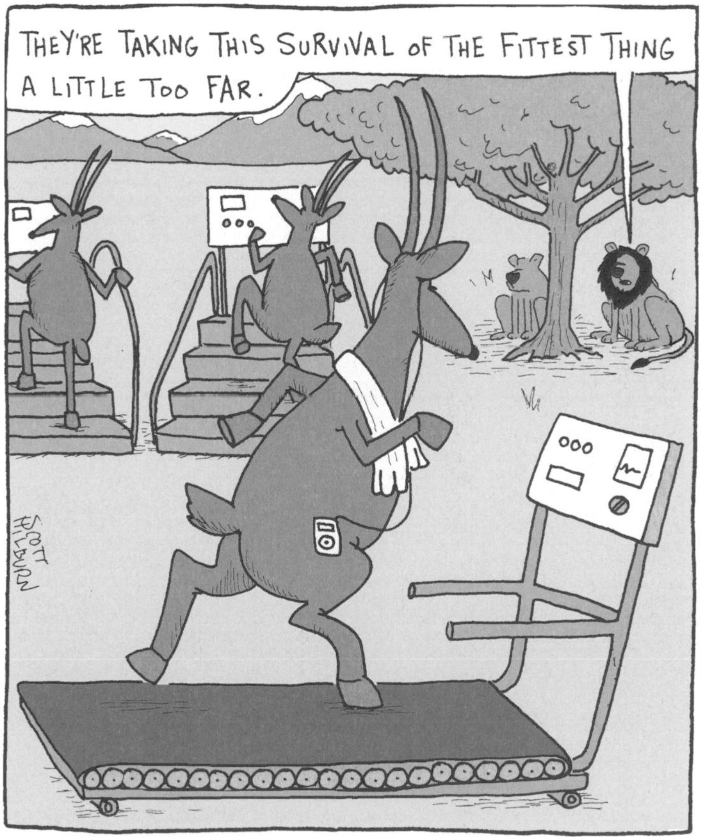
THEY'RE TAKING THIS SURVIVAL OF THE FITTEST THING A LITTLE TOO FAR.
SCOTT HILBURN

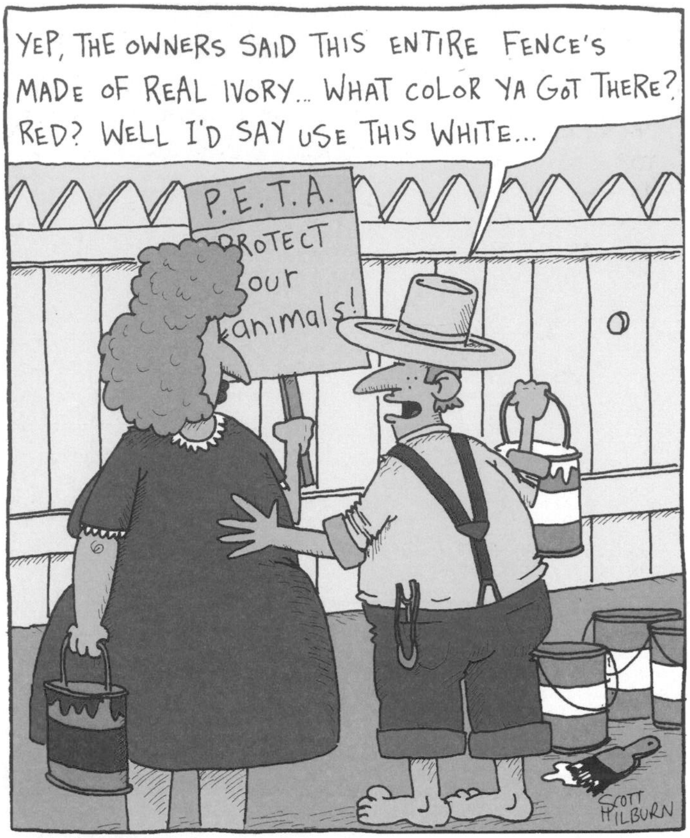
YEP, THE OWNERS SAID THIS ENTIRE FENCE'S MADE OF REAL IVORY... WHAT COLOR YA GOT THERE? RED? WELL I'D SAY USE THIS WHITE...
P.E.T.A.
PROTECT our animals!
SCOTT HILBURN

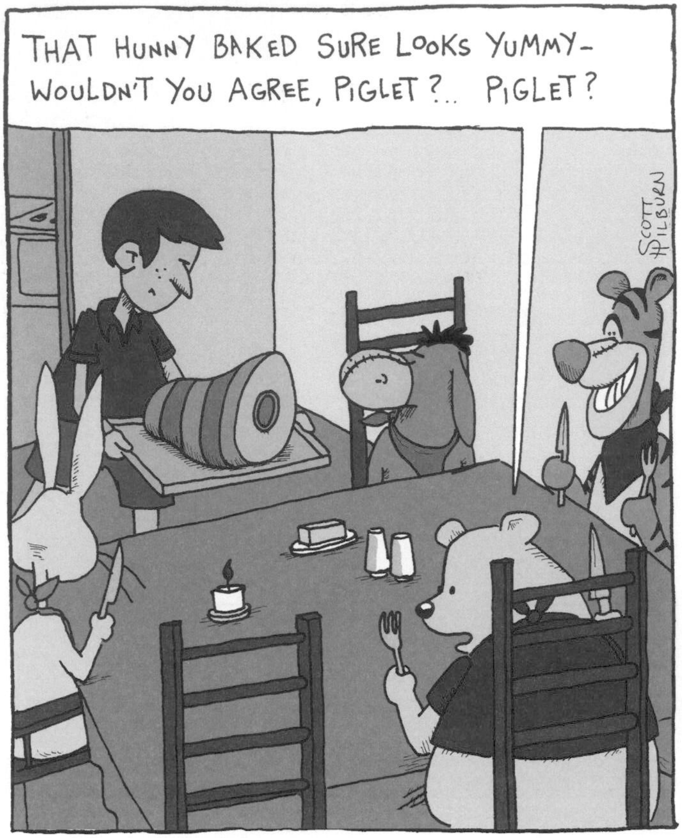
THAT HUNNY BAKED SURE LOOKS YUMMY- WOULDN'T YOU AGREE, PIGLET?.. PIGLET?
SCOTT HILBURN

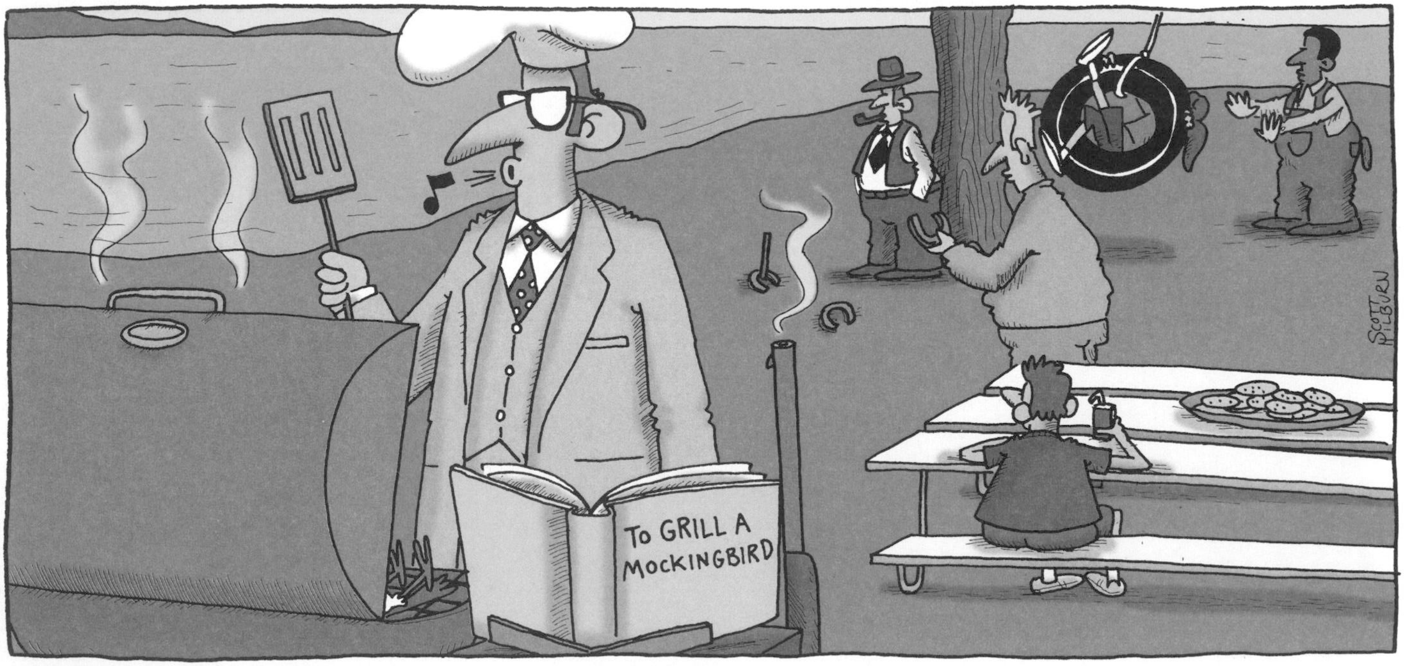
To GRILL A MOCKINGBIRD
SCOTT HILBURN

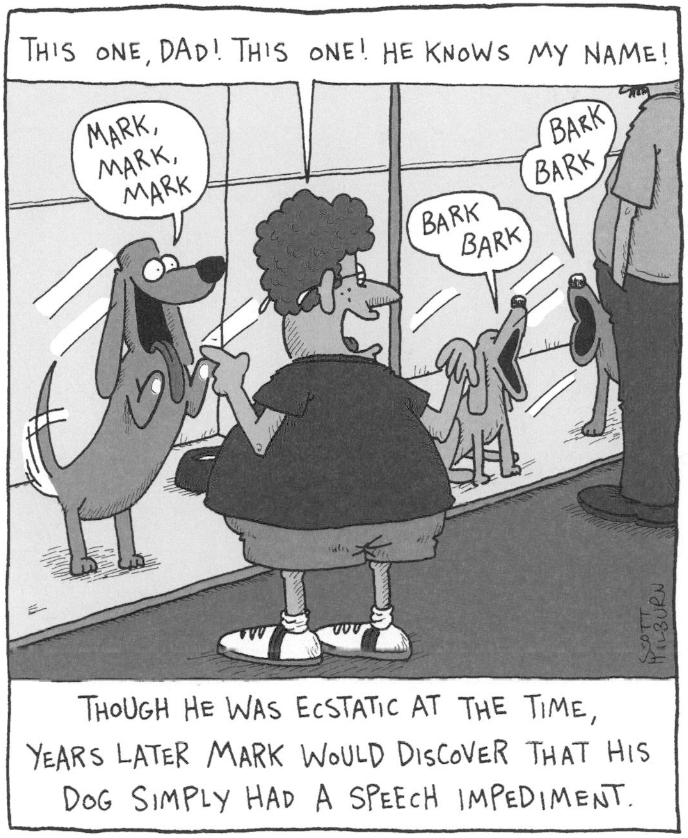
THIS ONE, DAD! THIS ONE! HE KNOWS MY NAME!
MARK, MARK, MARK
BARK BARK
BARK BARK
THOUGH HE WAS ECSTATIC AT THE TIME, YEARS LATER MARK WOULD DISCOVER THAT HIS DOG SIMPLY HAD A SPEECH IMPEDIMENT.

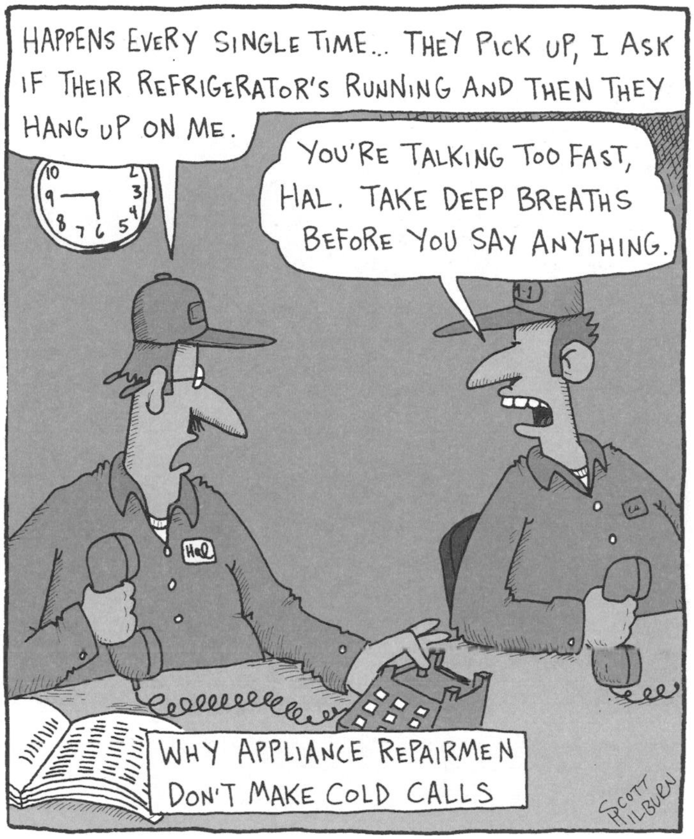
HAPPENS EVERY SINGLE TIME... THEY PICK UP, I ASK IF THEIR REFRIGERATOR'S RUNNING AND THEN THEY HANG UP ON ME.
YOU'RE TALKING TOO FAST, HAL. TAKE DEEP BREATHS BEFORE YOU SAY ANYTHING.
WHY APPLIANCE REPAIRMEN DON'T MAKE COLD CALLS

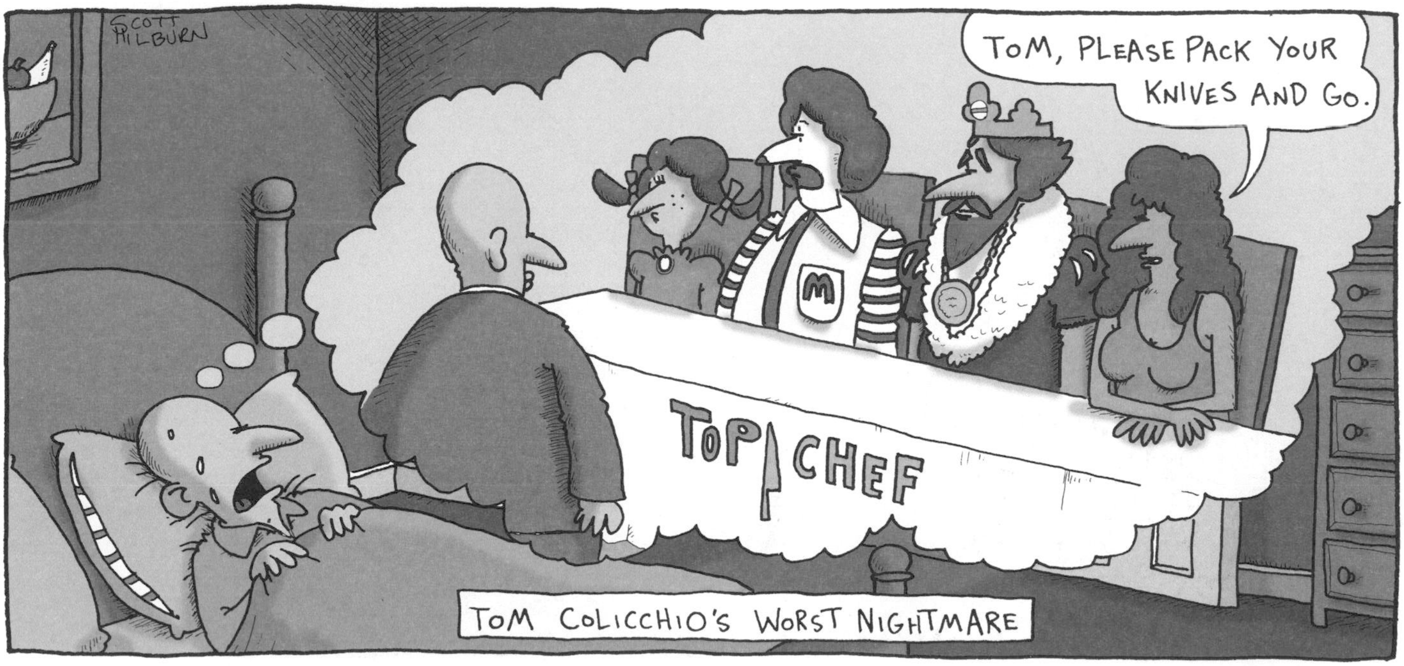
TOM, PLEASE PACK YOUR KNIVES AND GO.
TOP CHEF
TOM COLICCHIO'S WORST NIGHTMARE

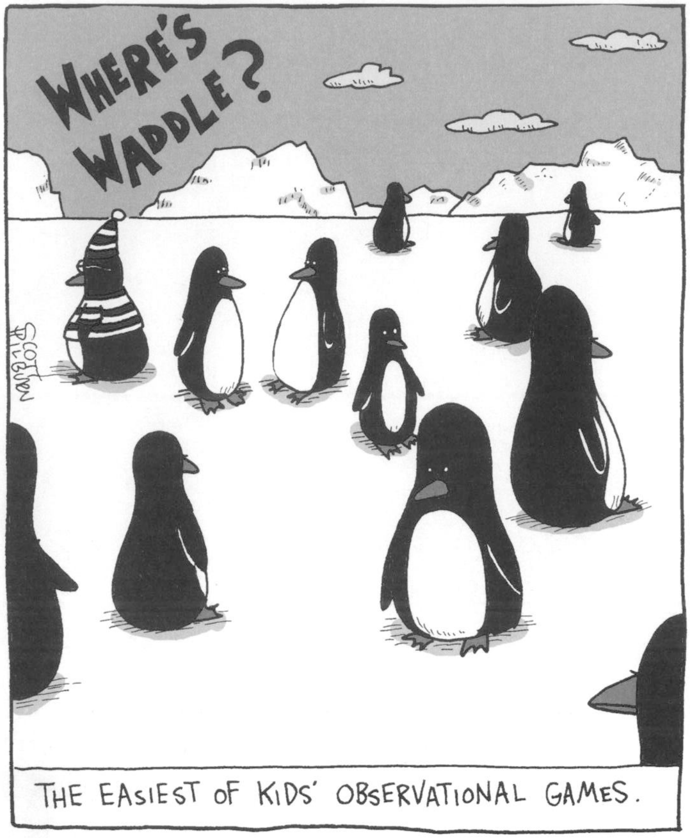
WHERE'S WADDLE?
SCOTT HILBURN
THE EASIEST OF KIDS' OBSERVATIONAL GAMES.

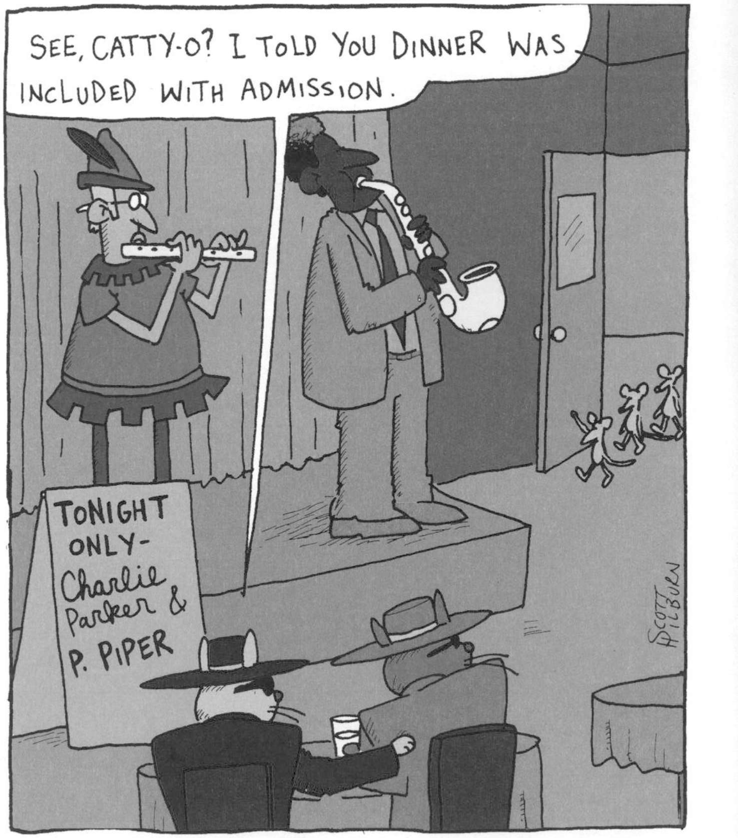
SEE, CATTY-O? I TOLD YOU DINNER WAS INCLUDED WITH ADMISSION.
TONIGHT ONLY- Charlie Parker & P. PIPER
SCOTT HILBURN

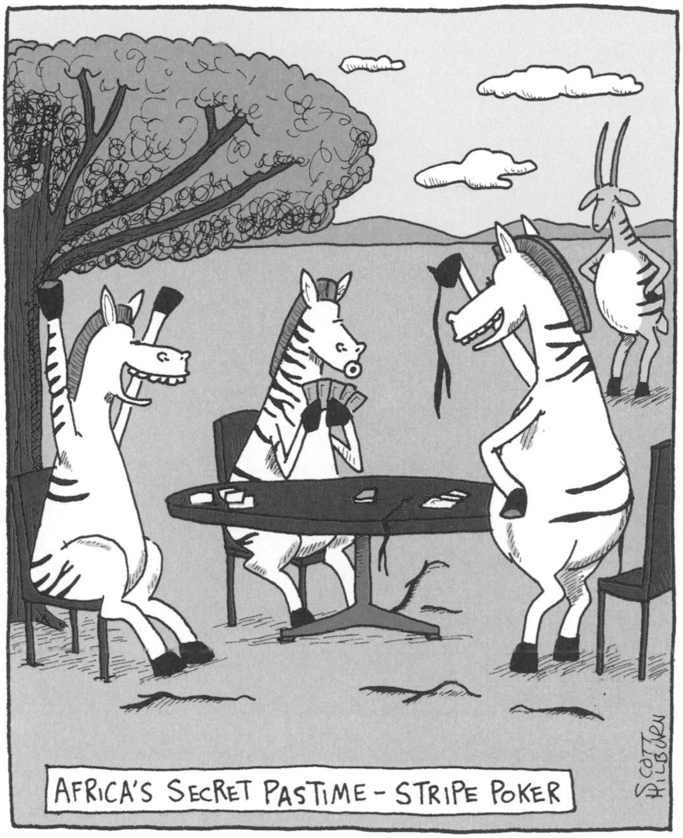
SCOTT HILBURN

AFRICA'S SECRET PASTIME - STRIPE POKER

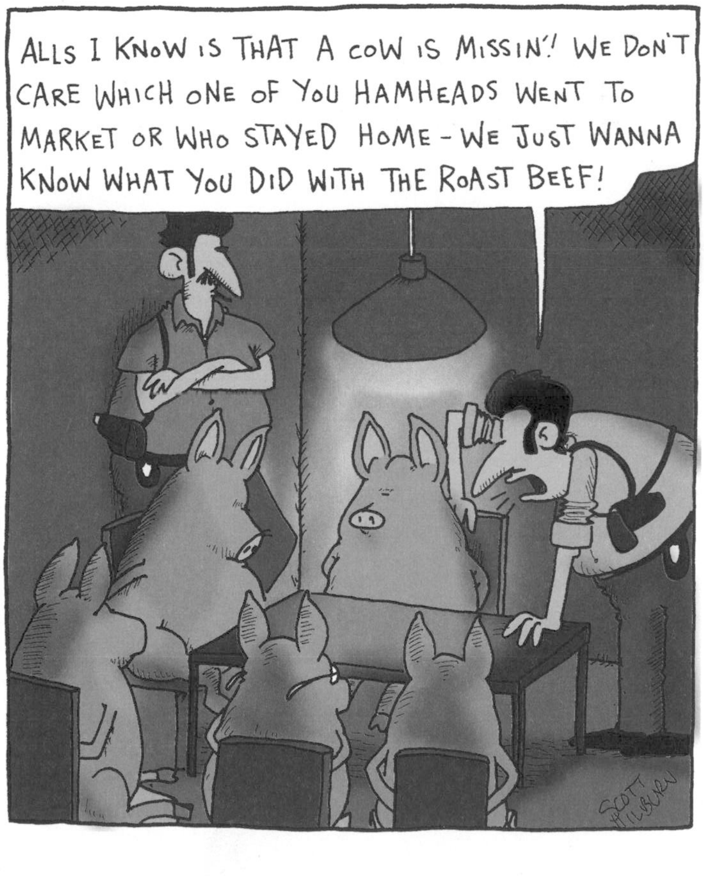
ALLS I KNOW IS THAT A COW IS MISSIN'! WE DON'T CARE WHICH ONE OF YOU HAMHEADS WENT TO MARKET OR WHO STAYED HOME - WE JUST WANNA KNOW WHAT YOU DID WITH THE ROAST BEEF!
SCOTT HILBURN

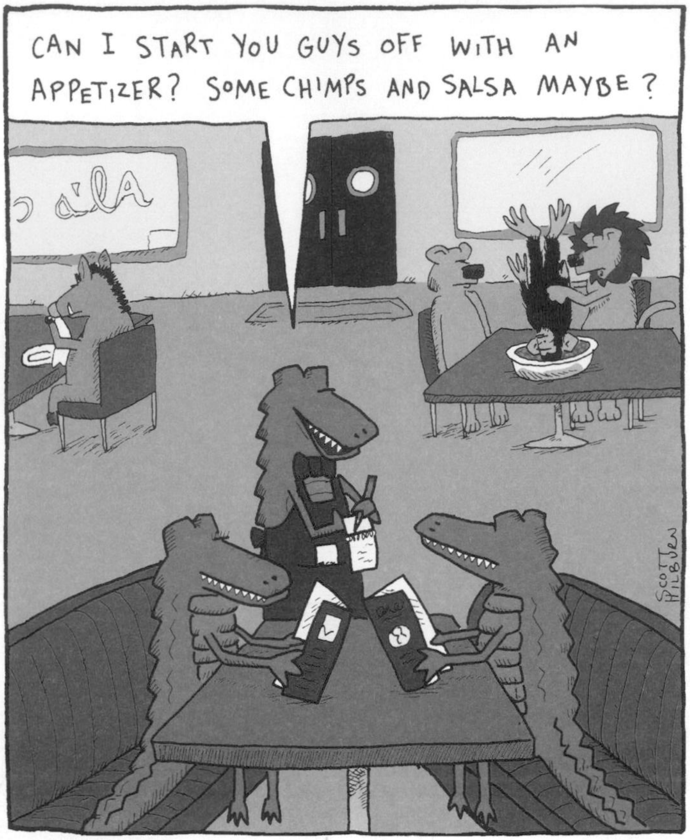
CAN I START YOU GUYS OFF WITH AN APPETIZER? SOME CHIMPS AND SALSA MAYBE?
SCOTT HILBURN

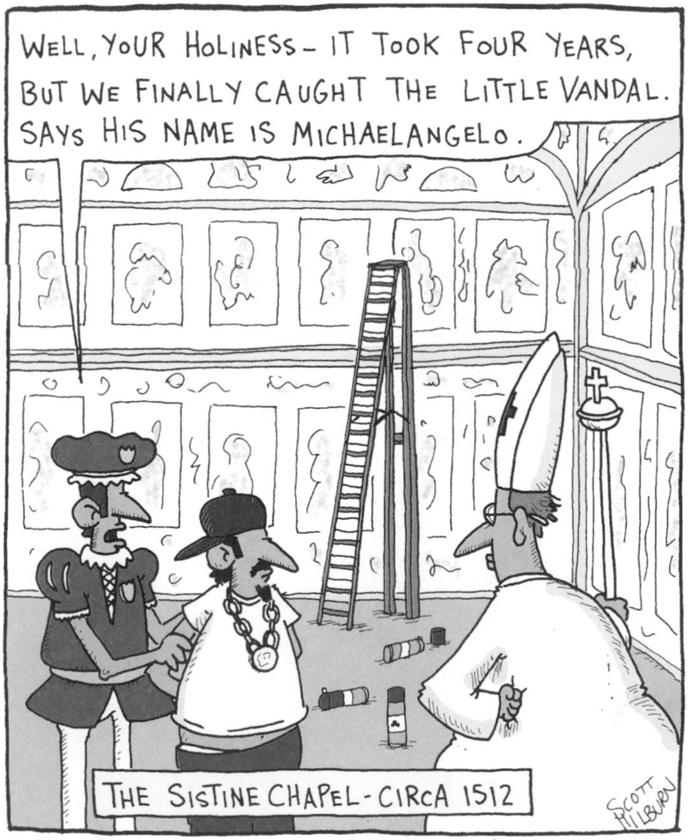
WELL, YOUR HOLINESS - IT TOOK FOUR YEARS, BUT WE FINALLY CAUGHT THE LITTLE VANDAL. SAYS HIS NAME IS MICHAELANGELO.
THE SISTINE CHAPEL - CIRCA 1512
SCOTT HILBURN

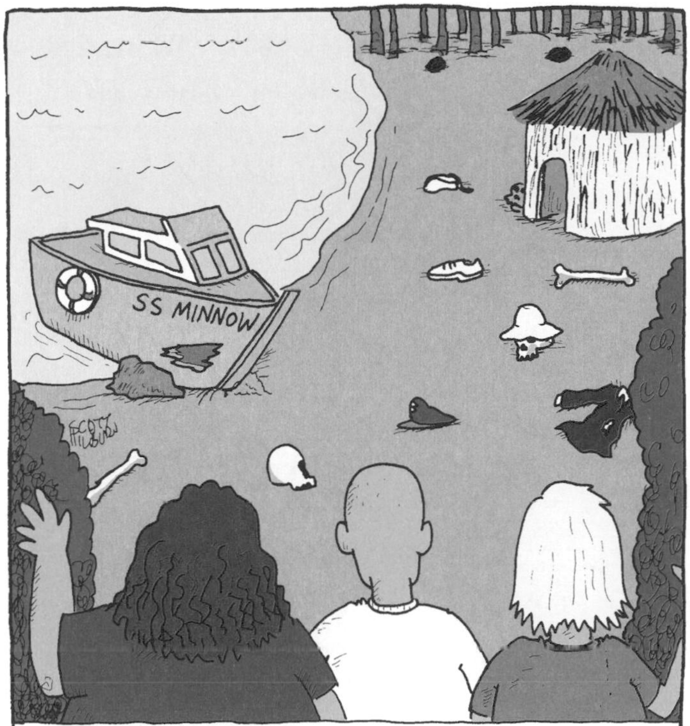
SS MINNOW
SCOTT HILBURN

LOCKE, HURLEY AND SAWYER STUMBLE UPON ANOTHER ABANDONED CAMPSITE AND MAKE A HORRIBLE DISCOVERY.

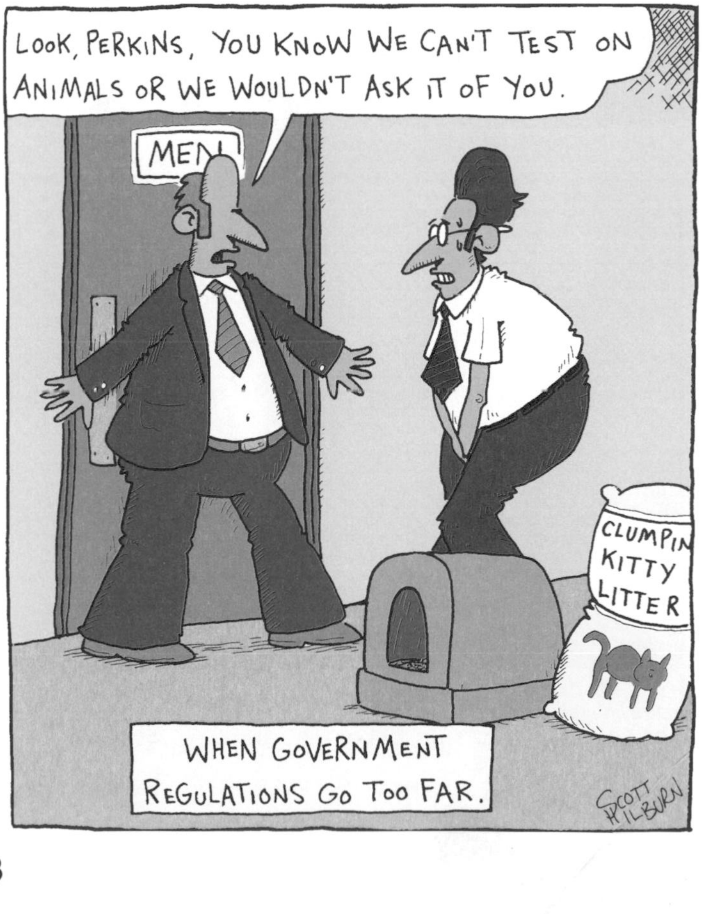
LOOK, PERKINS, YOU KNOW WE CAN'T TEST ON ANIMALS OR WE WOULDN'T ASK IT OF YOU.
MEN
CLUMPIN KITTY LITTER
SCOTT HILBURN

WHEN GOVERNMENT REGULATIONS GO TOO FAR.

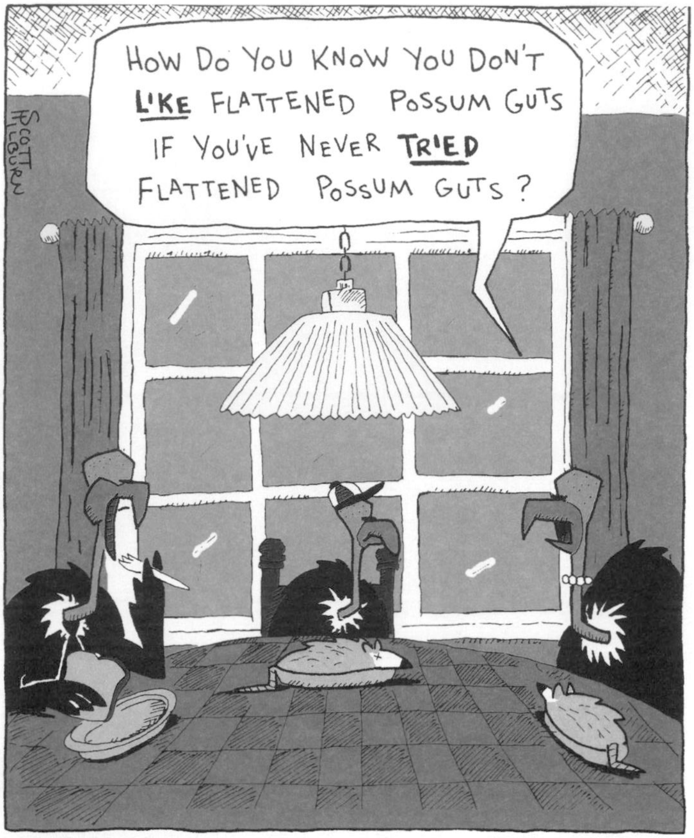
HOW DO YOU KNOW YOU DON'T LIKE FLATTENED POSSUM GUTS IF YOU'VE NEVER TRIED FLATTENED POSSUM GUTS?
SCOTT HILBURN

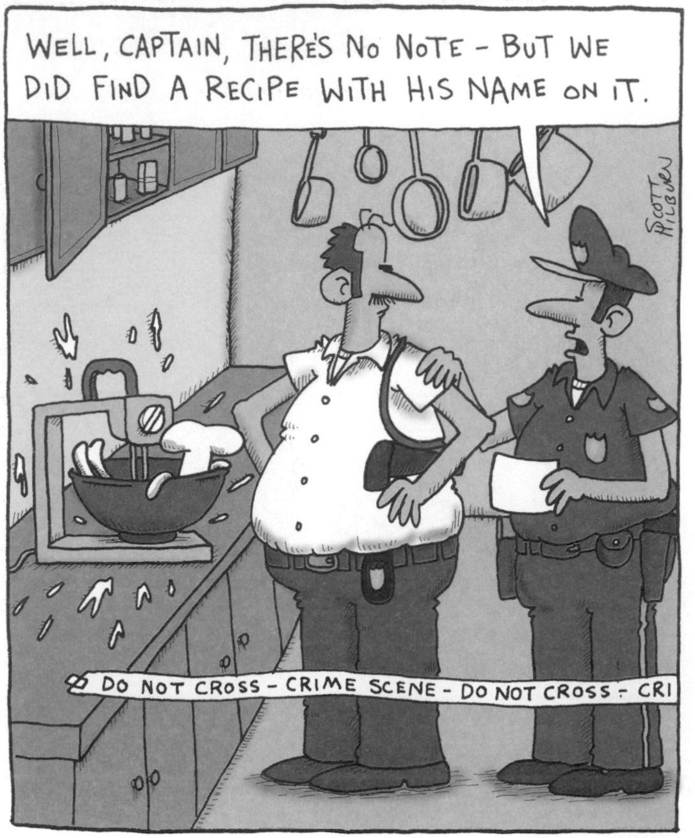
WELL, CAPTAIN, THERE'S NO NOTE - BUT WE DID FIND A RECIPE WITH HIS NAME ON IT.
DO NOT CROSS - CRIME SCENE - DO NOT CROSS - CRI
SCOTT HILBURN

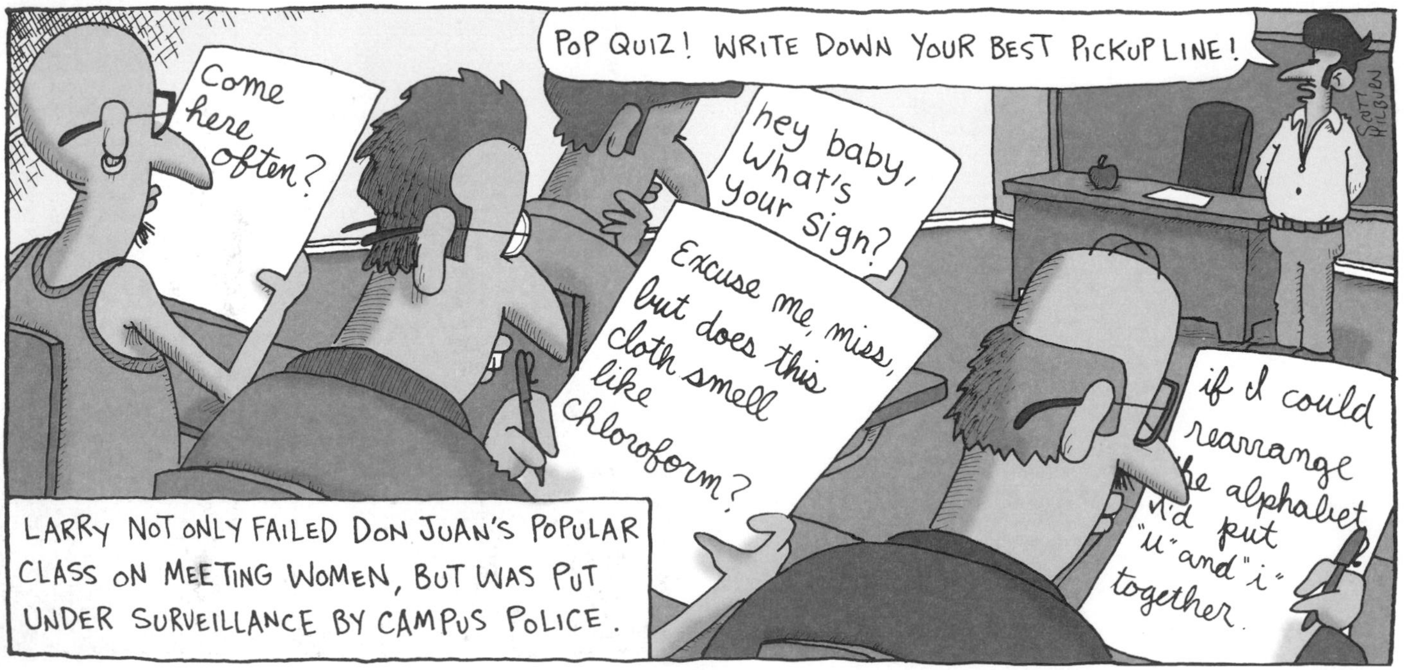
POP QUIZ! WRITE DOWN YOUR BEST PICKUP LINE!
Come here often?
hey baby, What's your sign?
Excuse me, miss, but does this cloth smell like chloroform?
if I could rearrange the alphabet I'd put "u" and "i" together.
SCOTT HILBURN
LARRY NOT ONLY FAILED DON JUAN'S POPULAR CLASS ON MEETING WOMEN, BUT WAS PUT UNDER SURVEILLANCE BY CAMPUS POLICE.

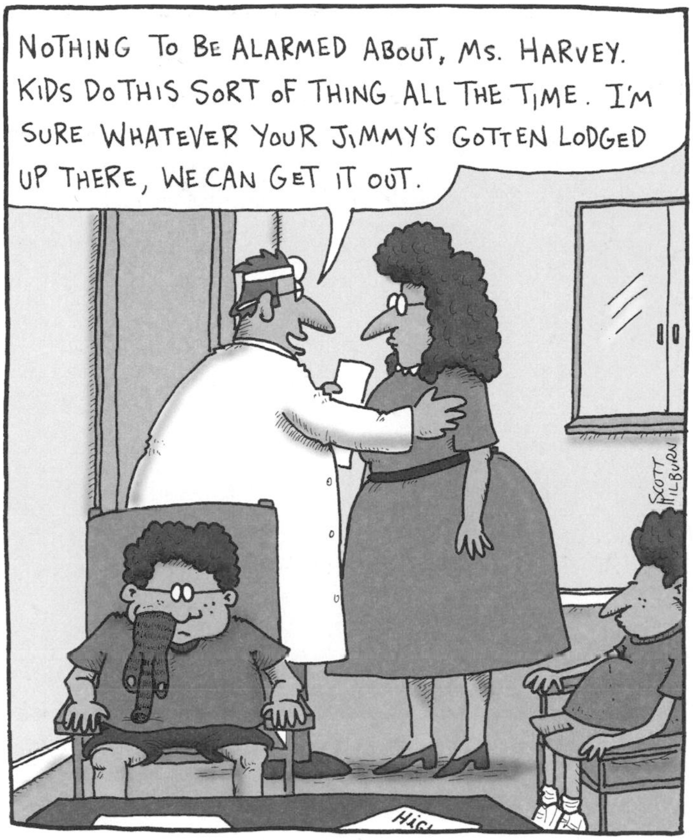
NOTHING TO BE ALARMED ABOUT, MS. HARVEY. KIDS DO THIS SORT OF THING ALL THE TIME. I'M SURE WHATEVER YOUR JIMMY'S GOTTEN LODGED UP THERE, WE CAN GET IT OUT.
SCOTT HILBURN

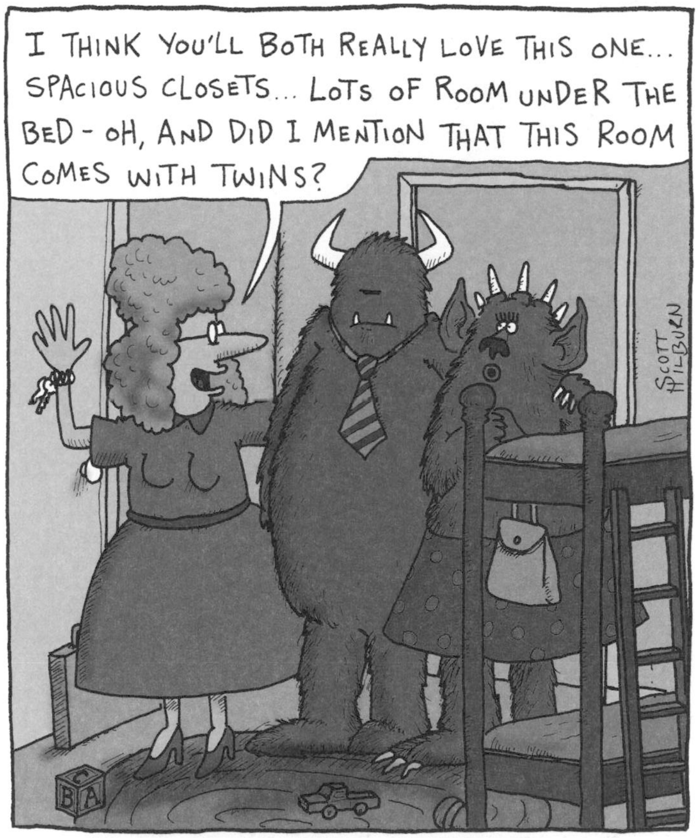
I THINK YOU'LL BOTH REALLY LOVE THIS ONE... SPACIOUS CLOSETS... LOTS OF ROOM UNDER THE BED - OH, AND DID I MENTION THAT THIS ROOM COMES WITH TWINS?
SCOTT HILBURN

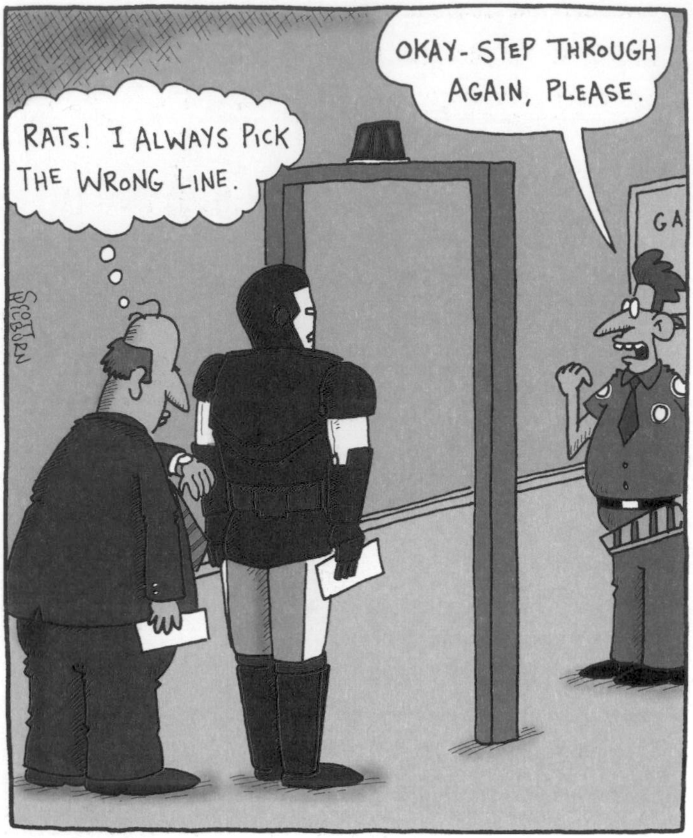
RATS! I ALWAYS PICK THE WRONG LINE.
OKAY- STEP THROUGH AGAIN, PLEASE.
GA
SCOTT HILBURN

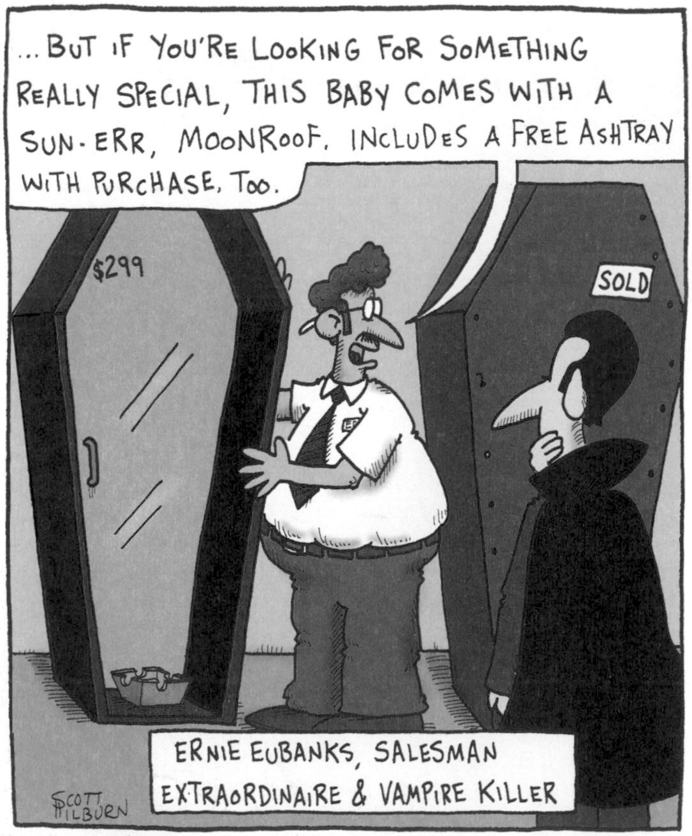
...BUT IF YOU'RE LOOKING FOR SOMETHING REALLY SPECIAL, THIS BABY COMES WITH A SUN-ERR, MOONROOF. INCLUDES A FREE ASHTRAY WITH PURCHASE, TOO.
$299
SOLD
SCOTT HILBURN

ERNIE EUBANKS, SALESMAN EXTRAORDINAIRE & VAMPIRE KILLER

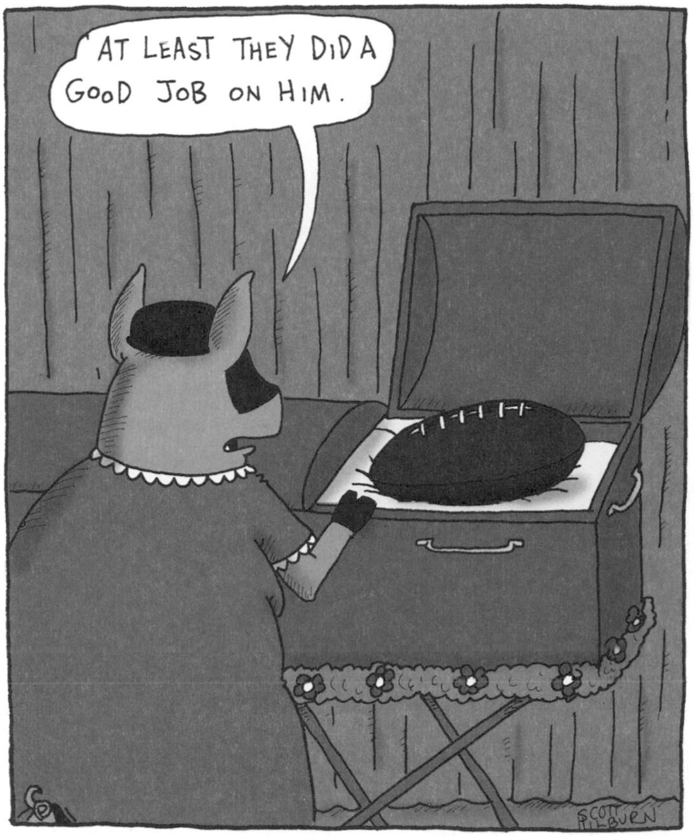
AT LEAST THEY DID A GOOD JOB ON HIM.
SCOTT HILBURN

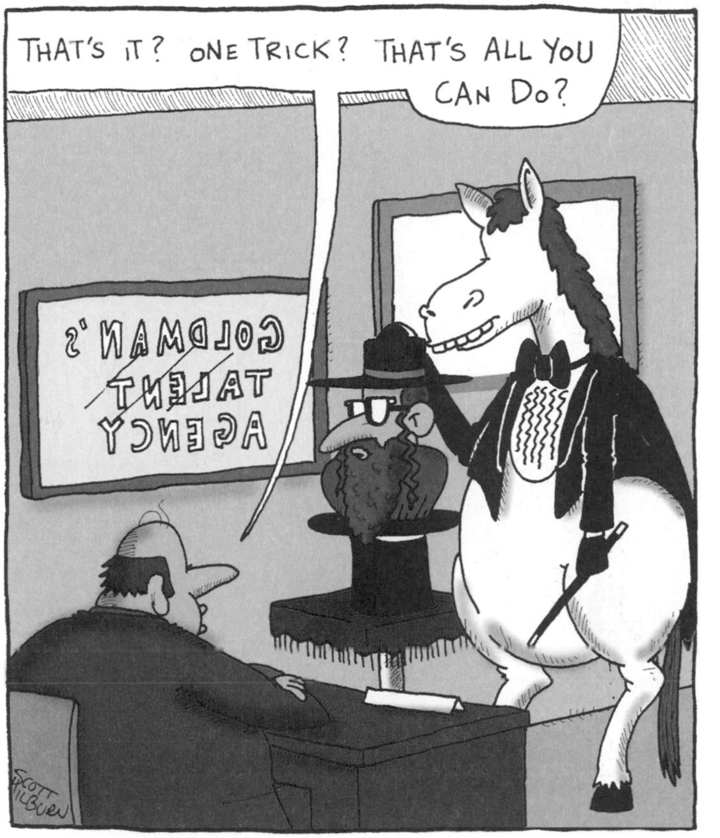
THAT'S IT? ONE TRICK? THAT'S ALL YOU CAN DO?
GOLDMAN'S
TALENT
AGENCY
SCOTT HILBURN

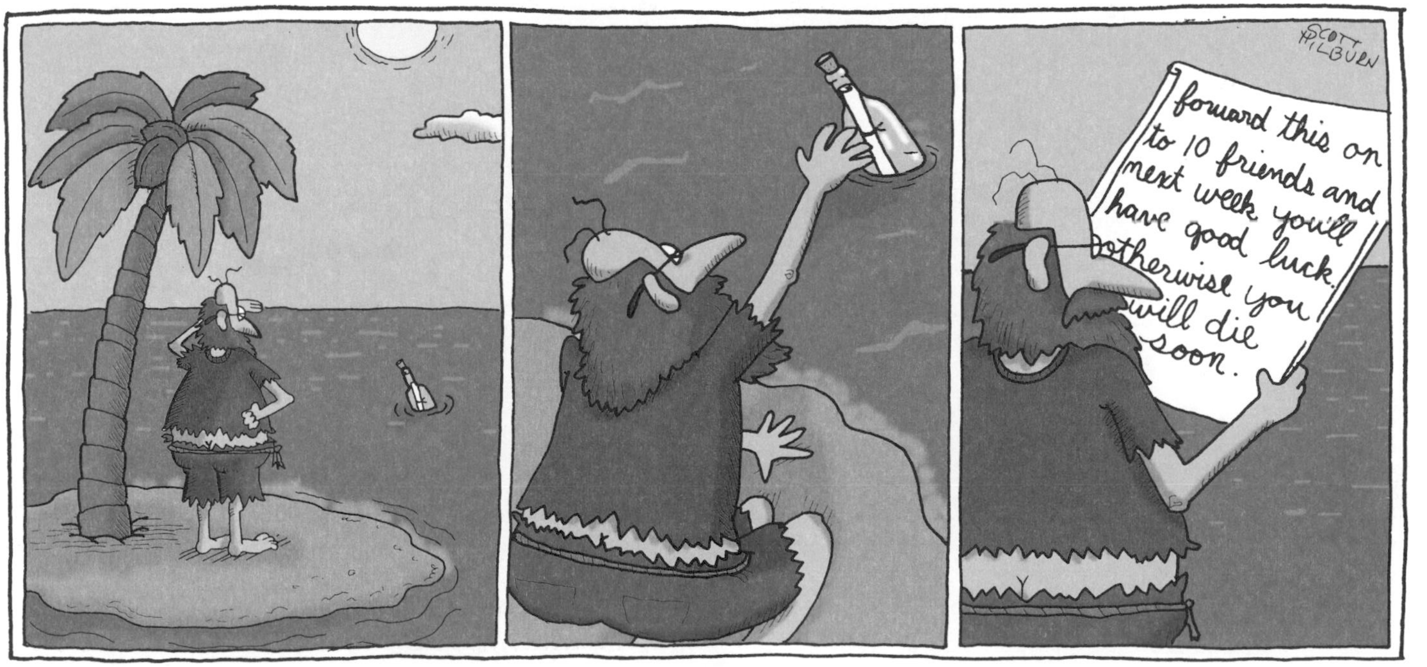
SCOTT HILBURN
forward this on to 10 friends and next week you'll have good luck. otherwise you will die soon.

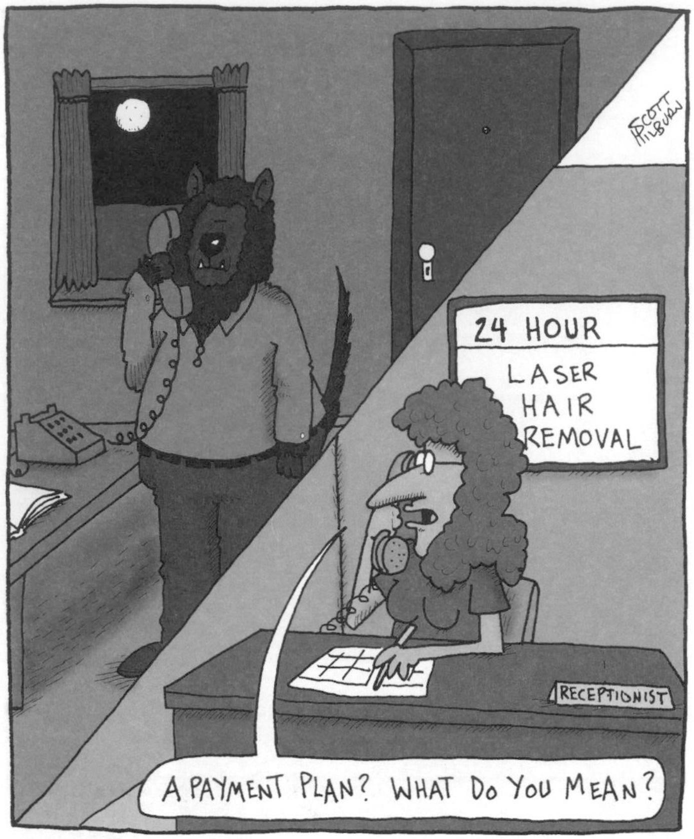
24 HOUR
LASER HAIR REMOVAL
RECEPTIONIST
A PAYMENT PLAN? WHAT DO YOU MEAN?

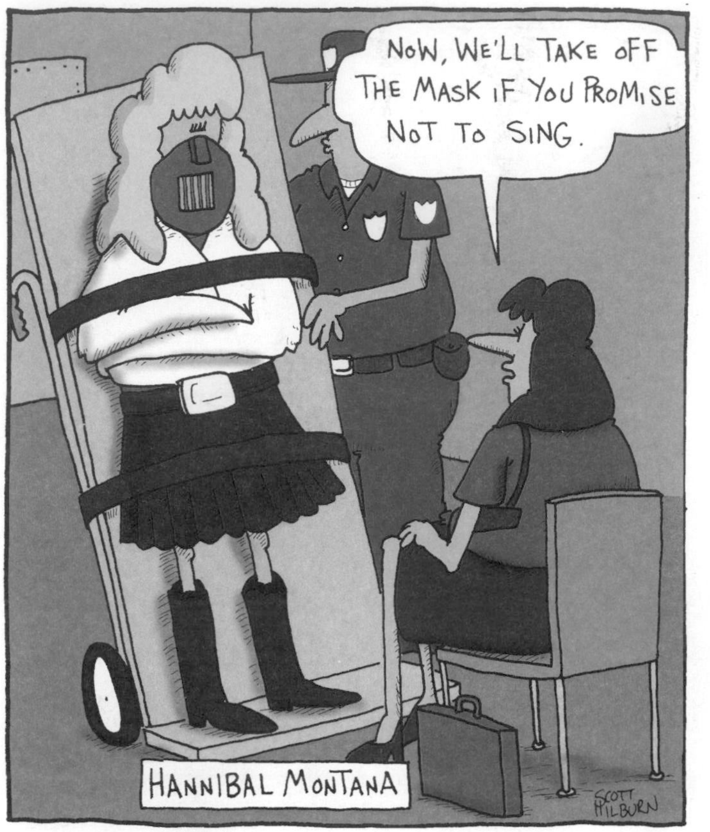
NOW, WE'LL TAKE OFF THE MASK IF YOU PROMISE NOT TO SING.
HANNIBAL MONTANA

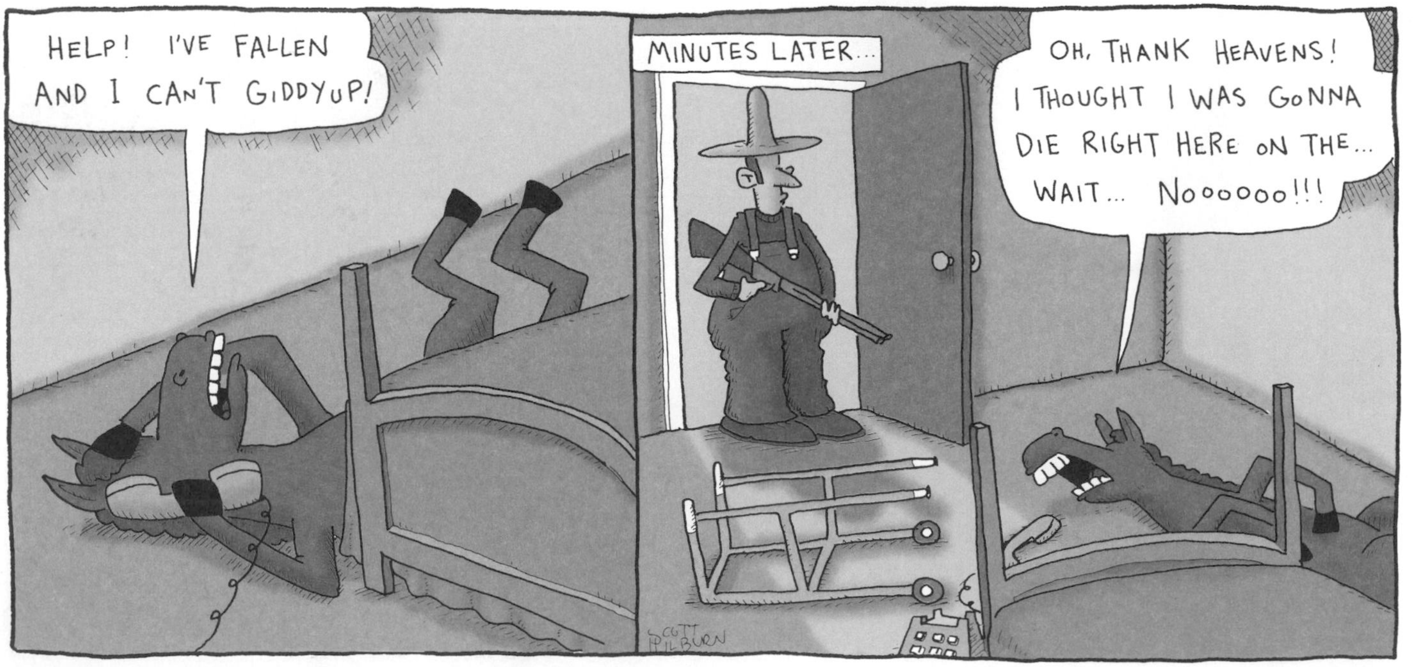
HELP! I'VE FALLEN AND I CAN'T GIDDYUP!
MINUTES LATER...
OH, THANK HEAVENS! I THOUGHT I WAS GONNA DIE RIGHT HERE ON THE... WAIT... Noooooo!!!

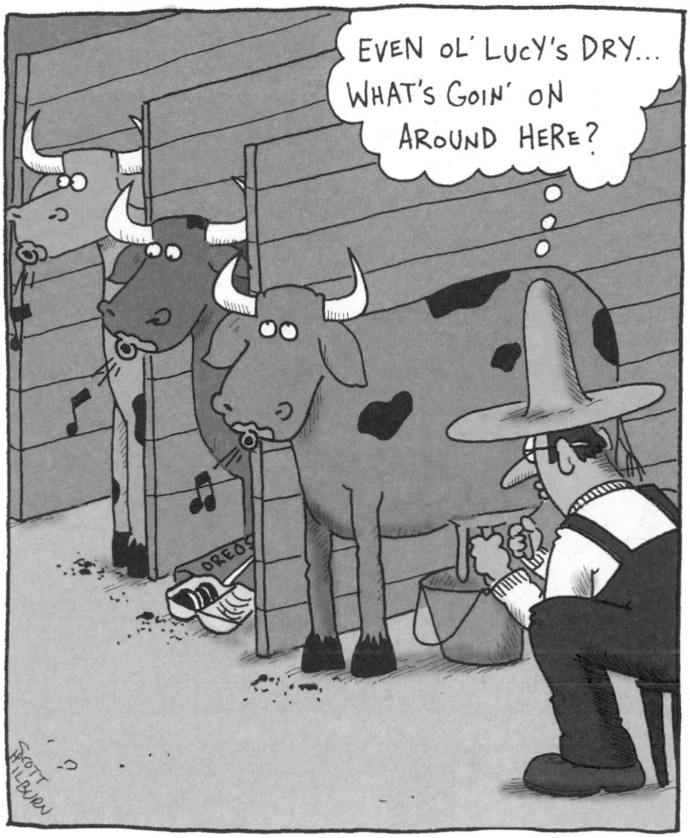
EVEN OL' LUCY'S DRY... WHAT'S GOIN' ON AROUND HERE?
OREOS
SCOTT HILBURN

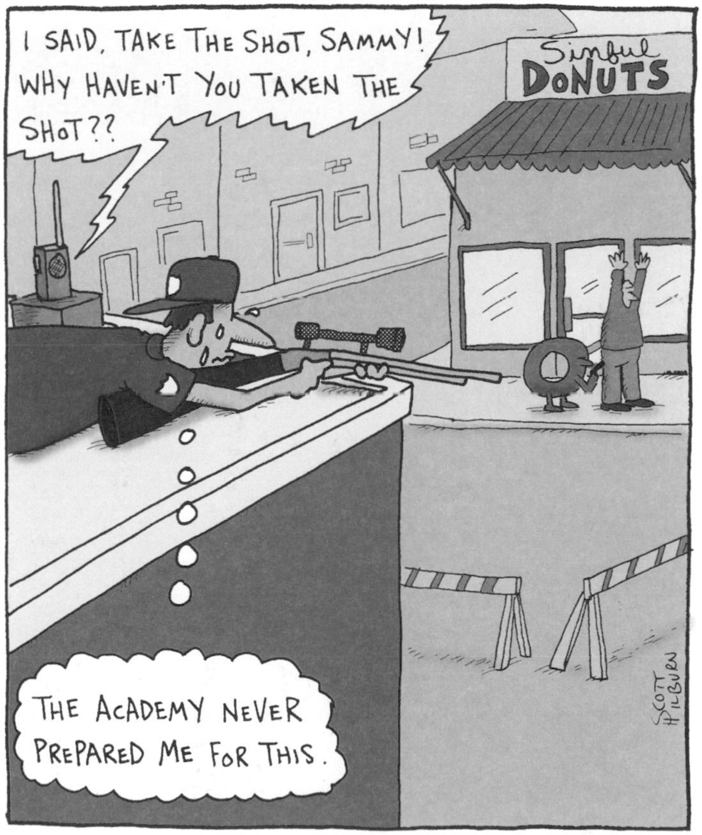
I SAID, TAKE THE SHOT, SAMMY! WHY HAVEN'T YOU TAKEN THE SHOT??
Sinful DONUTS
THE ACADEMY NEVER PREPARED ME FOR THIS.
SCOTT HILBURN

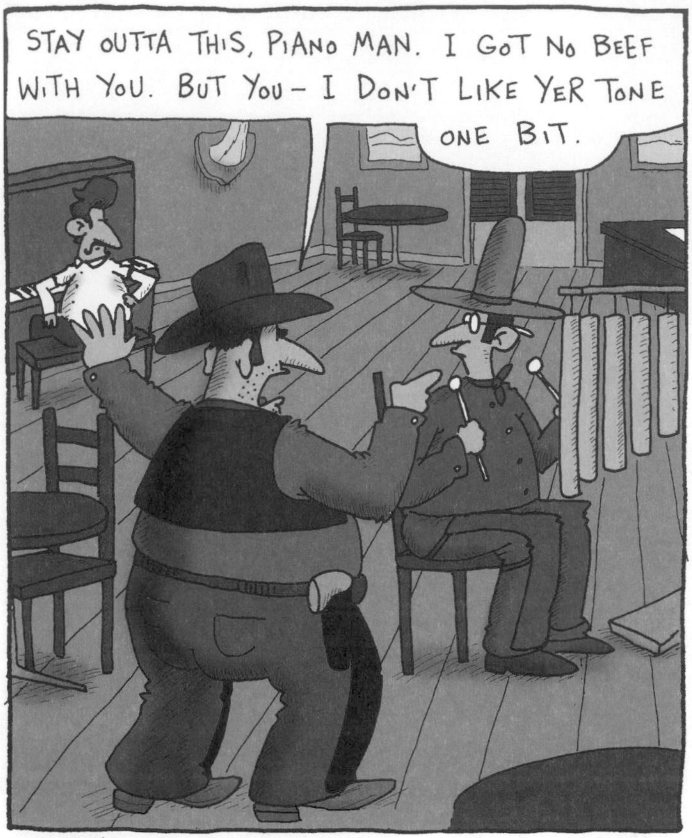
STAY OUTTA THIS, PIANO MAN. I GOT NO BEEF WITH YOU. BUT YOU – I DON'T LIKE YER TONE ONE BIT.

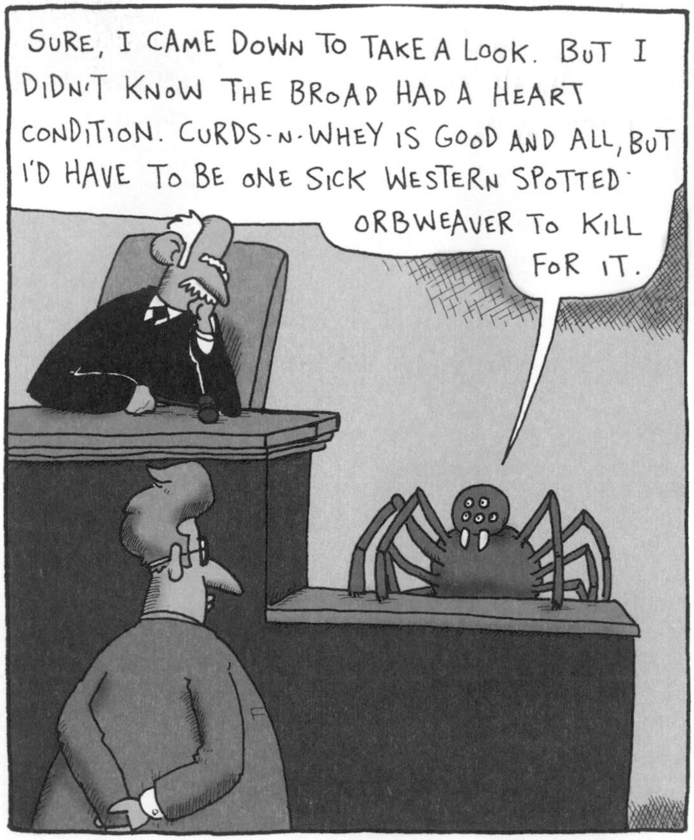
SURE, I CAME DOWN TO TAKE A LOOK. BUT I DIDN'T KNOW THE BROAD HAD A HEART CONDITION. CURDS-N-WHEY IS GOOD AND ALL, BUT I'D HAVE TO BE ONE SICK WESTERN SPOTTED-ORBWEAVER TO KILL FOR IT.

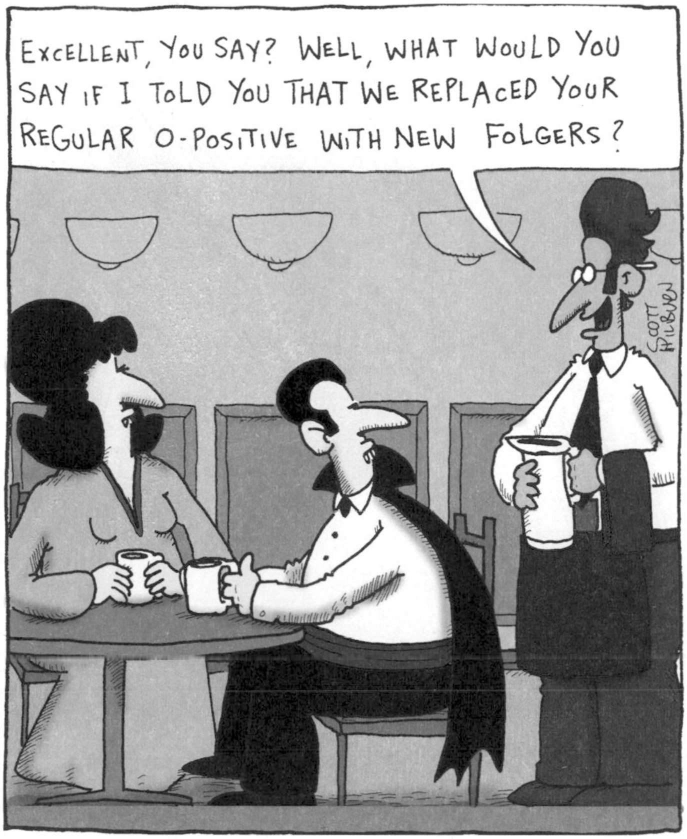
EXCELLENT, YOU SAY? WELL, WHAT WOULD YOU SAY IF I TOLD YOU THAT WE REPLACED YOUR REGULAR O-POSITIVE WITH NEW FOLGERS?
SCOTT HILBURN

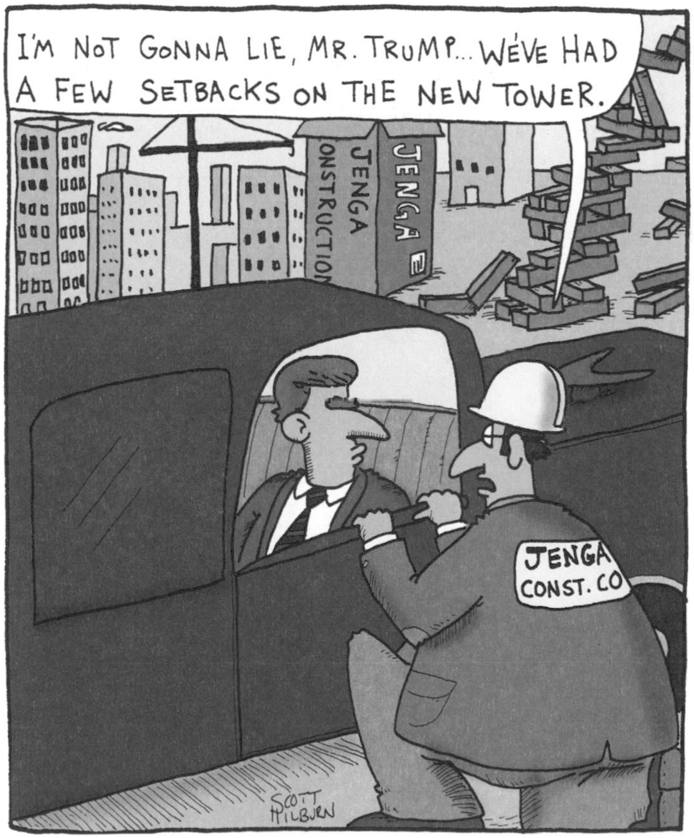
I'M NOT GONNA LIE, MR. TRUMP... WE'VE HAD A FEW SETBACKS ON THE NEW TOWER.
JENGA
JENGA
JENGA CONSTRUCTION
JENGA CONST. CO
SCOTT HILBURN

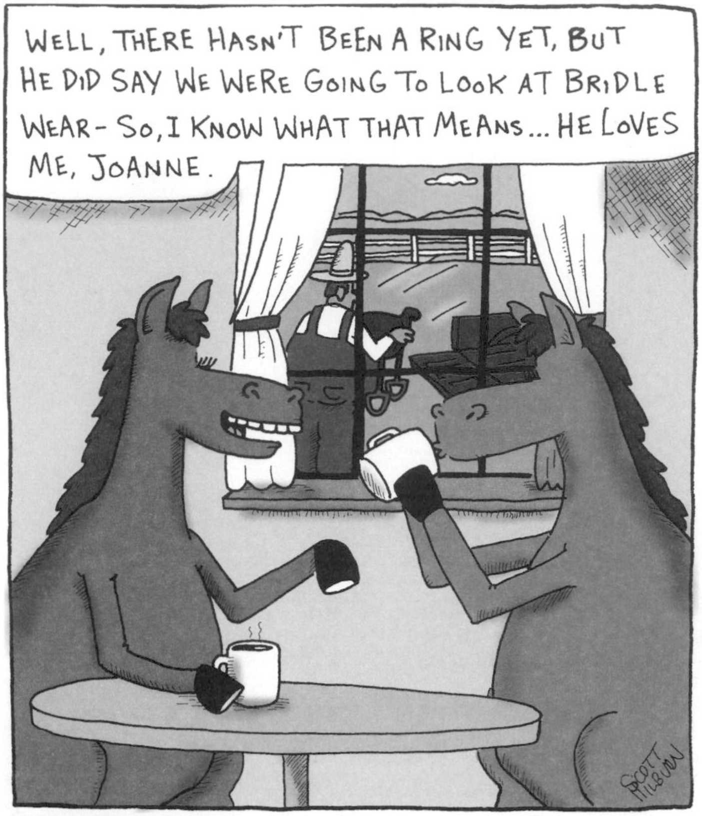
WELL, THERE HASN'T BEEN A RING YET, BUT HE DID SAY WE WERE GOING TO LOOK AT BRIDLE WEAR- SO, I KNOW WHAT THAT MEANS... HE LOVES ME, JOANNE.
SCOTT HILBURN

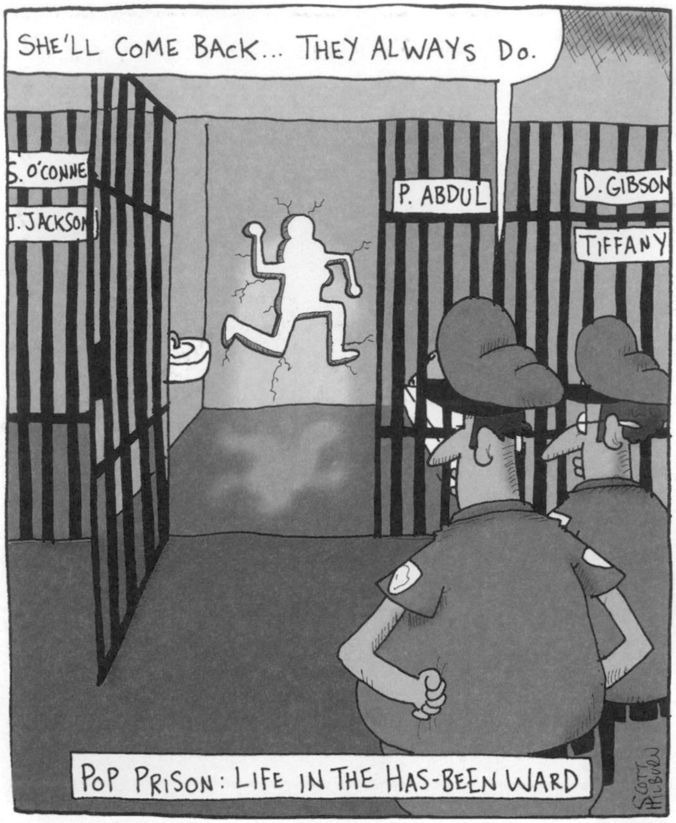
SHE'LL COME BACK... THEY ALWAYS DO.
S. O'CONNE
J. JACKSON
P. ABDUL
D. GIBSON
TIFFANY
SCOTT HILBURN

POP PRISON: LIFE IN THE HAS-BEEN WARD

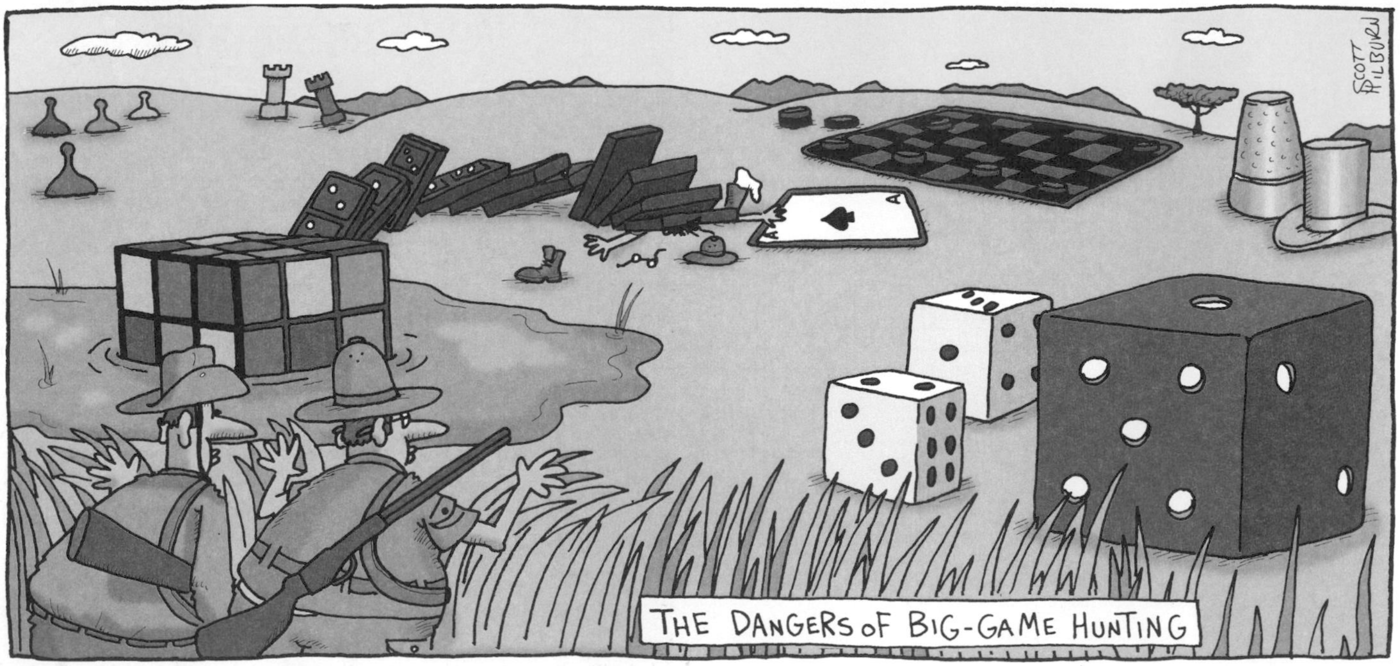
SCOTT HILBURN

THE DANGERS OF BIG-GAME HUNTING

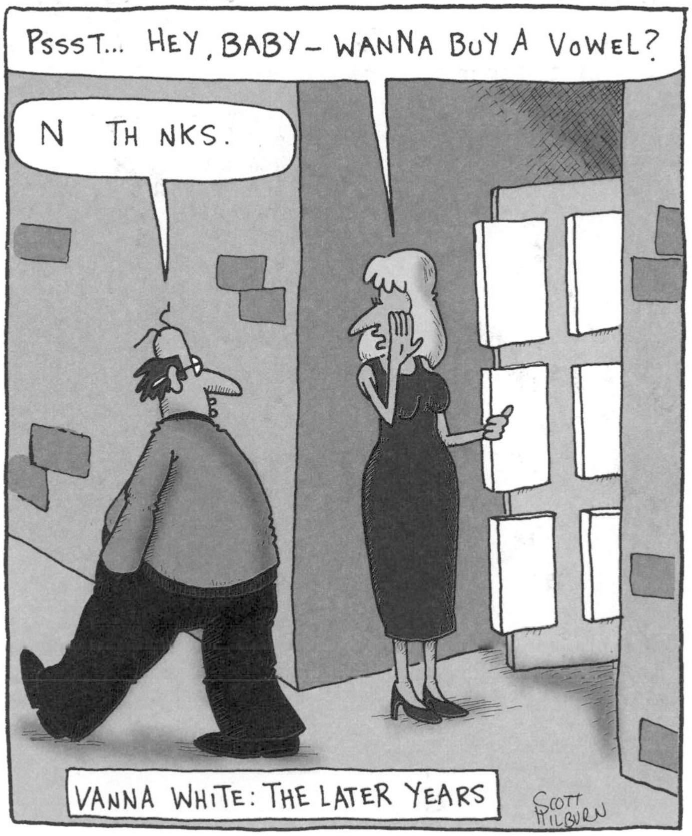
PSSST... HEY, BABY– WANNA BUY A VOWEL?
N TH NKS.
VANNA WHITE: THE LATER YEARS
SCOTT HILBURN

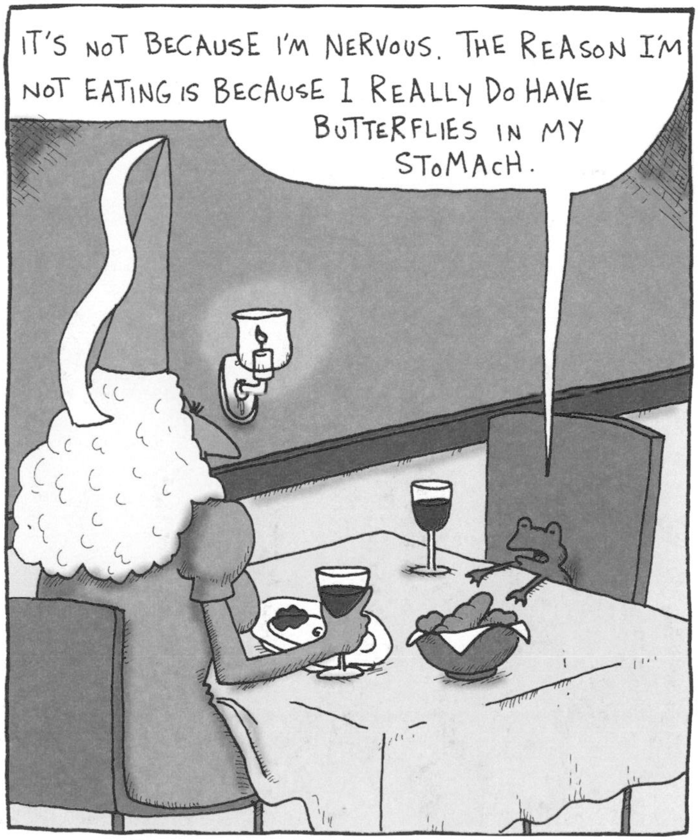
IT'S NOT BECAUSE I'M NERVOUS. THE REASON I'M NOT EATING IS BECAUSE I REALLY DO HAVE BUTTERFLIES IN MY STOMACH.

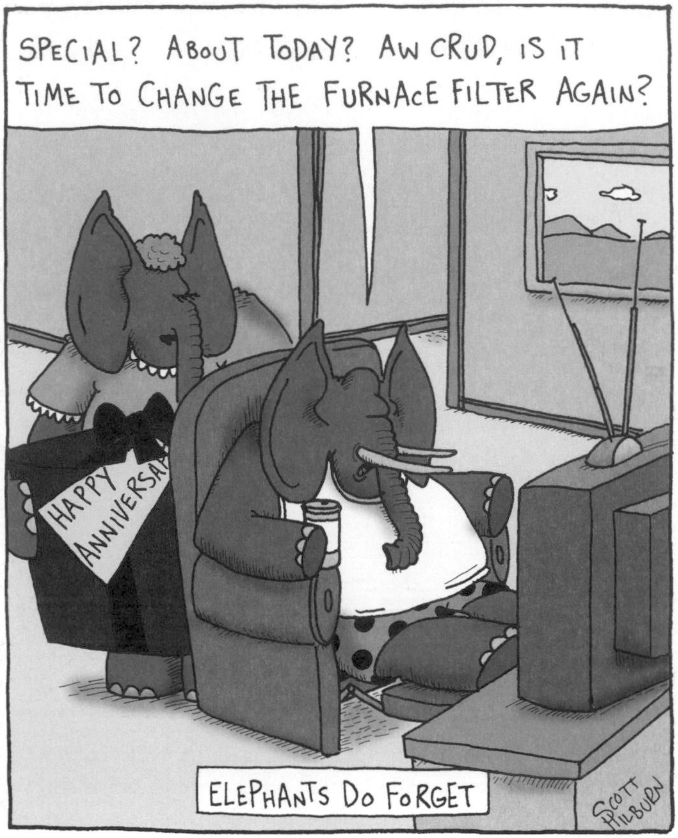
SPECIAL? ABOUT TODAY? AW CRUD, IS IT TIME TO CHANGE THE FURNACE FILTER AGAIN?
HAPPY ANNIVERSA
SCOTT HILBURN
ELEPHANTS DO FORGET

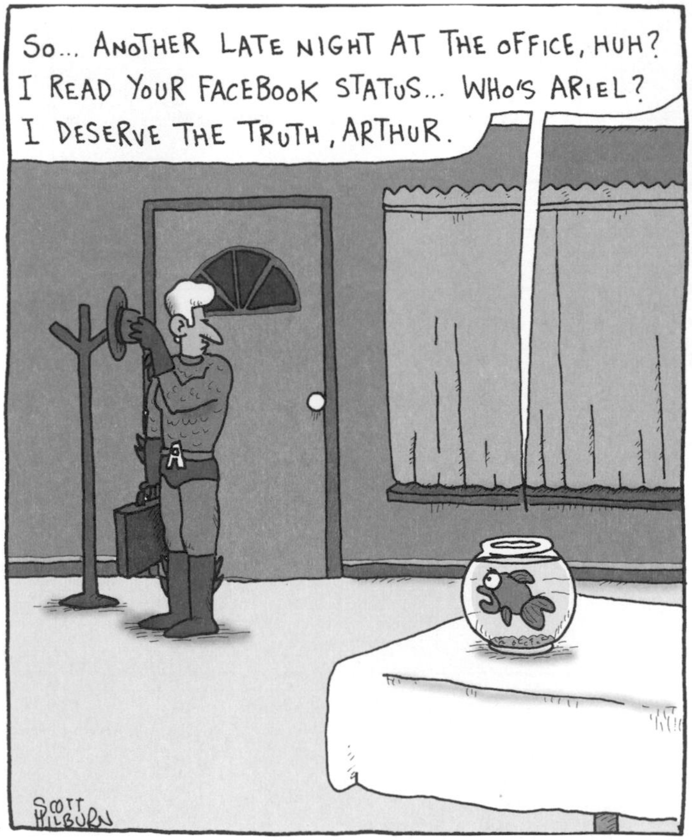
SO... ANOTHER LATE NIGHT AT THE OFFICE, HUH? I READ YOUR FACEBOOK STATUS... WHO'S ARIEL? I DESERVE THE TRUTH, ARTHUR.
A
SCOTT HILBURN

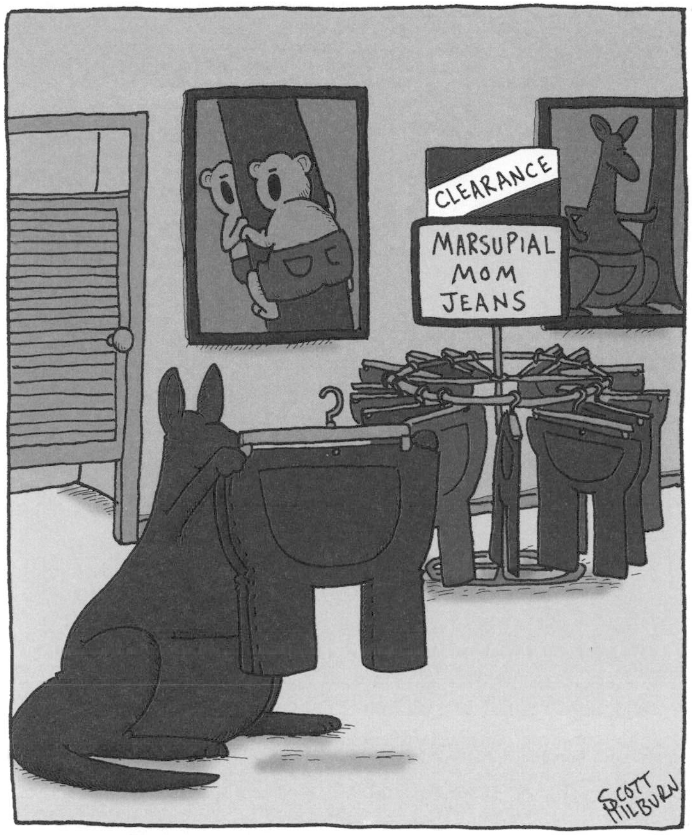
CLEARANCE
MARSUPIAL MOM JEANS
SCOTT HILBURN

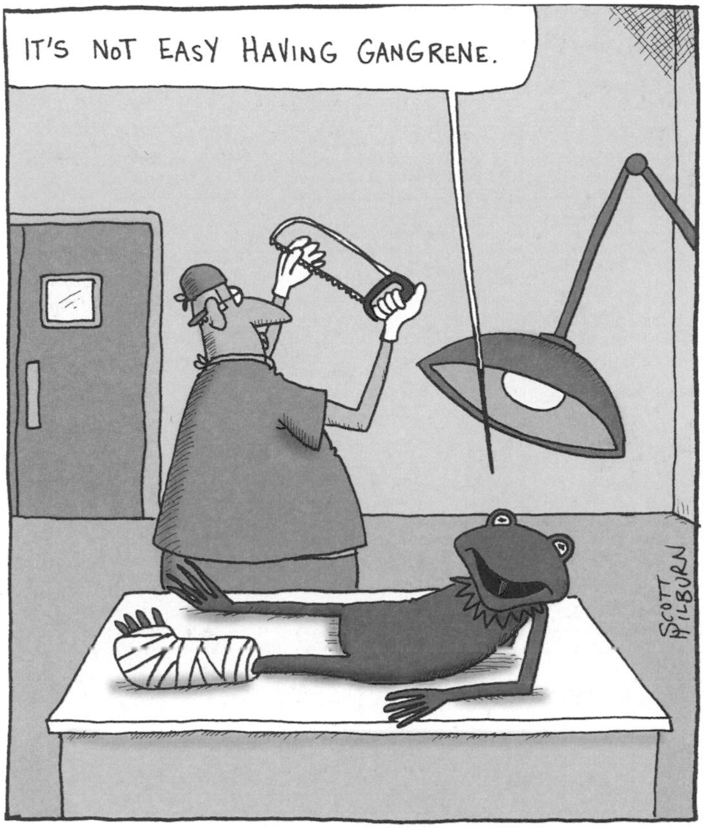
IT'S NOT EASY HAVING GANGRENE.
SCOTT HILBURN

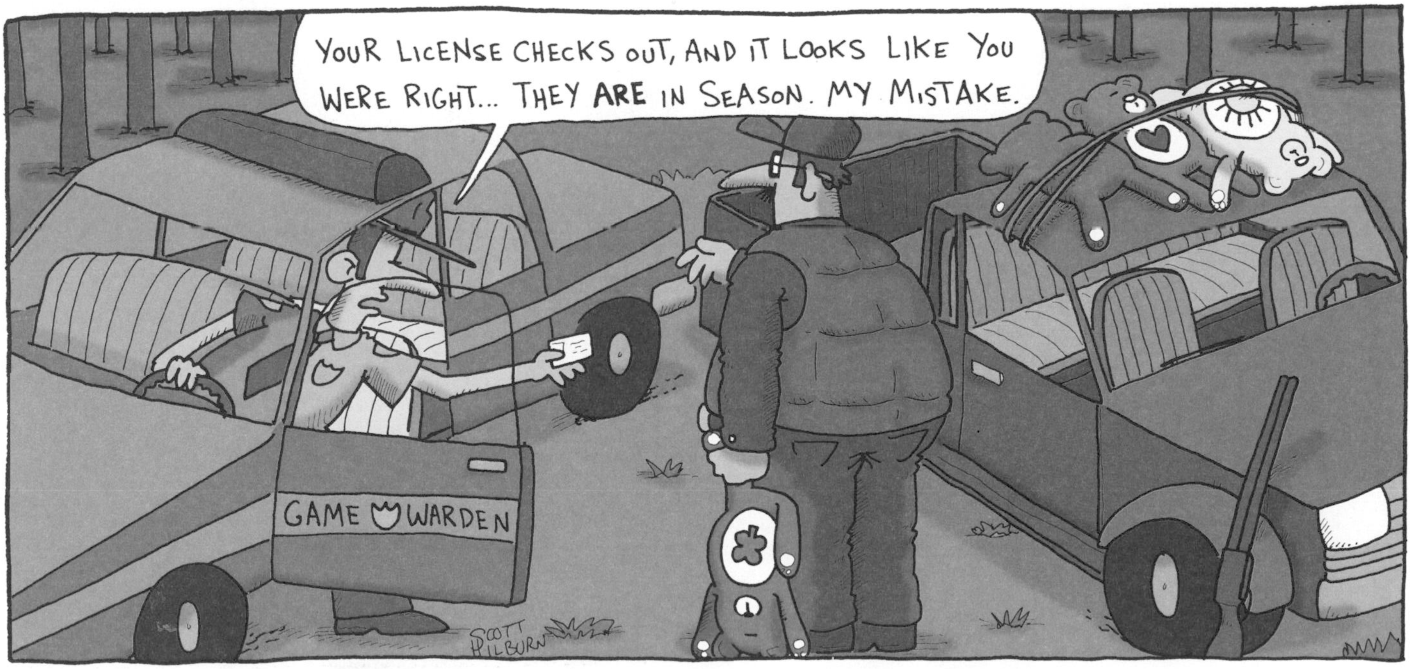
YOUR LICENSE CHECKS OUT, AND IT LOOKS LIKE YOU WERE RIGHT... THEY ARE IN SEASON. MY MISTAKE.
GAME WARDEN
SCOTT HILBURN

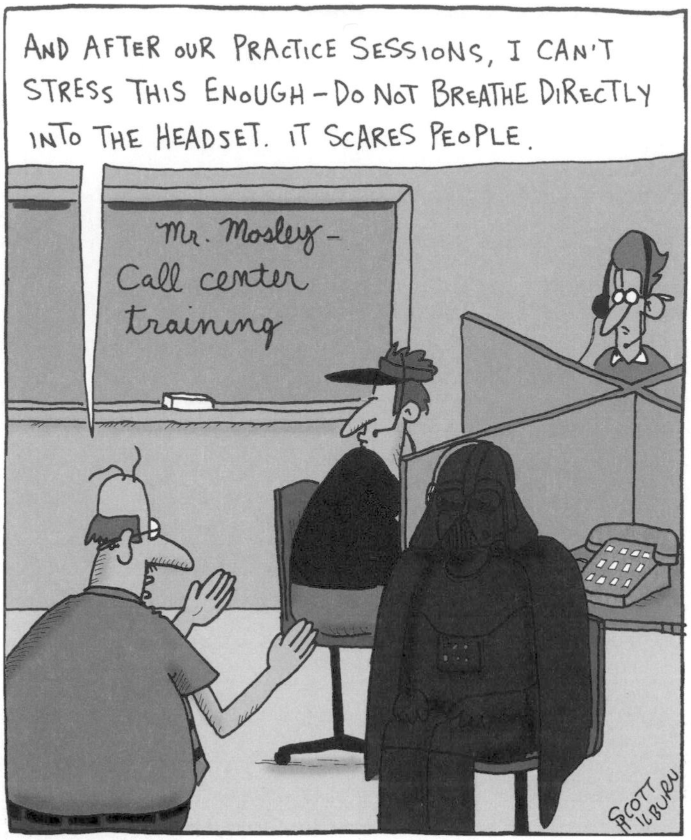
AND AFTER OUR PRACTICE SESSIONS, I CAN'T STRESS THIS ENOUGH – DO NOT BREATHE DIRECTLY INTO THE HEADSET. IT SCARES PEOPLE.
Mr. Mosley – Call center training
SCOTT HILBURN

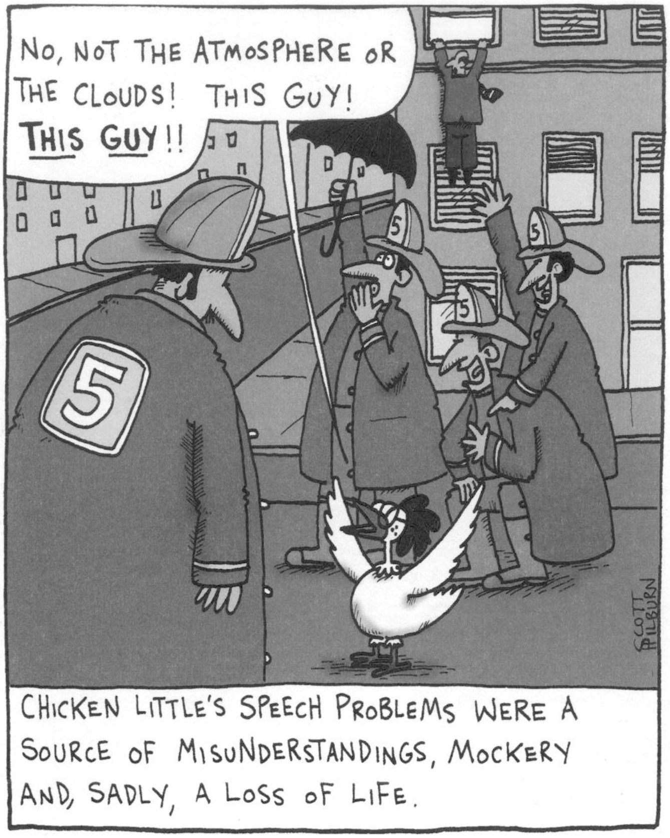
NO, NOT THE ATMOSPHERE OR THE CLOUDS! THIS GUY! THIS GUY!!
5
SCOTT HILBURN
CHICKEN LITTLE'S SPEECH PROBLEMS WERE A SOURCE OF MISUNDERSTANDINGS, MOCKERY AND, SADLY, A LOSS OF LIFE.

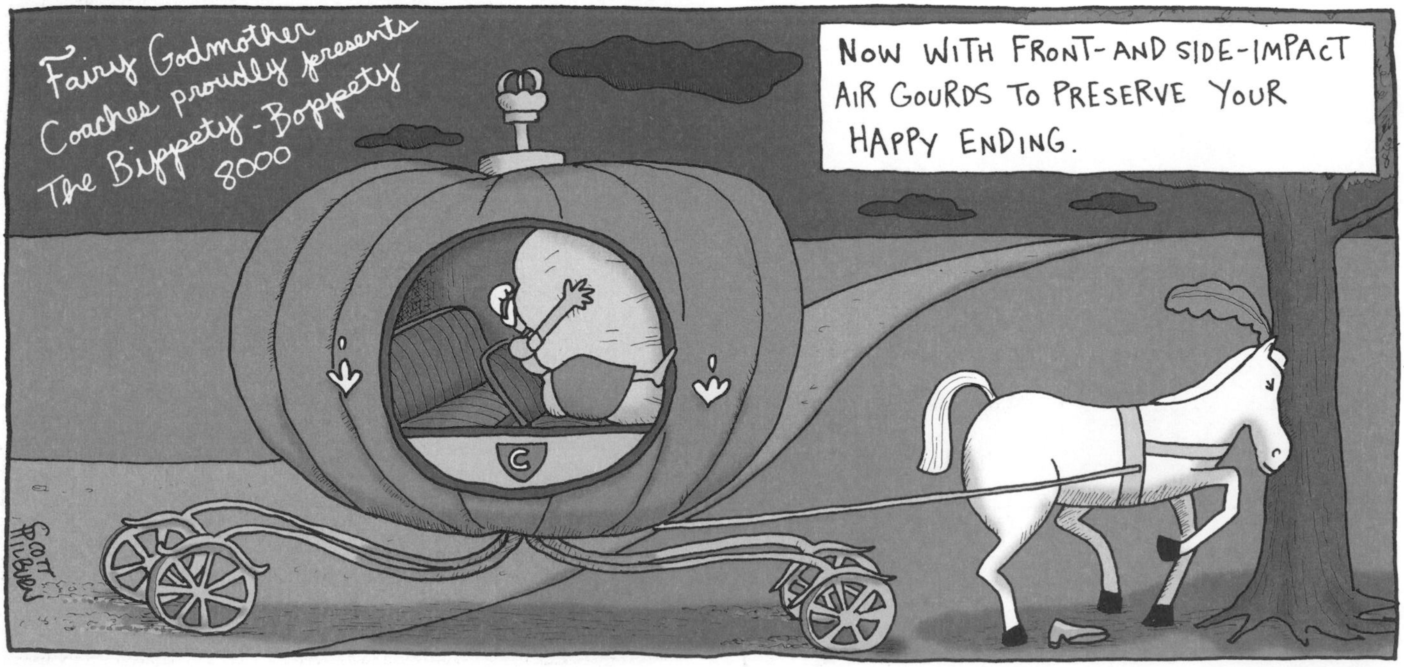
Fairy Godmother Coaches proudly presents The Bippety-Boppety 8000
NOW WITH FRONT- AND SIDE-IMPACT AIR GOURDS TO PRESERVE YOUR HAPPY ENDING.
C
SCOTT HILBURN

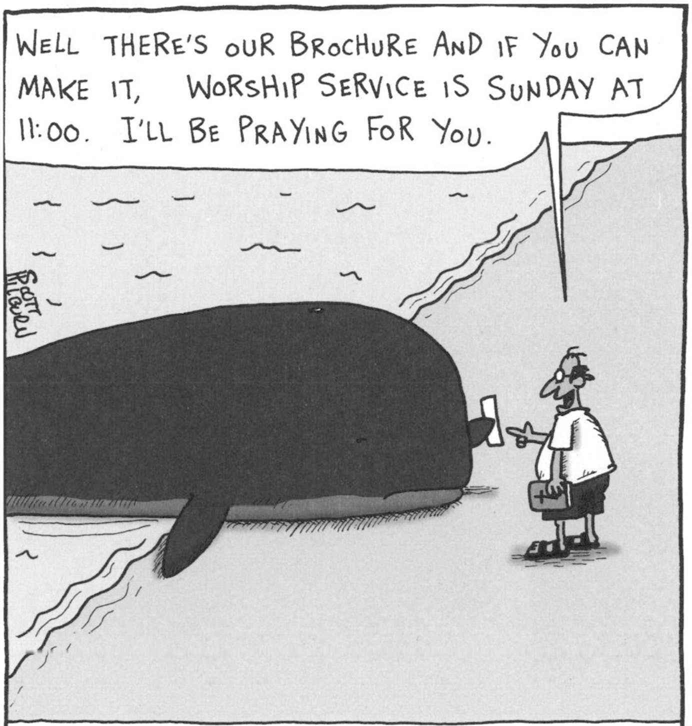
WELL THERE'S OUR BROCHURE AND IF YOU CAN MAKE IT, WORSHIP SERVICE IS SUNDAY AT 11:00. I'LL BE PRAYING FOR YOU.

IN HIS OWN WAY, TODD DOES HIS PART TO SAVE THE WHALES.

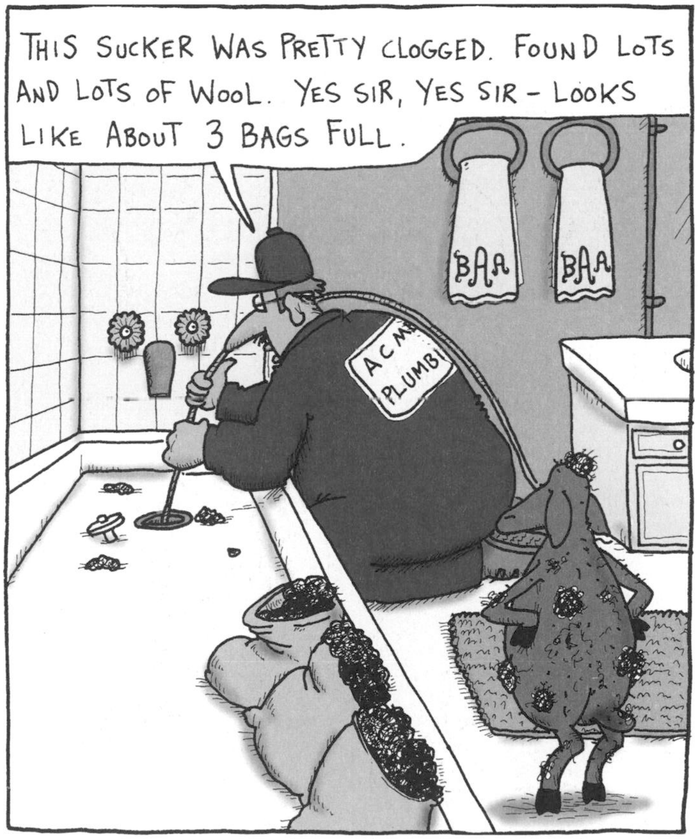
THIS SUCKER WAS PRETTY CLOGGED. FOUND LOTS AND LOTS OF WOOL. YES SIR, YES SIR - LOOKS LIKE ABOUT 3 BAGS FULL.
BAA
BAA

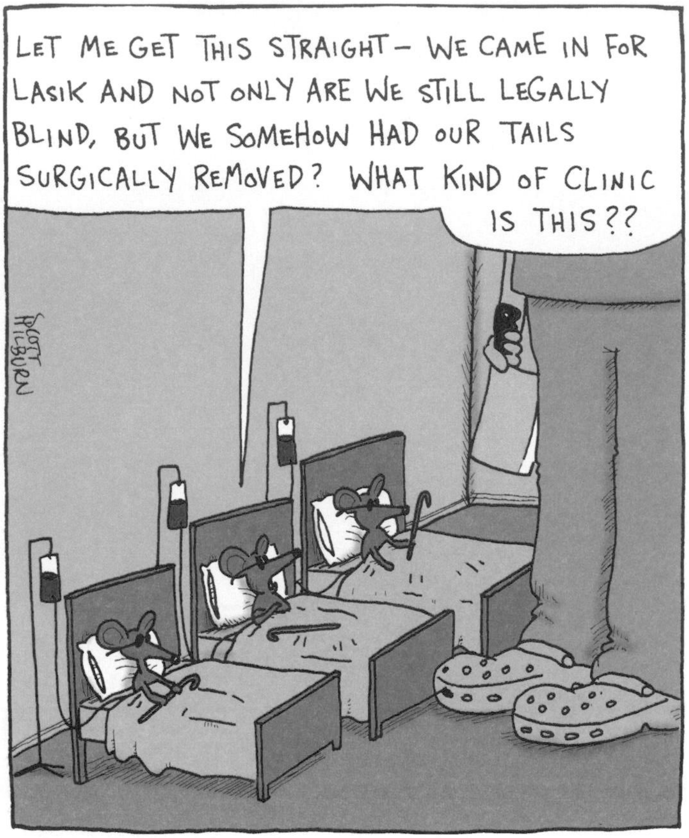
LET ME GET THIS STRAIGHT– WE CAME IN FOR LASIK AND NOT ONLY ARE WE STILL LEGALLY BLIND, BUT WE SOMEHOW HAD OUR TAILS SURGICALLY REMOVED? WHAT KIND OF CLINIC IS THIS??
SCOTT HILBURN

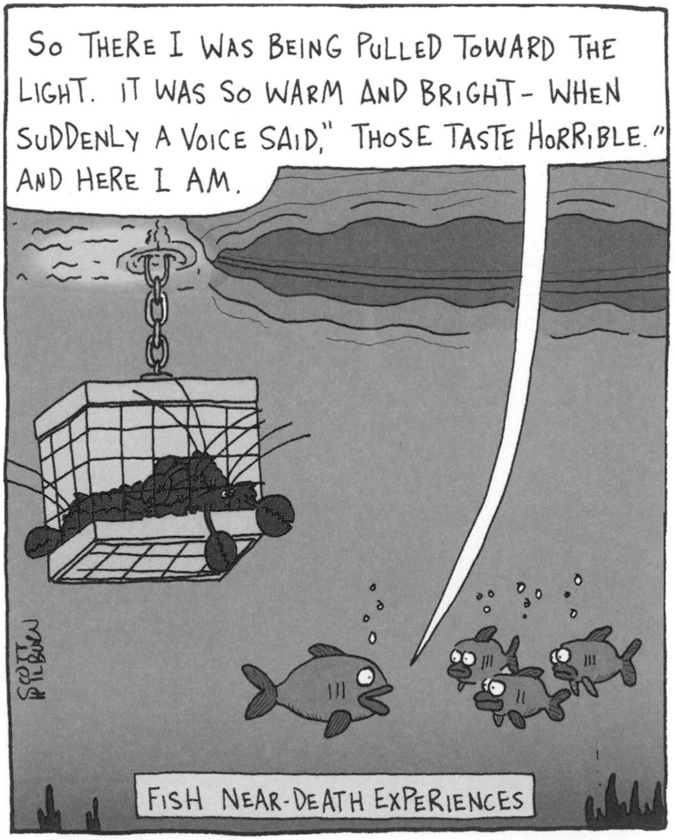
SO THERE I WAS BEING PULLED TOWARD THE LIGHT. IT WAS SO WARM AND BRIGHT– WHEN SUDDENLY A VOICE SAID," THOSE TASTE HORRIBLE." AND HERE I AM.
SCOTT HILBURN
FISH NEAR-DEATH EXPERIENCES

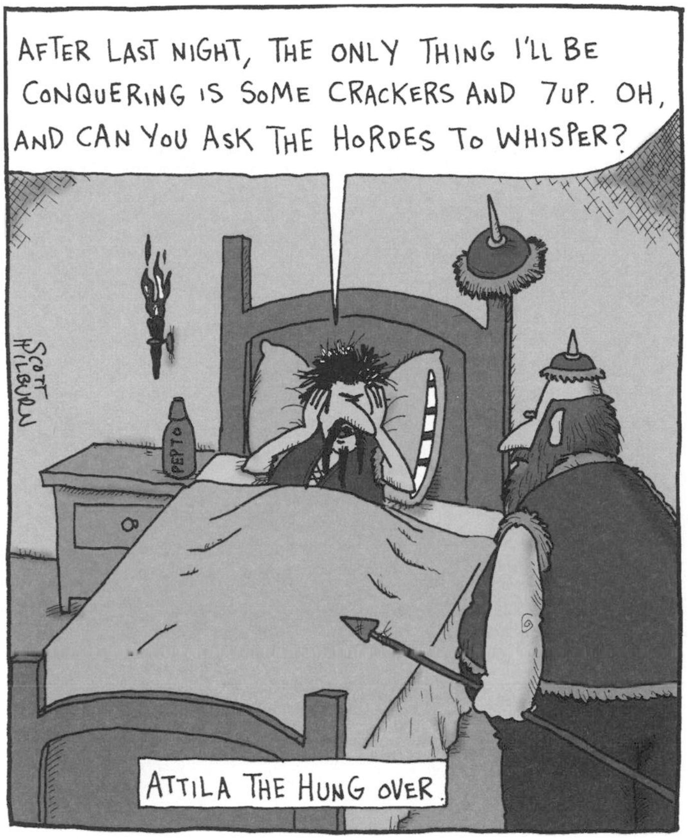
AFTER LAST NIGHT, THE ONLY THING I'LL BE CONQUERING IS SOME CRACKERS AND 7UP. OH, AND CAN YOU ASK THE HORDES TO WHISPER?
SCOTT HILBURN
PEPTO
ATTILA THE HUNG OVER.

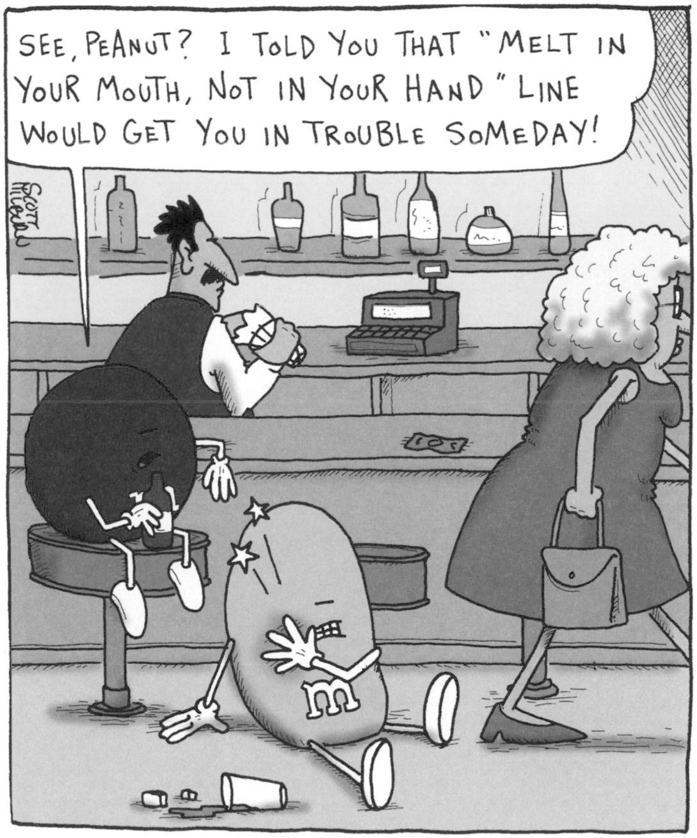
SEE, PEANUT? I TOLD YOU THAT "MELT IN YOUR MOUTH, NOT IN YOUR HAND" LINE WOULD GET YOU IN TROUBLE SOMEDAY!
SCOTT HILBURN
m

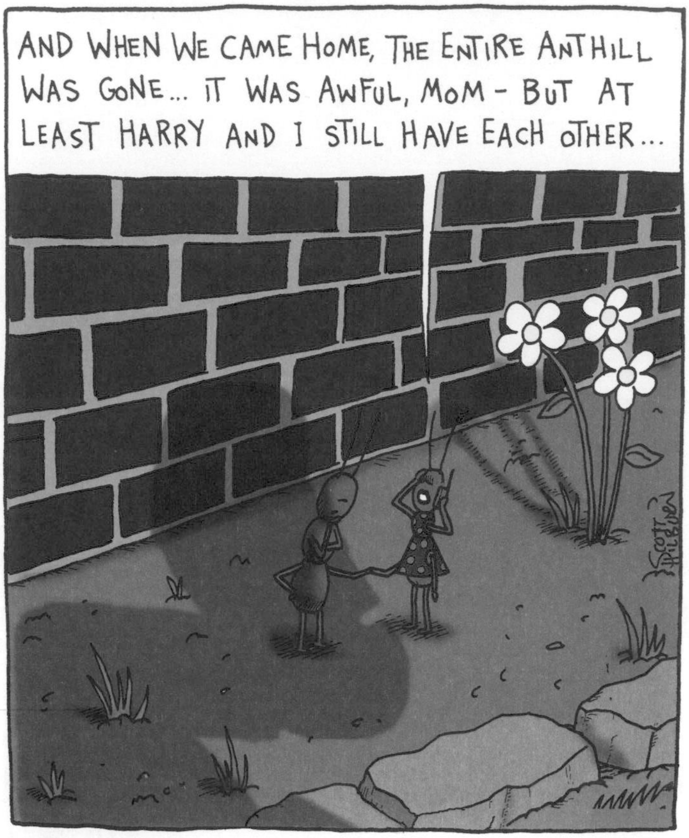
AND WHEN WE CAME HOME, THE ENTIRE ANTHILL WAS GONE... IT WAS AWFUL, MOM - BUT AT LEAST HARRY AND I STILL HAVE EACH OTHER...

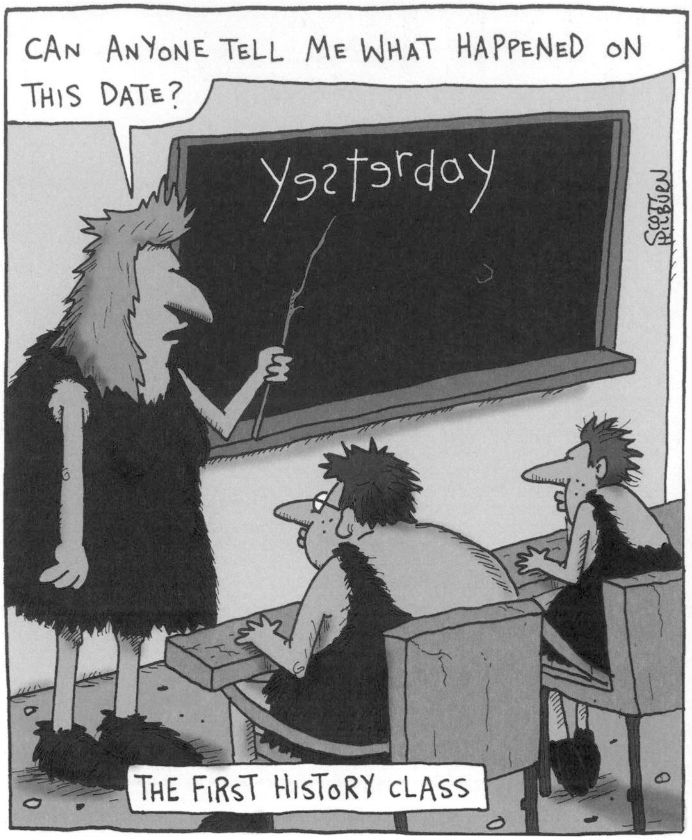
CAN ANYONE TELL ME WHAT HAPPENED ON THIS DATE?
yesterday
THE FIRST HISTORY CLASS

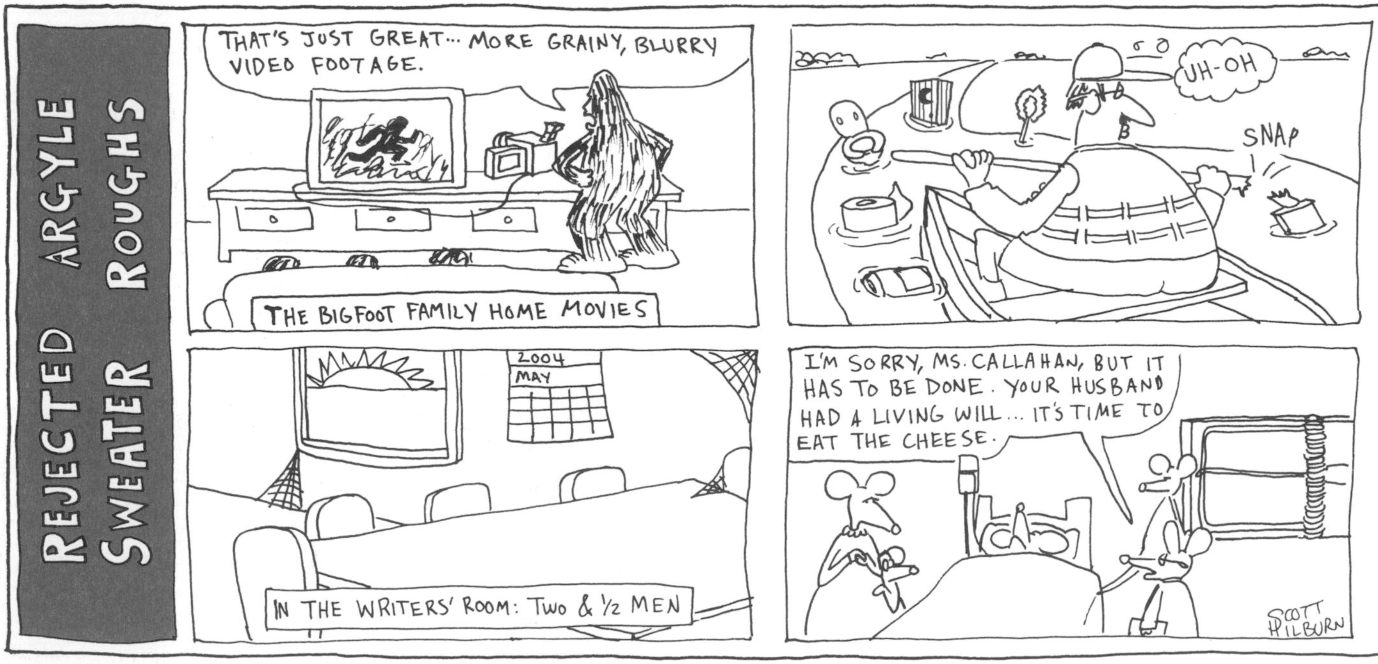
REJECTED ARGYLE SWEATER ROUGHS
THAT'S JUST GREAT... MORE GRAINY, BLURRY VIDEO FOOTAGE.
THE BIGFOOT FAMILY HOME MOVIES
UH-OH
SNAP
2004
MAY
IN THE WRITERS' ROOM: TWO & 1/2 MEN
I'M SORRY, MS. CALLAHAN, BUT IT HAS TO BE DONE. YOUR HUSBAND HAD A LIVING WILL... IT'S TIME TO EAT THE CHEESE.

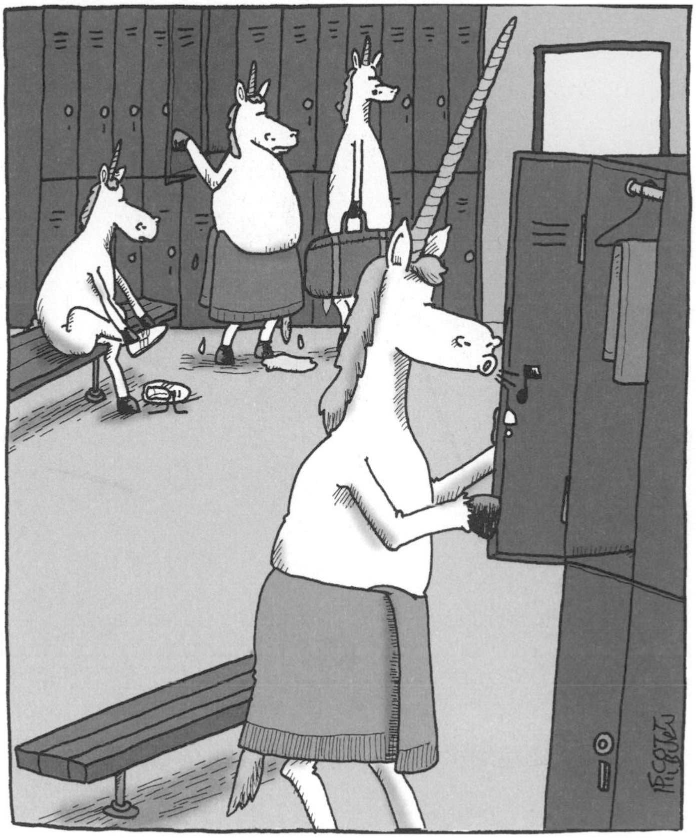

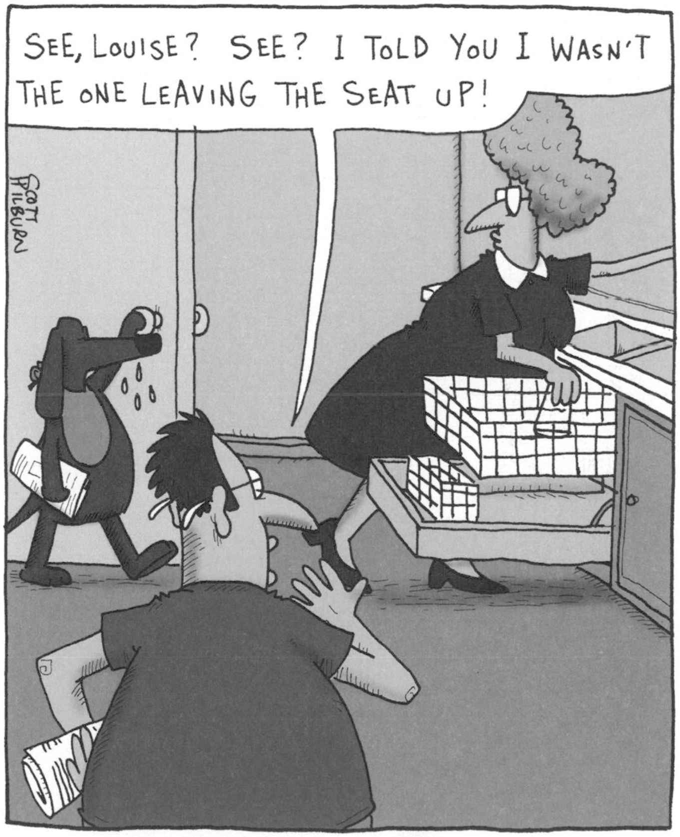
SEE, LOUISE? SEE? I TOLD YOU I WASN'T THE ONE LEAVING THE SEAT UP!

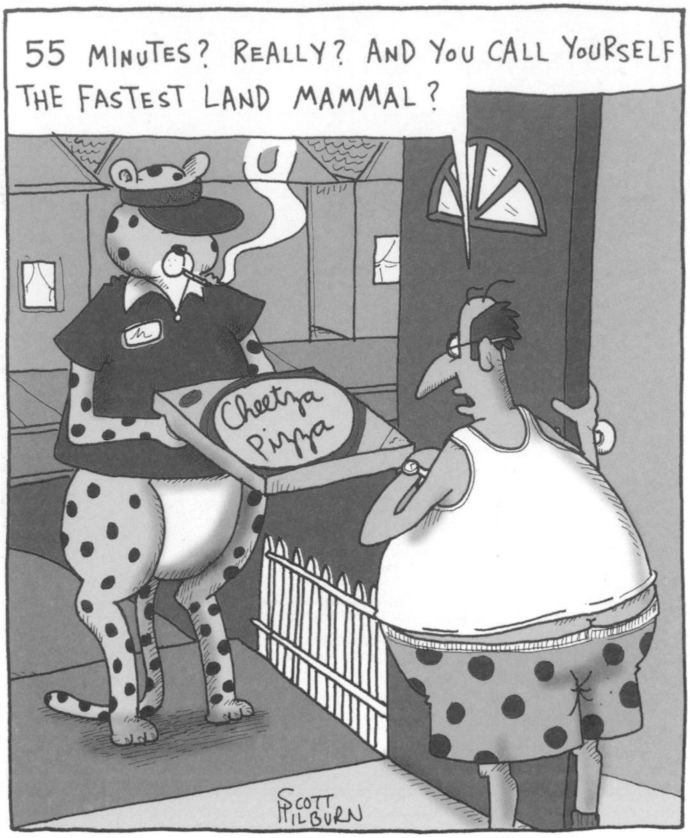
55 MINUTES? REALLY? AND YOU CALL YOURSELF THE FASTEST LAND MAMMAL?
Cheetza Pizza
SCOTT HILBURN

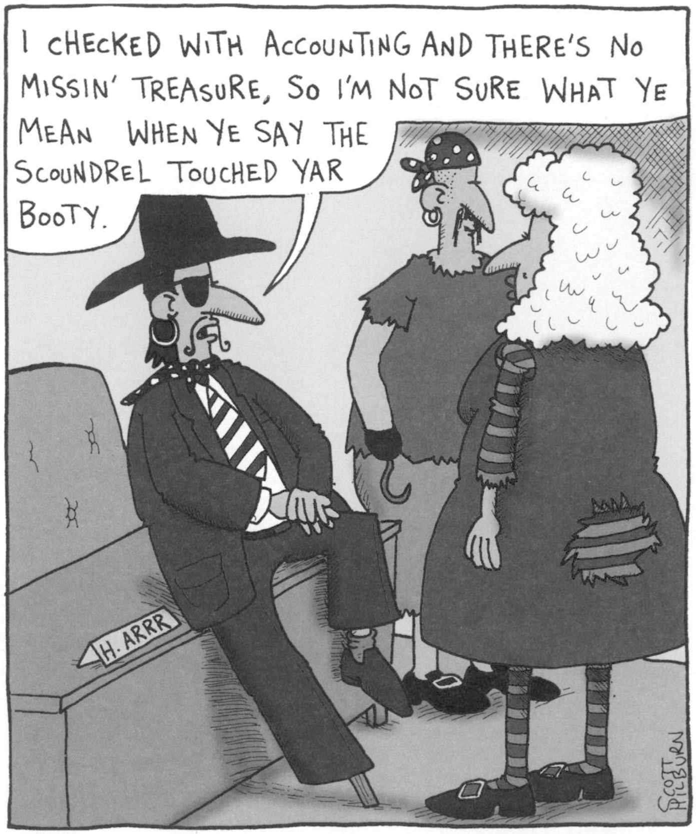
I CHECKED WITH ACCOUNTING AND THERE'S NO MISSIN' TREASURE, SO I'M NOT SURE WHAT YE MEAN WHEN YE SAY THE SCOUNDREL TOUCHED YAR BOOTY.
H. ARRR
SCOTT HILBURN

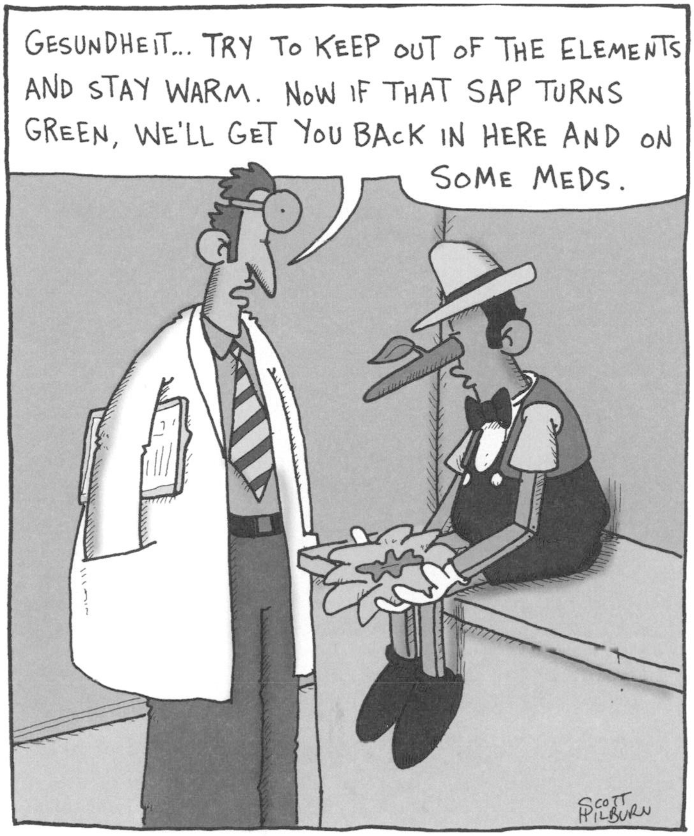
GESUNDHEIT... TRY TO KEEP OUT OF THE ELEMENTS AND STAY WARM. NOW IF THAT SAP TURNS GREEN, WE'LL GET YOU BACK IN HERE AND ON SOME MEDS.
SCOTT HILBURN

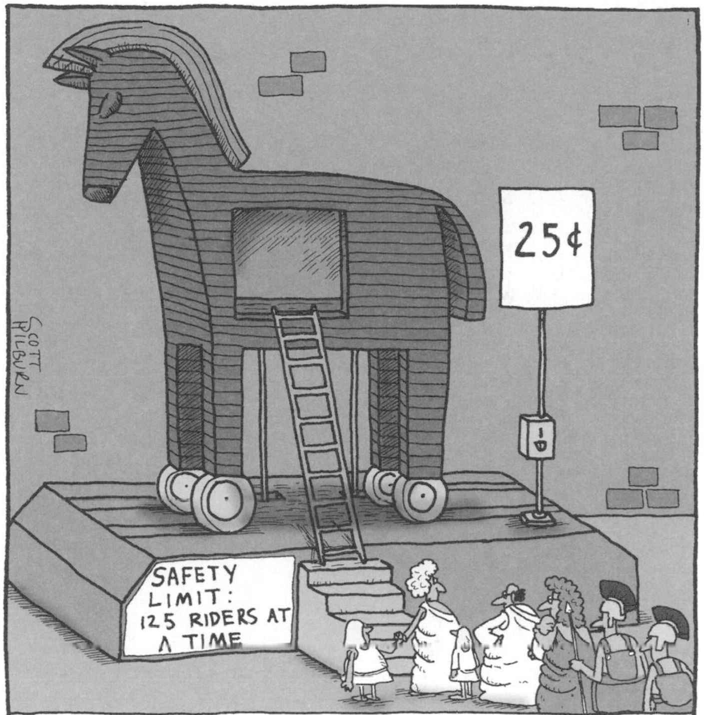
25¢
SAFETY LIMIT: 125 RIDERS AT A TIME
SCOTT HILBURN

YEARS AFTER IT WAS RETIRED FROM BATTLE, THE TROJAN HORSE KEPT RIGHT ON ROCKIN'.

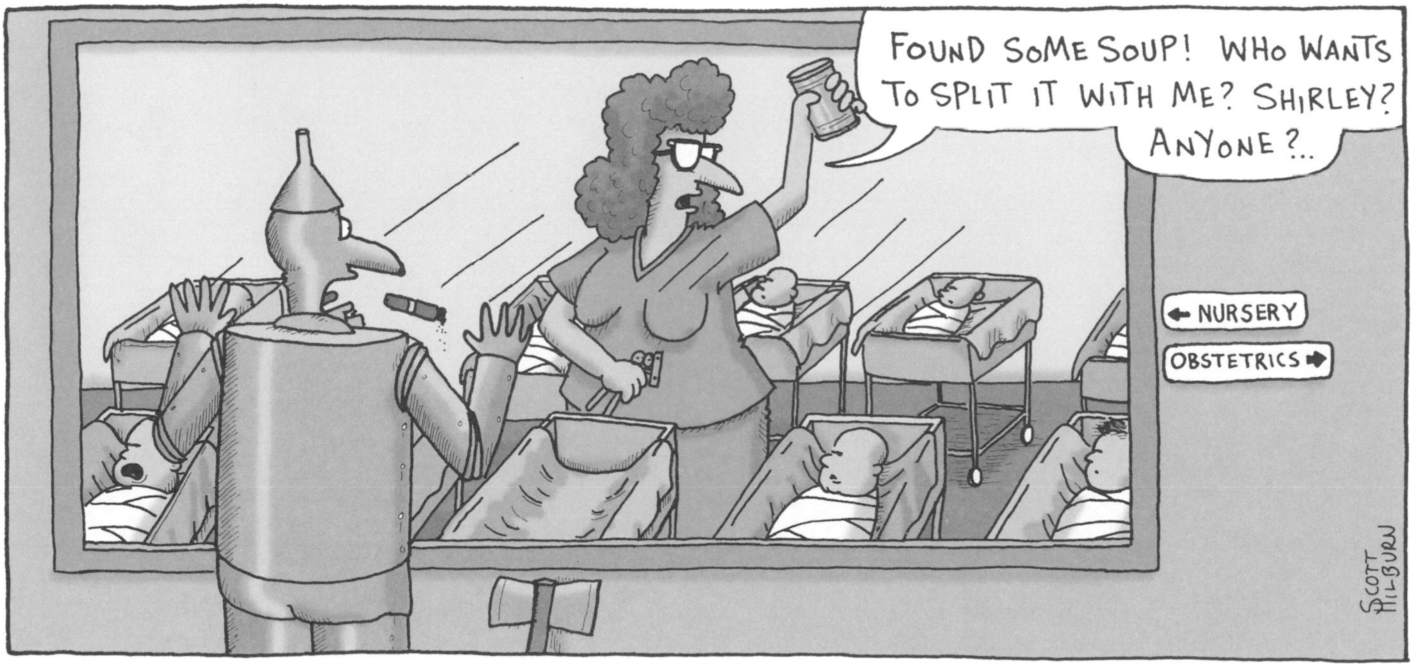
FOUND SOME SOUP! WHO WANTS TO SPLIT IT WITH ME? SHIRLEY? ANYONE?..
NURSERY
OBSTETRICS
SCOTT HILBURN

DANG.
SCOTT HILBURN

WITH PHONE BOOTHS NOW OBSOLETE IN METROPOLIS, SUPERMAN IS FORCED TO USE ANY AVAILABLE SPACE TO GET DRESSED - OFTEN IN THE DARK.

SCOTT HILBURN

WITH THEIR ENORMOUS WEALTH, GOOD LOOKS AND POWER, THE ENTIRE KENNEDY FAMILY WAS REVERED - EXCEPT FOR BRAD WHO WAS REGRETTABLY BORN WITH A SILVER SPOON IN HIS NOSE.

POKER? TONIGHT? I'M IN! WAIT- I CAN'T. I JUST REMEMBERED CHERYL'S OUTTA TOWN, AND I'M STUCK SITTIN' ON THIS EGG FOR 8 MORE WEEKS.
SCOTT HILBURN

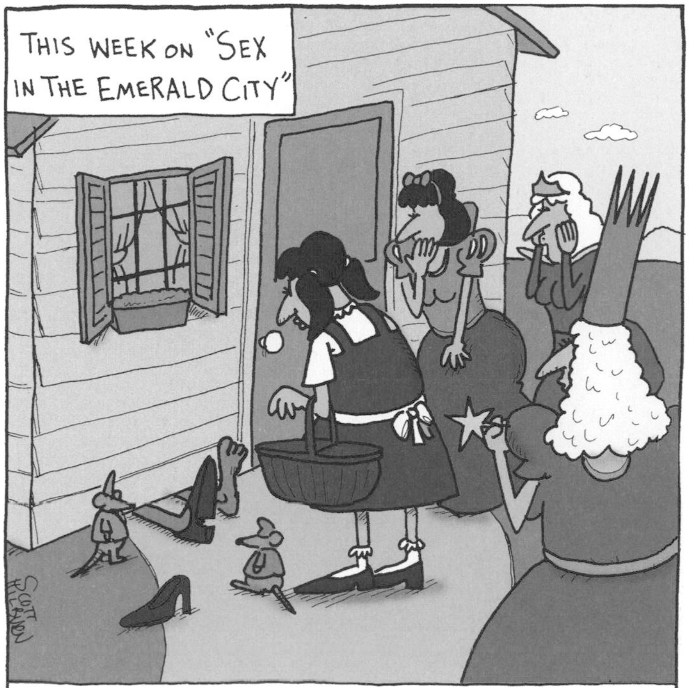
THIS WEEK ON "SEX IN THE EMERALD CITY"

FORTUNATELY FOR DOROTHY, EACH TORNADO SEASON BROUGHT A VERITABLE WINDFALL OF SHINY NEW FOOTWEAR.

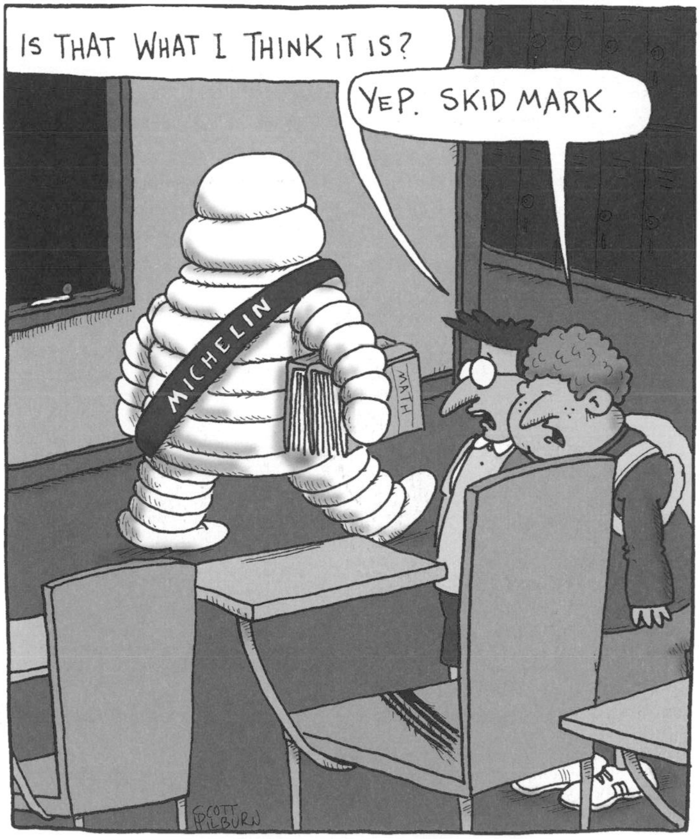
IS THAT WHAT I THINK IT IS?
YEP. SKID MARK.
MICHELIN
MATH
SCOTT HILBURN

YES, I REALIZE THAT A SALT WITH A DEADLY WEAPON IS FRIGHTENING, BUT I ONLY KEEP IT TO PROTECT MY FAMILY - AND I ALWAYS KEEP THE SAFETY ON.
SALT
SCOTT HILBURN

SOMEDAY, YOU HANDSOME SUNNUVA GUN, YOU'RE GONNA CREATE SOMETHING SO IMPORTANT TO CIVILIZED SOCIETY THAT YOUR NAME WILL FOREVER BE ASSOCIATED WITH PRESTIGE AND HONOR!
SIR THOMAS CRAPPER, CIRCA 1860
SCOTT HILBURN

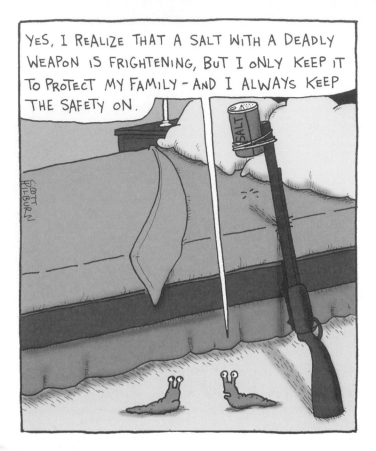

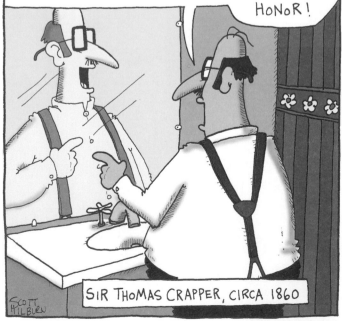

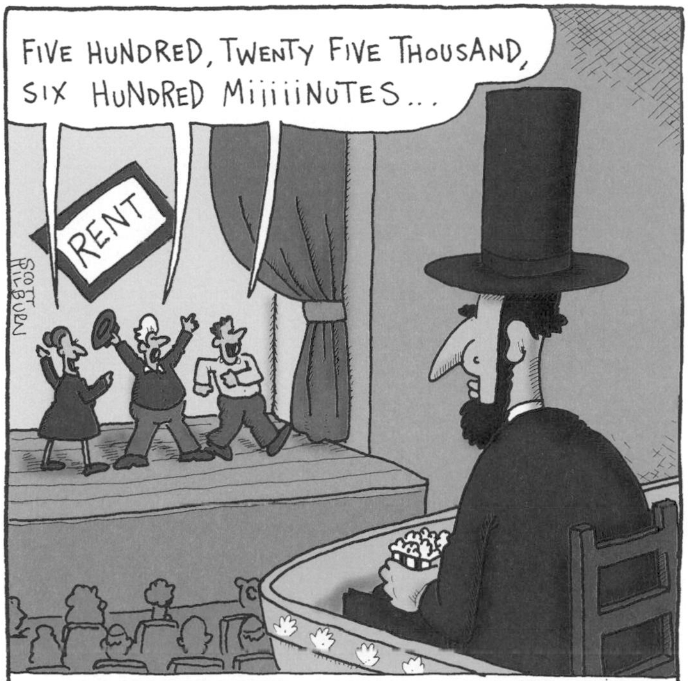
FIVE HUNDRED, TWENTY FIVE THOUSAND, SIX HUNDRED MIiiiiNUTES...
RENT
SCOTT HILBURN

FORENSIC EVIDENCE NOW PROVES THAT THE SHOTS IN THE BALCONY WEREN'T MEANT FOR THE PRESIDENT, BUT RATHER THE SHOW'S CAST.

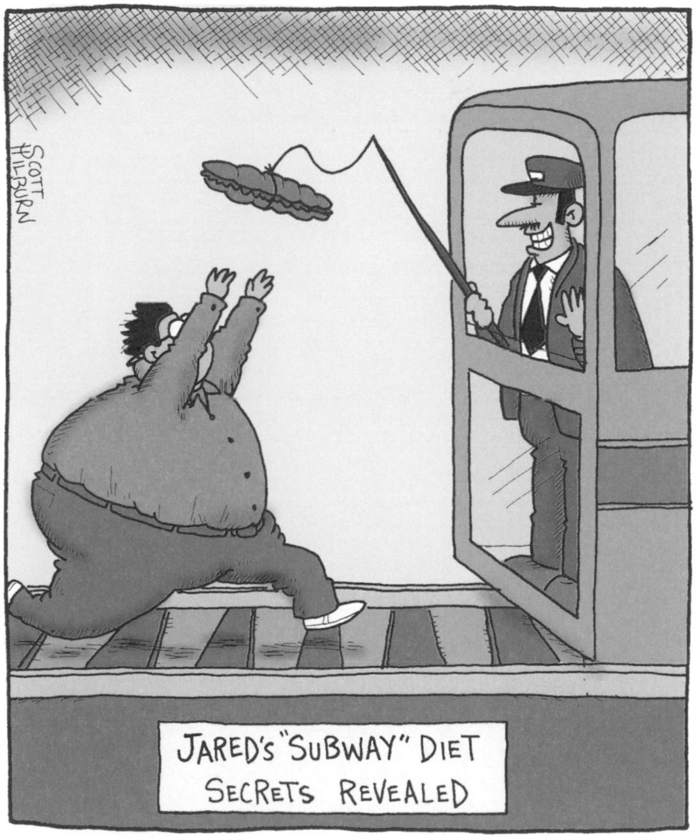
SCOTT HILBURN

JARED'S "SUBWAY" DIET SECRETS REVEALED

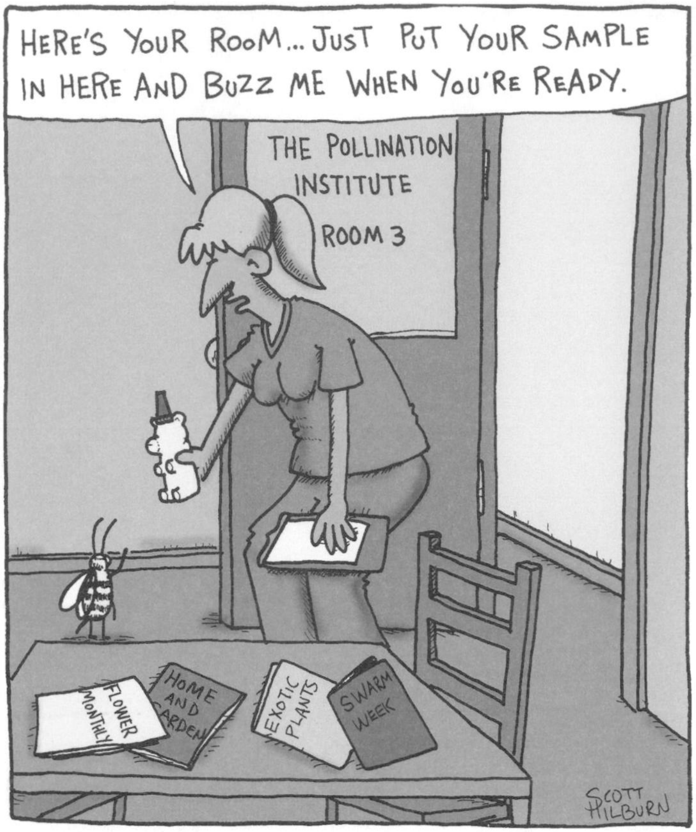
HERE'S YOUR ROOM... JUST PUT YOUR SAMPLE IN HERE AND BUZZ ME WHEN YOU'RE READY.
THE POLLINATION INSTITUTE
ROOM 3
FLOWER MONTHLY
HOME AND GARDEN
EXOTIC PLANTS
SWARM WEEK
SCOTT HILBURN

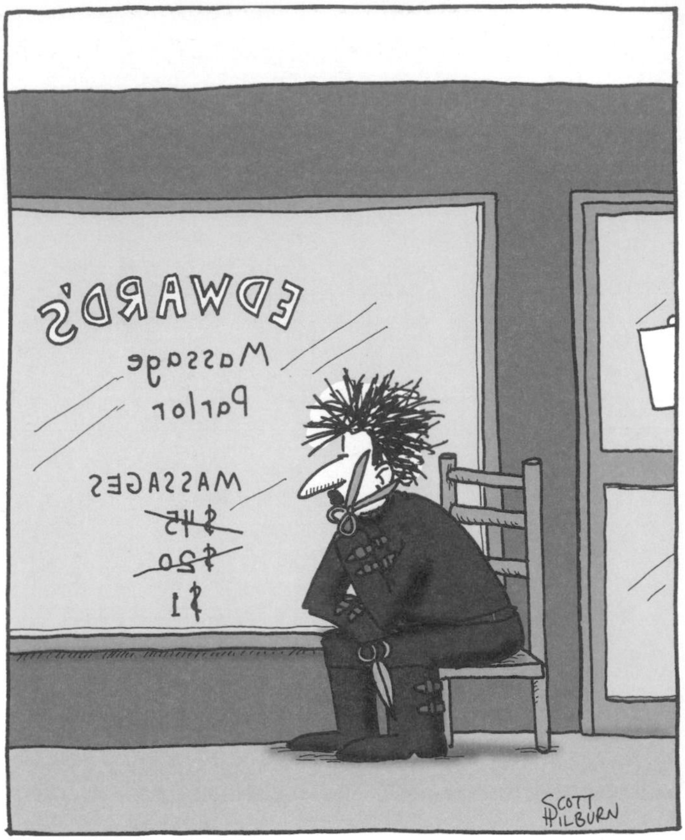
EDWARD'S
Massage Parlor
MASSAGES
$15
$20
$1
SCOTT HILBURN

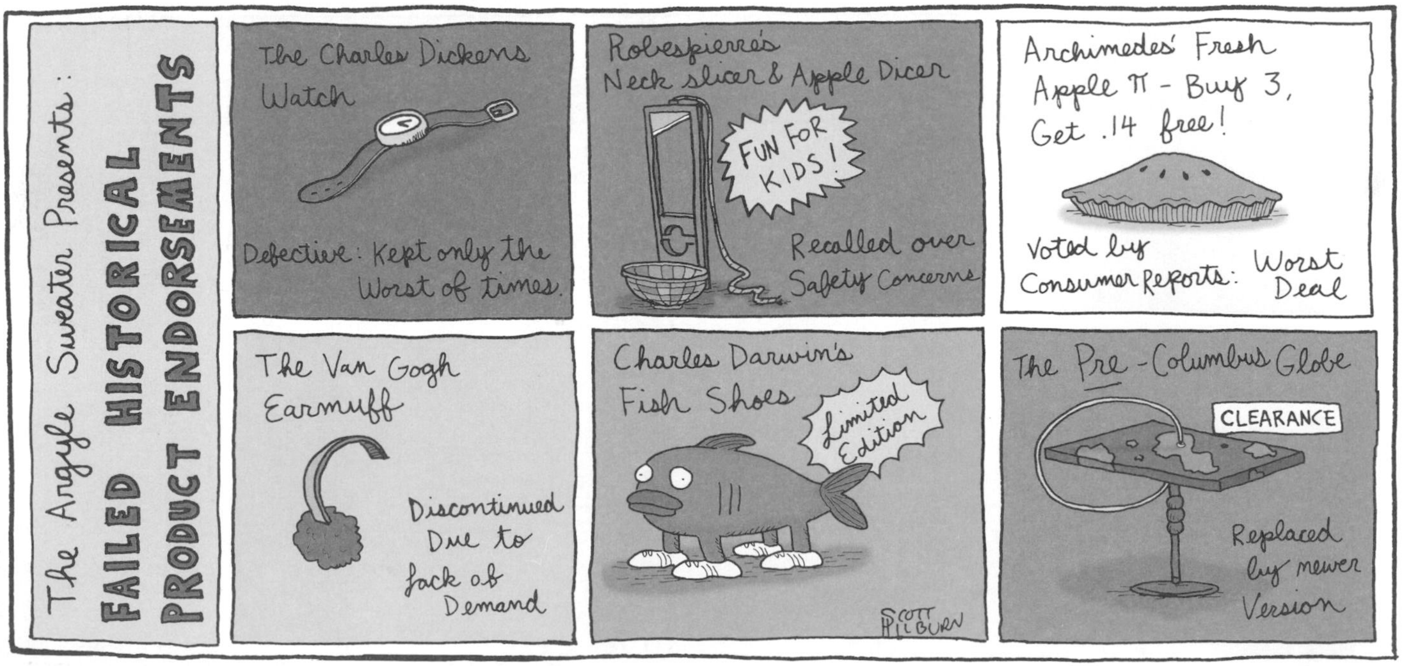
The Argyle Sweater Presents:
FAILED HISTORICAL PRODUCT ENDORSEMENTS
The Charles Dickens Watch
Defective: Kept only the Worst of times.
Robespierre's Neck slicer & Apple Dicer
FUN FOR KIDS!
Recalled over Safety Concerns
Archimedes' Fresh Apple π - Buy 3, Get .14 free!
Voted by Consumer Reports: Worst Deal
The Van Gogh Earmuff
Discontinued Due to Lack of Demand
Charles Darwin's Fish Shoes
Limited Edition
SCOTT HILBURN
The Pre-Columbus Globe
CLEARANCE
Replaced by newer Version

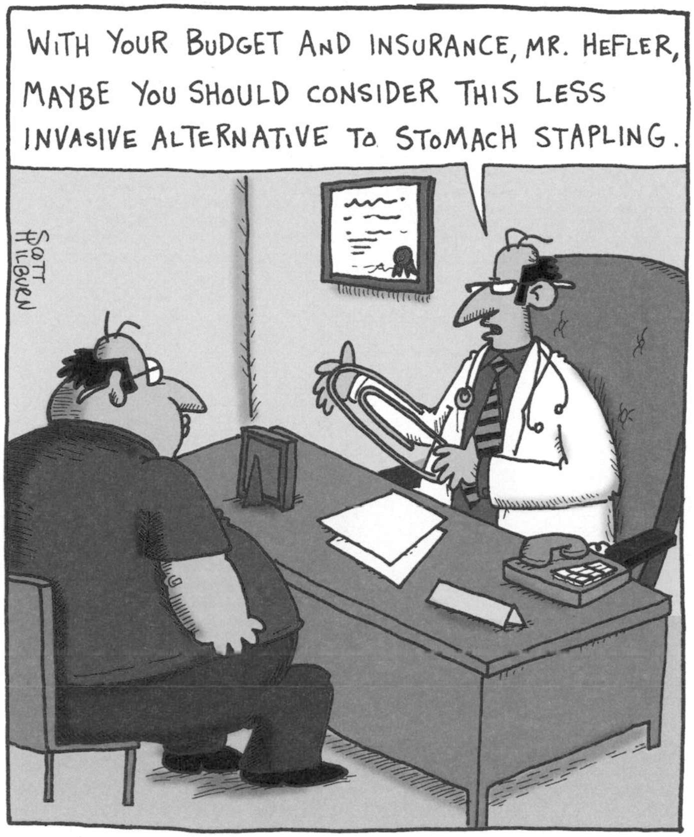
WITH YOUR BUDGET AND INSURANCE, MR. HEFLER, MAYBE YOU SHOULD CONSIDER THIS LESS INVASIVE ALTERNATIVE TO STOMACH STAPLING.

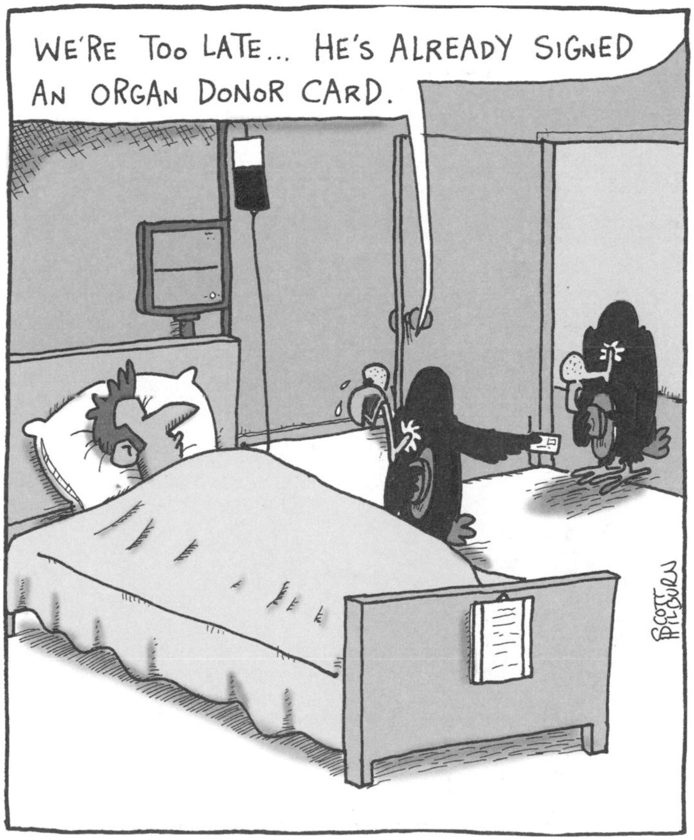
WE'RE TOO LATE... HE'S ALREADY SIGNED AN ORGAN DONOR CARD.

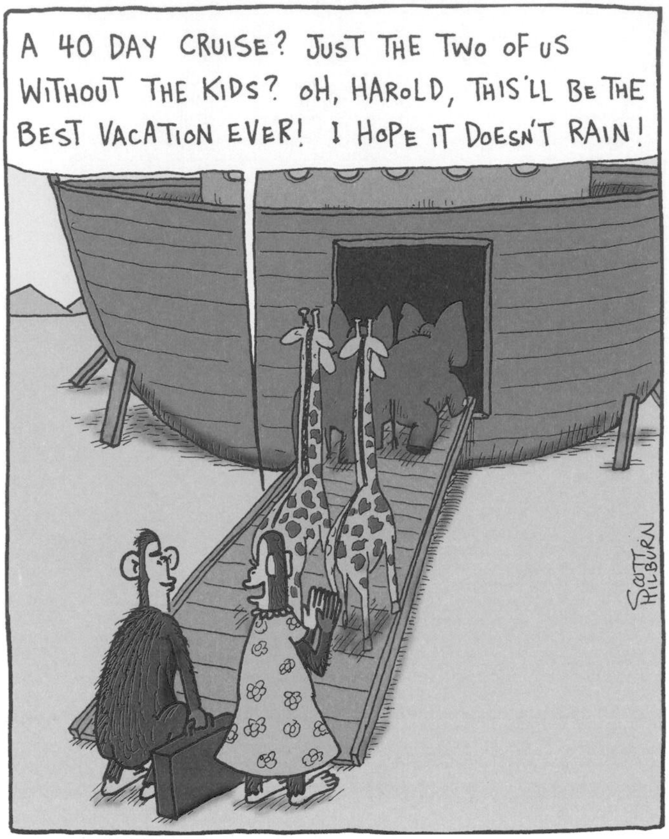
A 40 DAY CRUISE? JUST THE TWO OF US WITHOUT THE KIDS? OH, HAROLD, THIS'LL BE THE BEST VACATION EVER! I HOPE IT DOESN'T RAIN!
SCOTT HILBURN

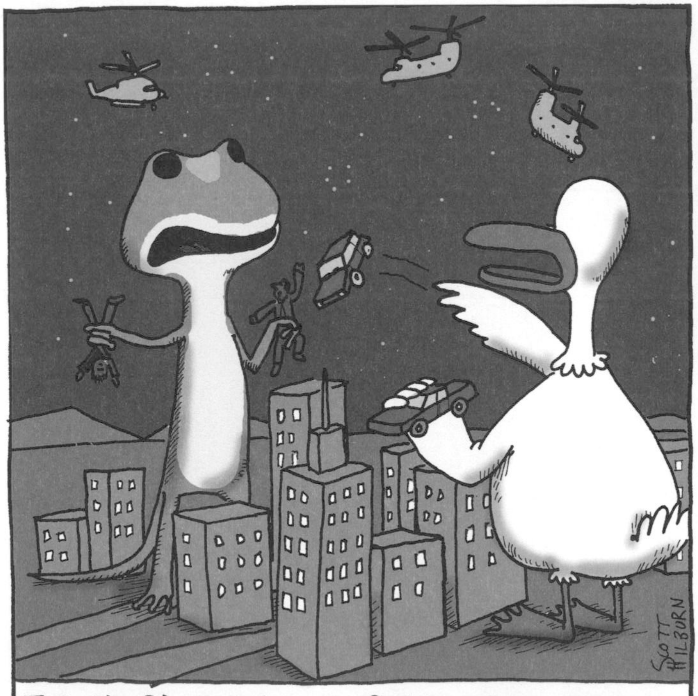
SCOTT HILBURN

THE INSURANCE GIANTS DO BATTLE, IRONICALLY COSTING THEIR OWN COMPANIES BILLIONS OF DOLLARS IN CLAIMS.

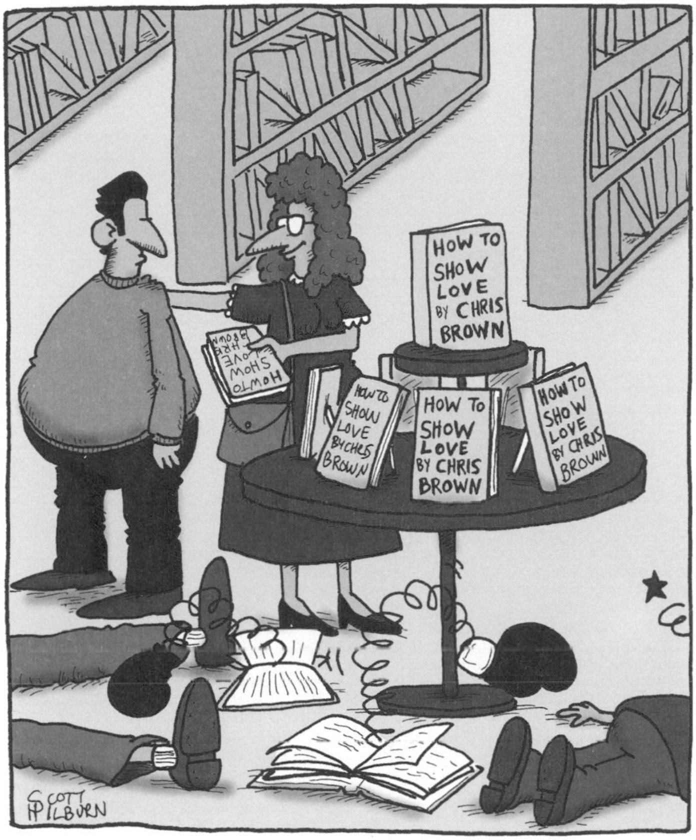
HOW TO SHOW LOVE BY CHRIS BROWN
HOW TO SHOW LOVE BY CHRIS BROWN
HOW TO SHOW LOVE BY CHRIS BROWN
HOW TO SHOW LOVE BY CHRIS BROWN
SCOTT HILBURN

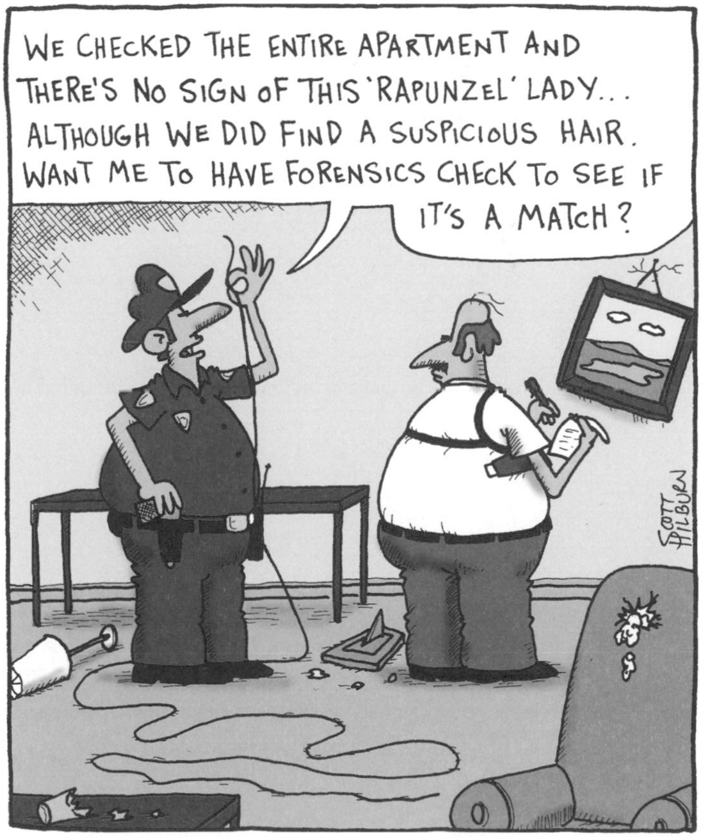
WE CHECKED THE ENTIRE APARTMENT AND THERE'S NO SIGN OF THIS 'RAPUNZEL' LADY... ALTHOUGH WE DID FIND A SUSPICIOUS HAIR. WANT ME TO HAVE FORENSICS CHECK TO SEE IF IT'S A MATCH?
SCOTT HILBURN

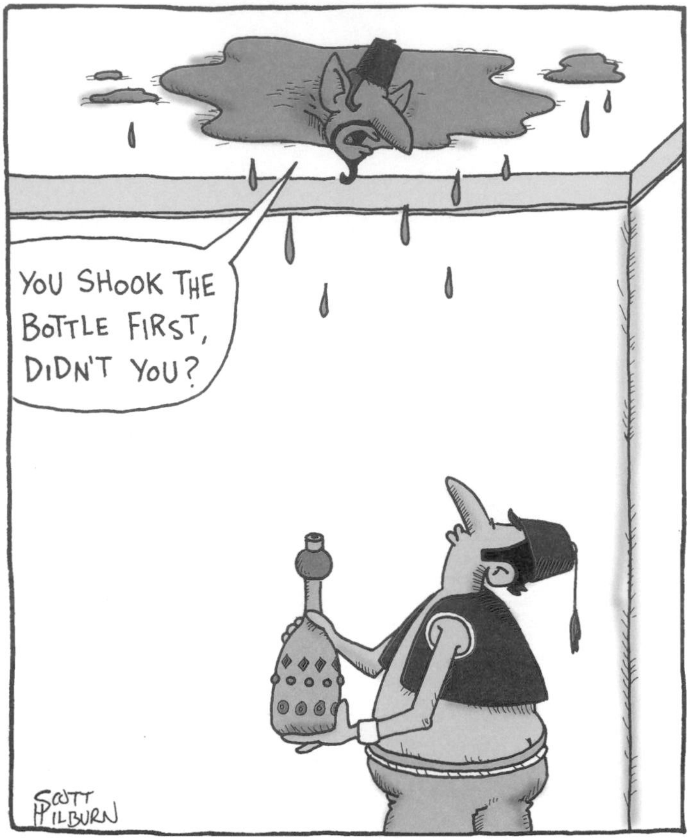
YOU SHOOK THE BOTTLE FIRST, DIDN'T YOU?
SCOTT HILBURN

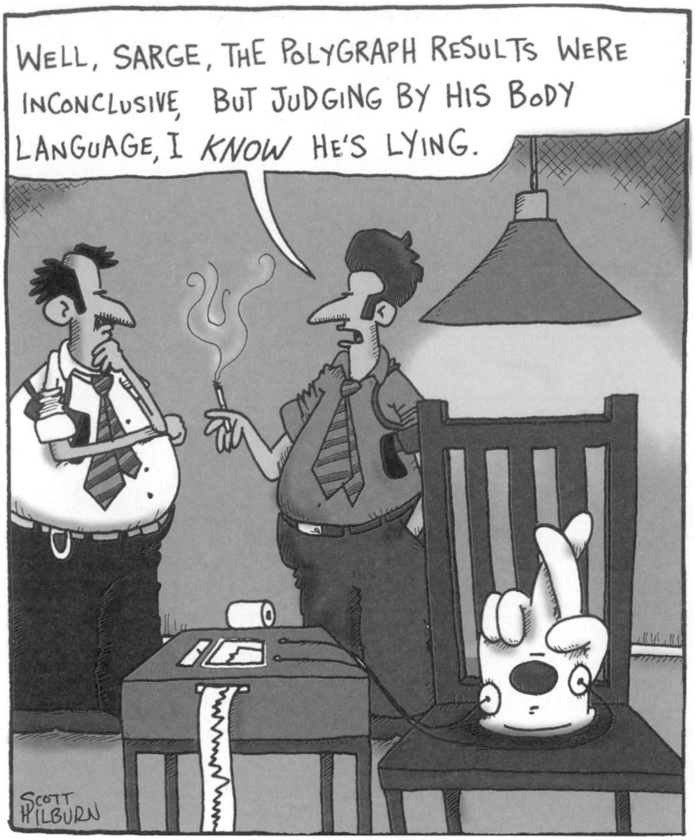
WELL, SARGE, THE POLYGRAPH RESULTS WERE INCONCLUSIVE, BUT JUDGING BY HIS BODY LANGUAGE, I *KNOW* HE'S LYING.
SCOTT HILBURN

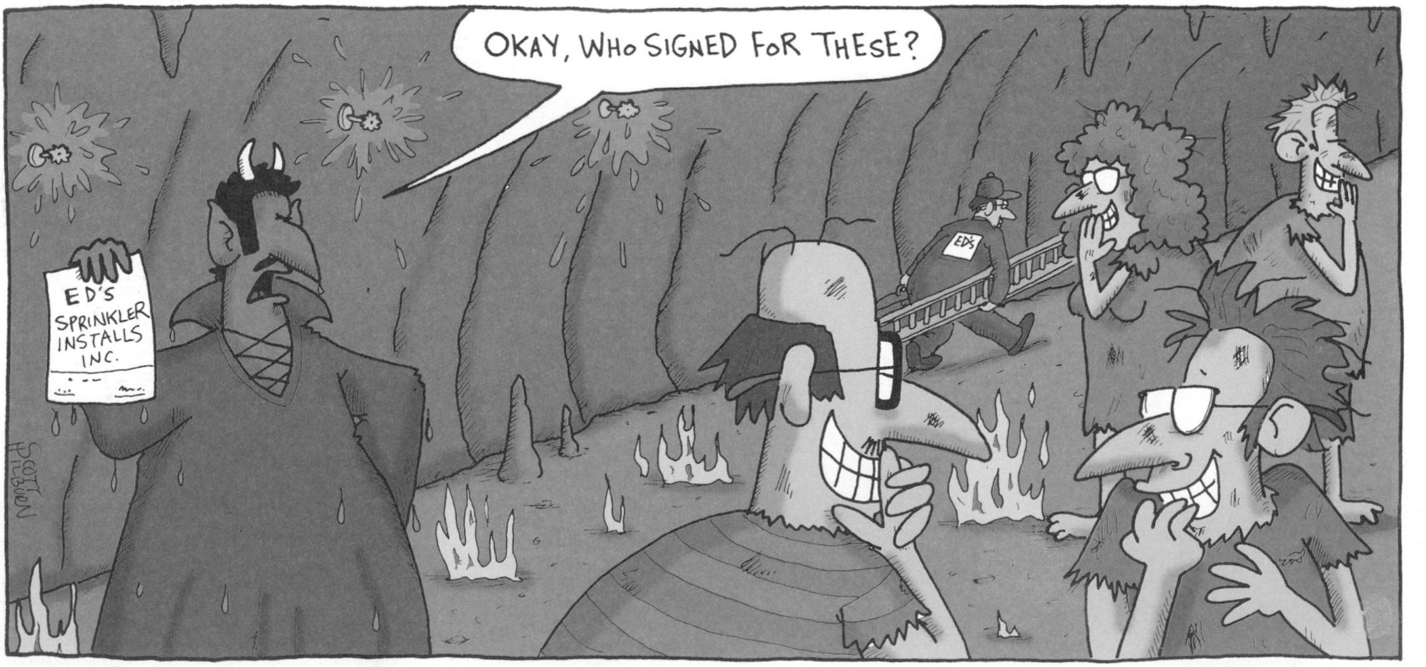
OKAY, WHO SIGNED FOR THESE?
ED'S SPRINKLER INSTALLS INC.
ED'S
SCOTT HILBURN

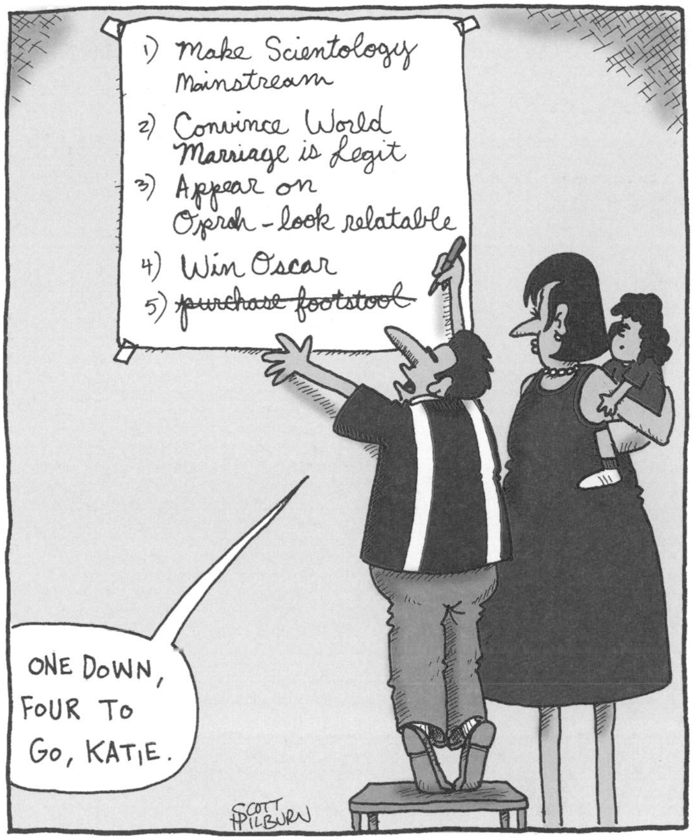
1) Make Scientology Mainstream
2) Convince World Marriage is Legit
3) Appear on Oprah - look relatable
4) Win Oscar
5) purchase footstool
ONE DOWN, FOUR TO GO, KATIE.
SCOTT HILBURN

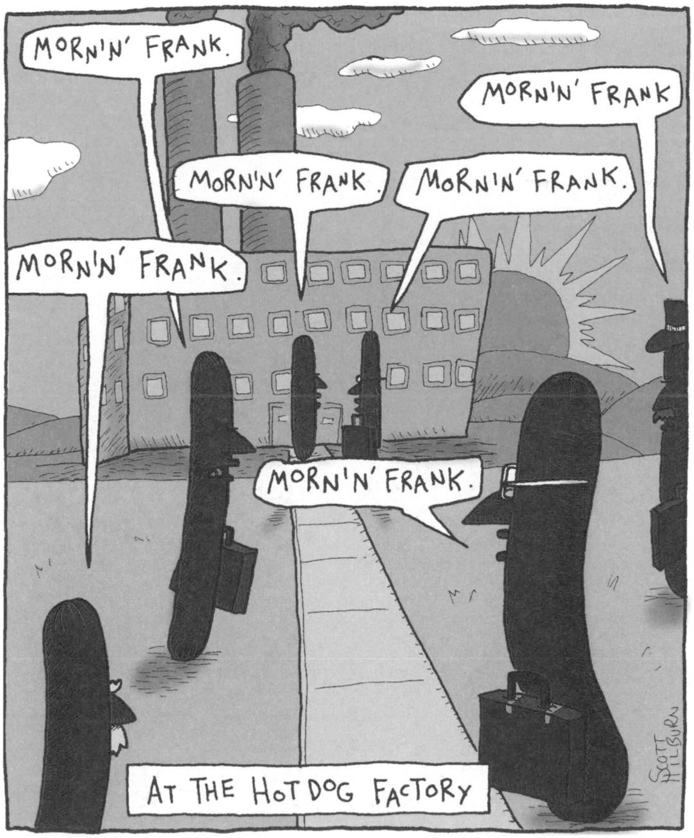
MORN'N' FRANK.
MORN'N' FRANK
MORN'N' FRANK.
MORN'N' FRANK.
MORN'N' FRANK.
MORN'N' FRANK.
AT THE HOT DOG FACTORY
SCOTT HILBURN

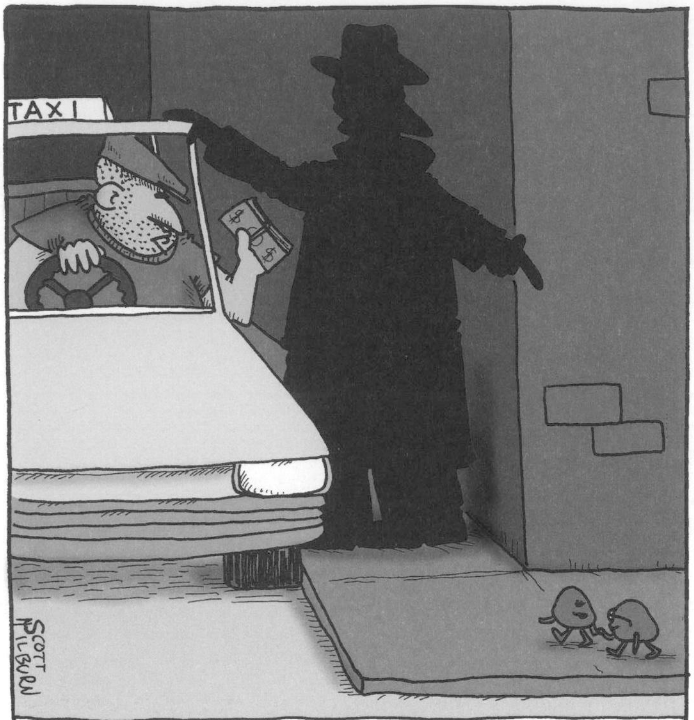
TAXI
SCOTT HILBURN

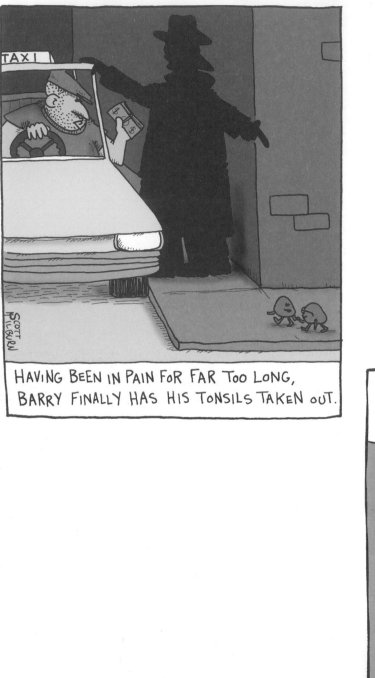

HAVING BEEN IN PAIN FOR FAR TOO LONG, BARRY FINALLY HAS HIS TONSILS TAKEN OUT.

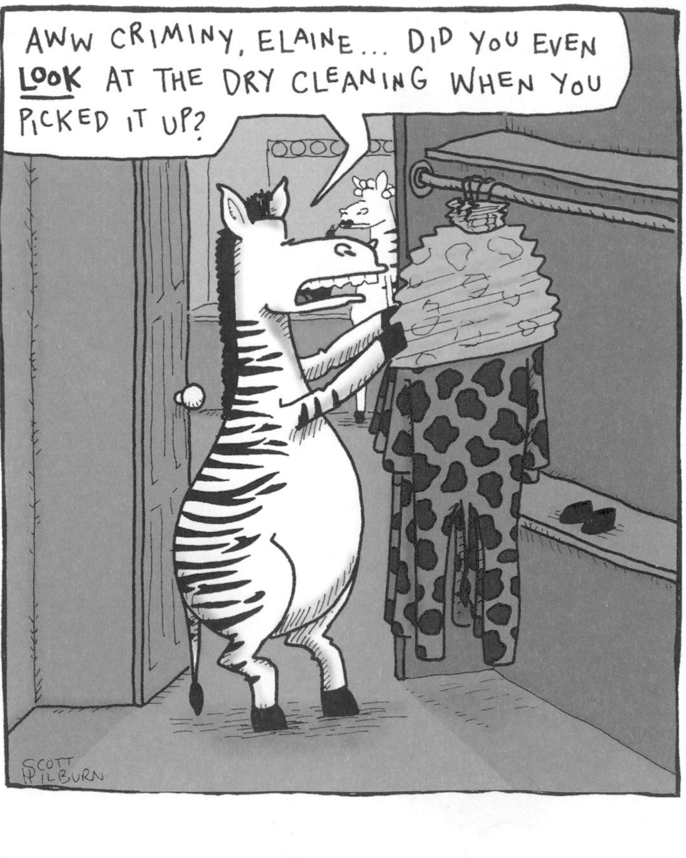
AWW CRIMINY, ELAINE... DID YOU EVEN LOOK AT THE DRY CLEANING WHEN YOU PICKED IT UP?
SCOTT HILBURN

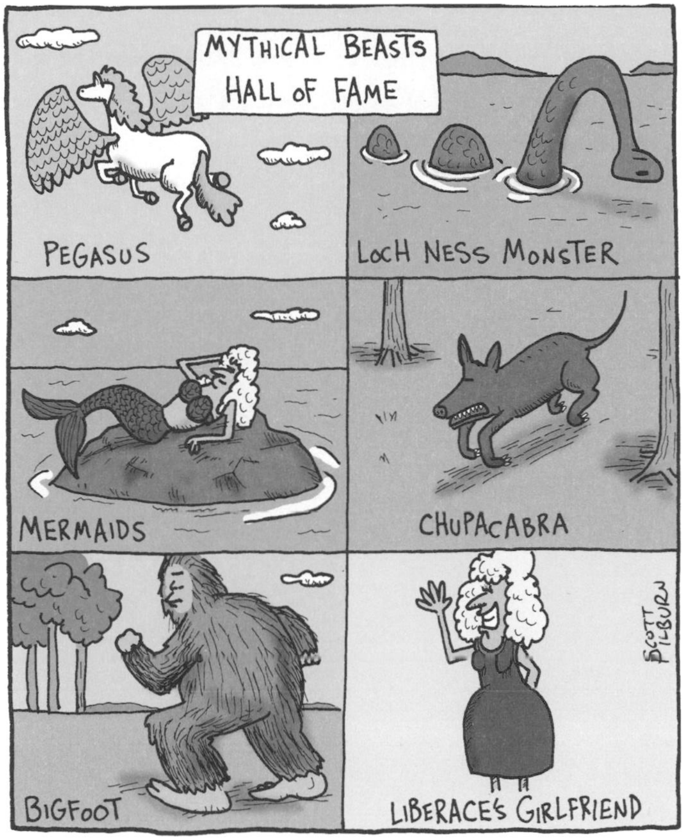
MYTHICAL BEASTS HALL OF FAME
PEGASUS
LOCH NESS MONSTER
MERMAIDS
CHUPACABRA
BIGFOOT
LIBERACE'S GIRLFRIEND
SCOTT HILBURN

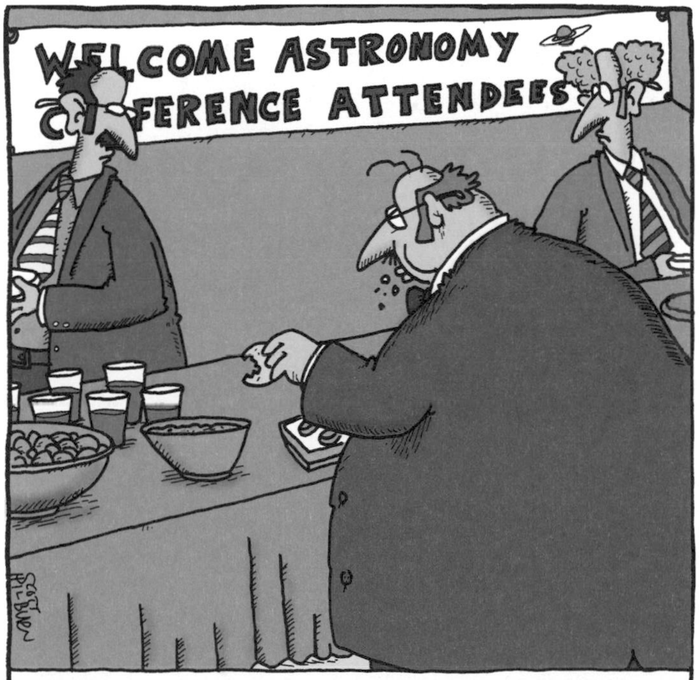
WELCOME ASTRONOMY CONFERENCE ATTENDEES
SCOTT HILBURN

WEINBERG'S EGREGIOUS ERROR WOULD DAMAGE HIS REPUTATION FOREVER. HIS COLLEAGUES WOULD THEREAFTER REFER TO HIM AS "THE BIG DOUBLE DIPPER."

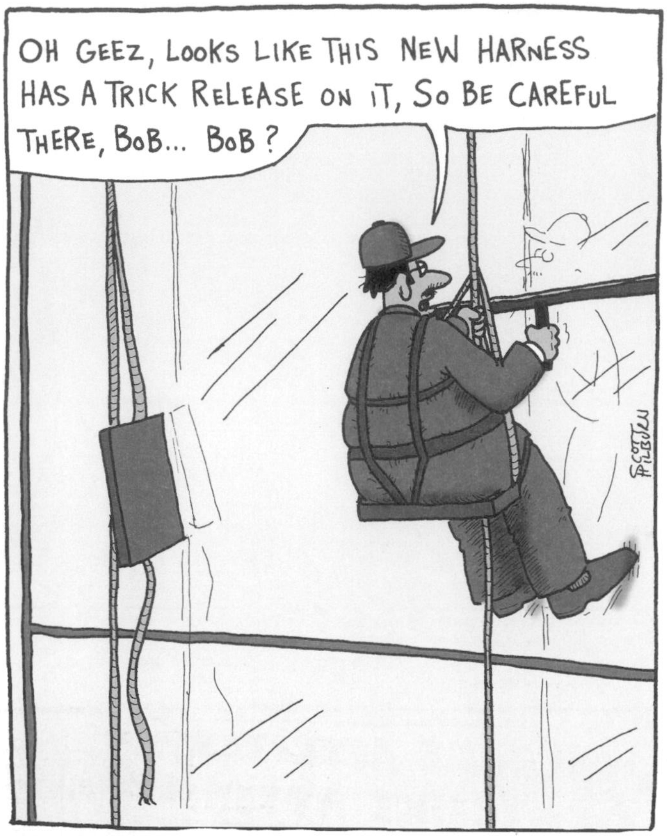
OH GEEZ, LOOKS LIKE THIS NEW HARNESS HAS A TRICK RELEASE ON IT, SO BE CAREFUL THERE, BOB... BOB?
SCOTT HILBURN

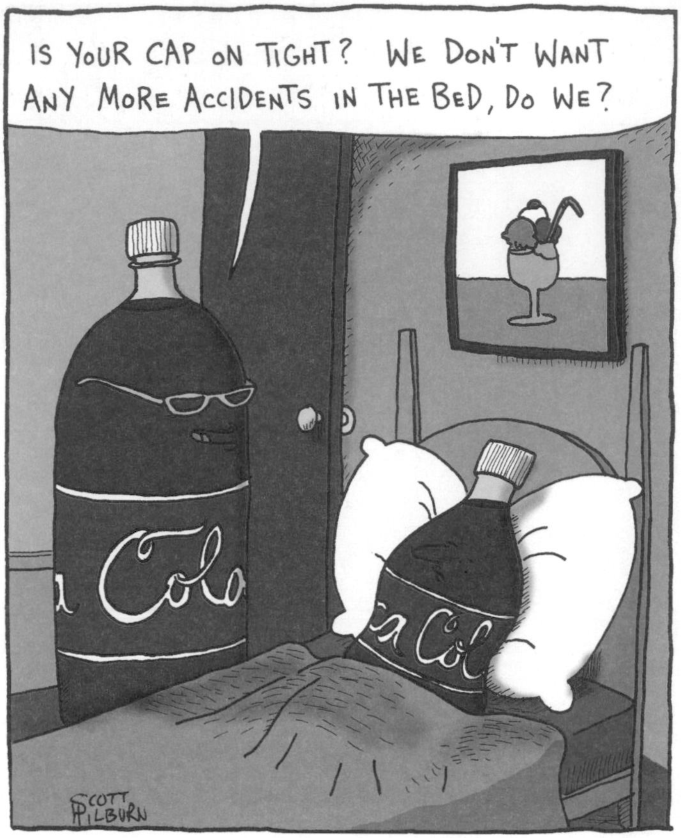
IS YOUR CAP ON TIGHT? WE DON'T WANT ANY MORE ACCIDENTS IN THE BED, DO WE?
SCOTT HILBURN

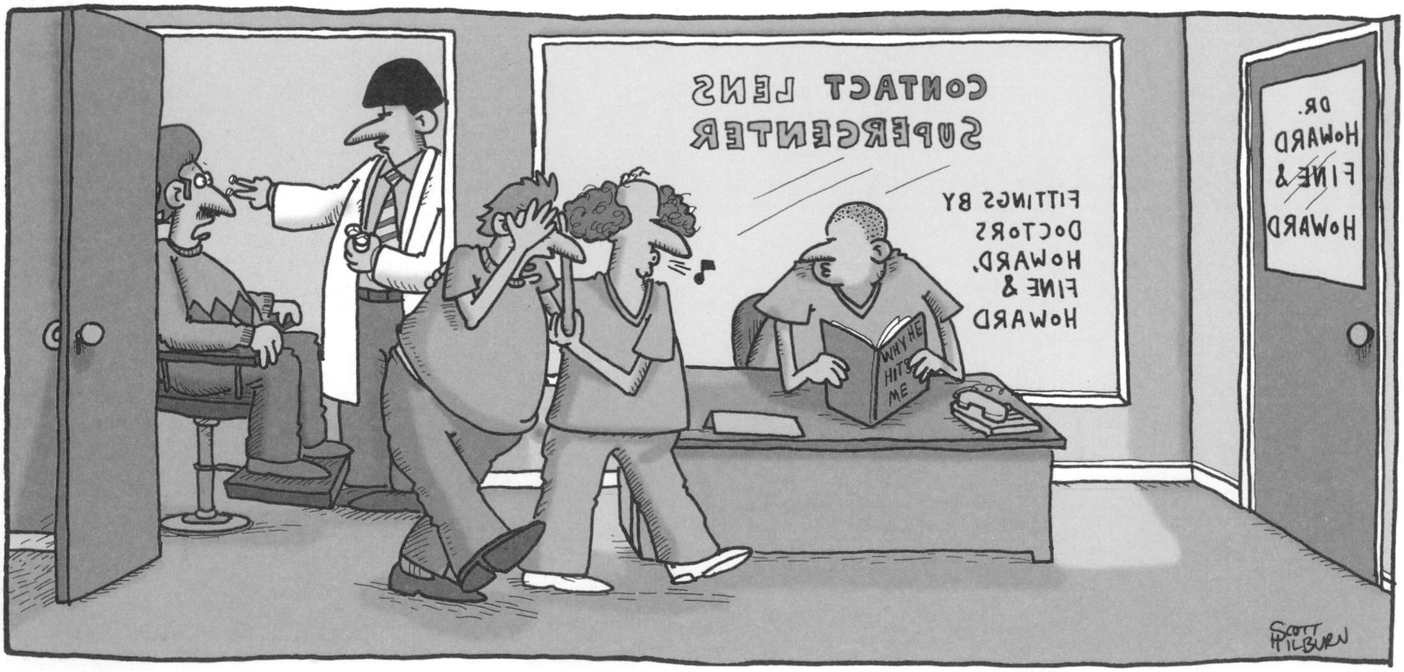
CONTACT LENS SUPERCENTER
FITTINGS BY DOCTORS HOWARD, FINE & HOWARD
DR. HOWARD FINE & HOWARD
WHY HE HITS ME
SCOTT HILBURN

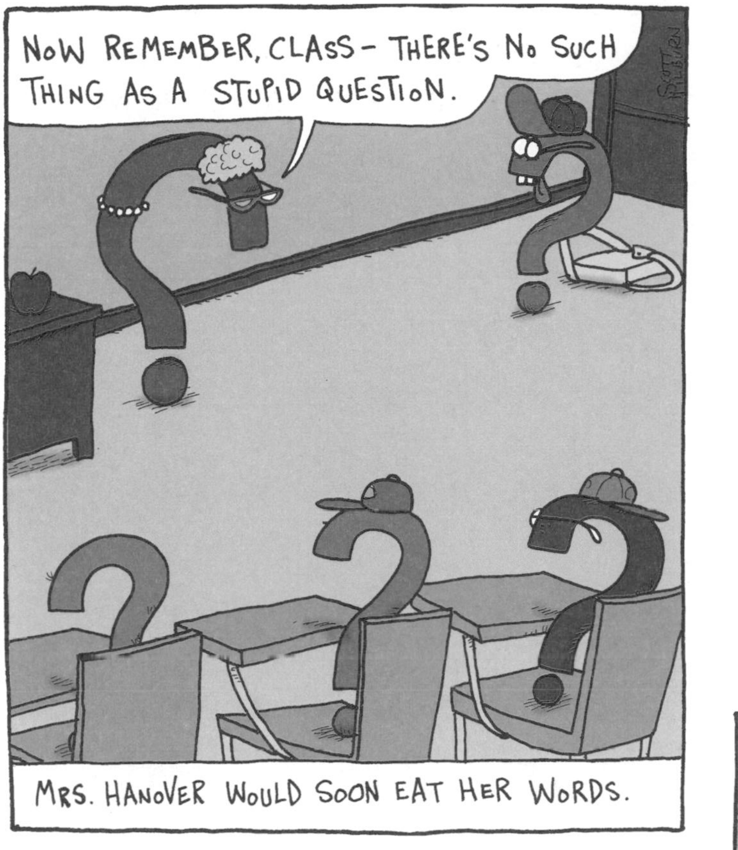
NOW REMEMBER, CLASS - THERE'S NO SUCH THING AS A STUPID QUESTION.

MRS. HANOVER WOULD SOON EAT HER WORDS.

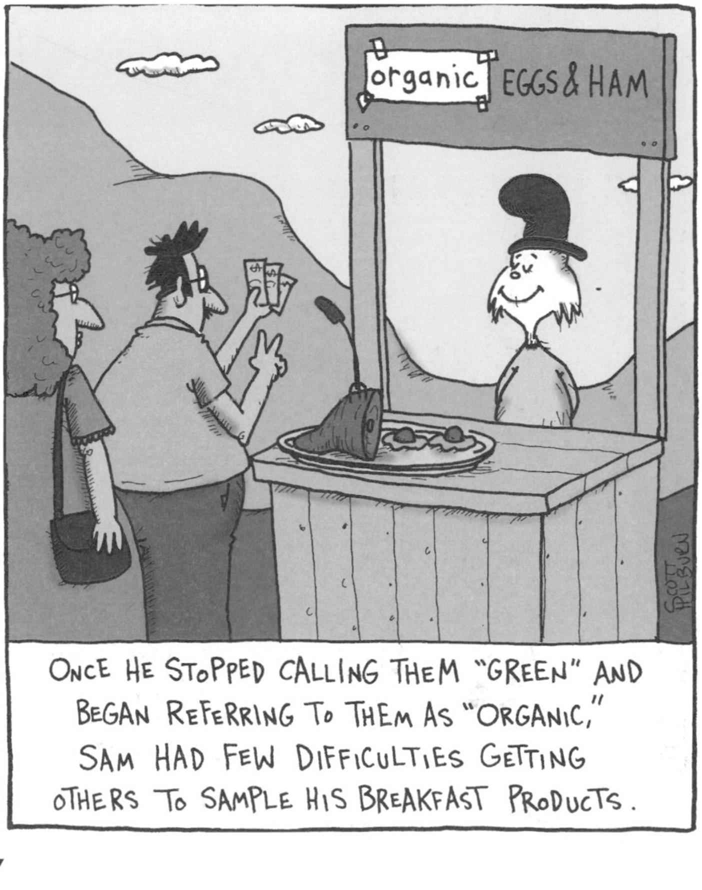
organic EGGS & HAM

ONCE HE STOPPED CALLING THEM "GREEN" AND BEGAN REFERRING TO THEM AS "ORGANIC," SAM HAD FEW DIFFICULTIES GETTING OTHERS TO SAMPLE HIS BREAKFAST PRODUCTS.

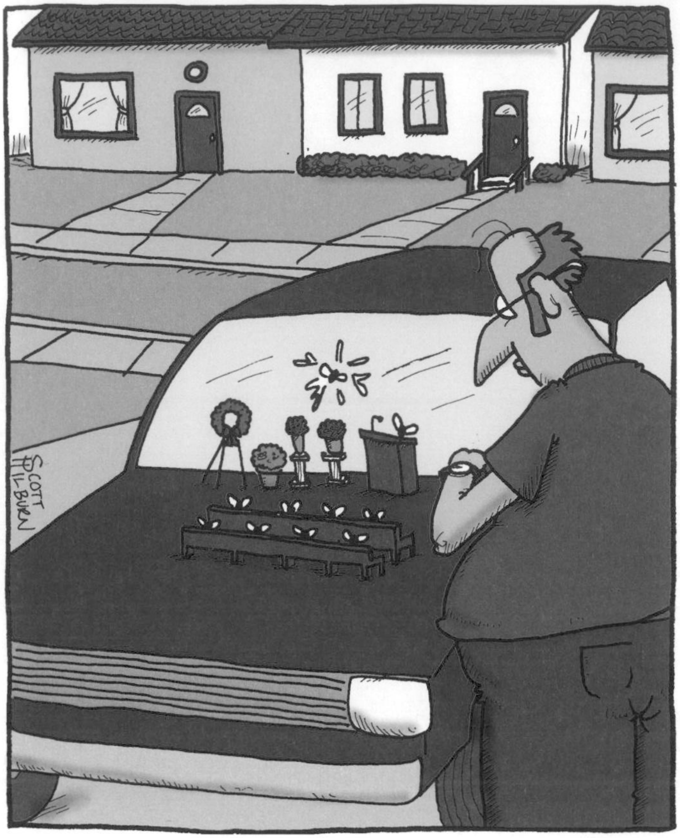
SCOTT HILBURN

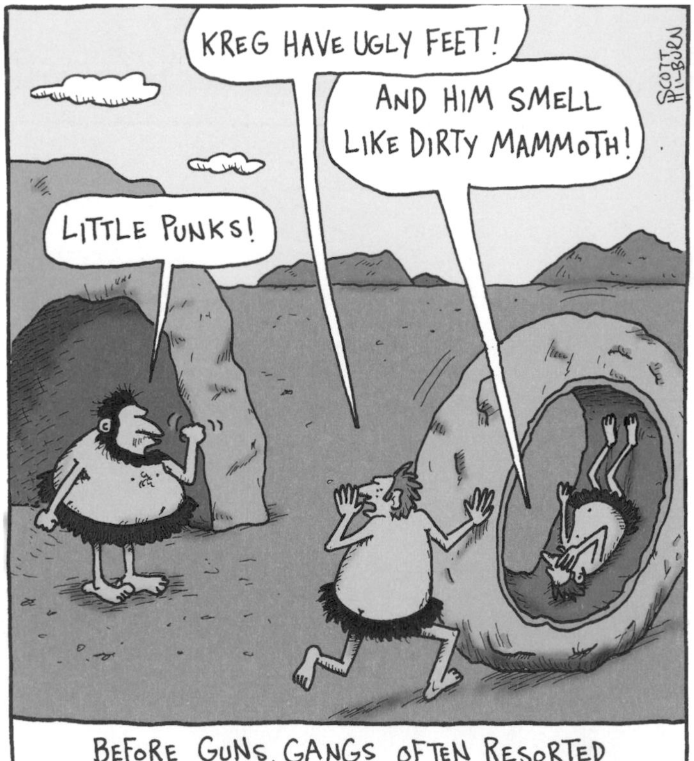
SCOTT HILBURN
LITTLE PUNKS!
KREG HAVE UGLY FEET!
AND HIM SMELL LIKE DIRTY MAMMOTH!

BEFORE GUNS, GANGS OFTEN RESORTED TO DRIVE-BY SHOUTINGS.

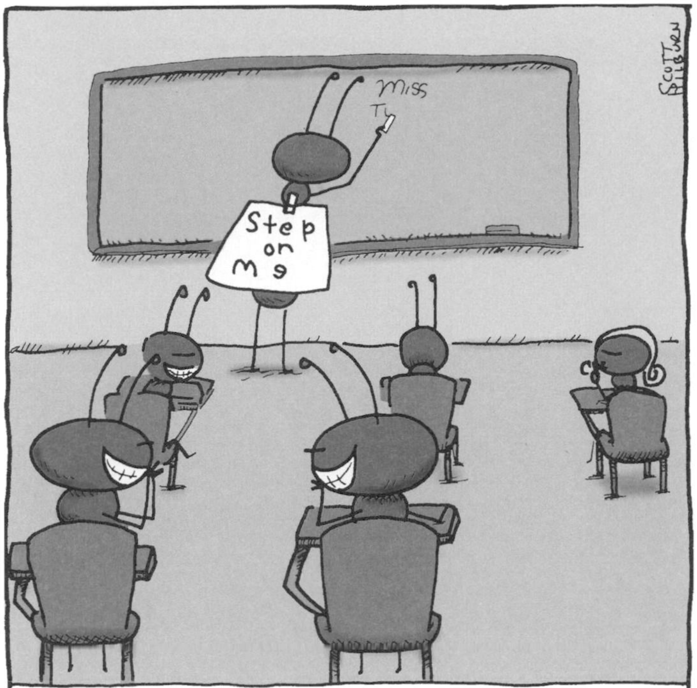
Miss
Step on Me
SCOTT HILBURN

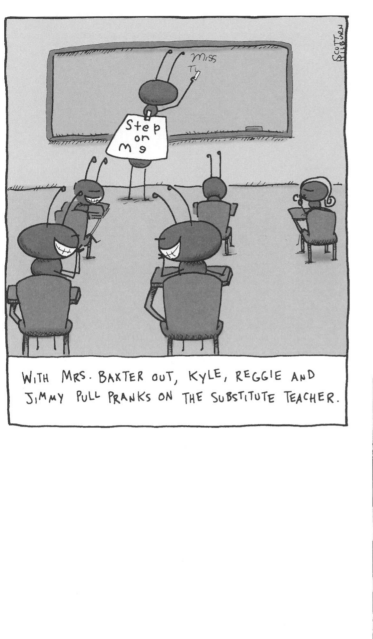

WITH MRS. BAXTER OUT, KYLE, REGGIE AND JIMMY PULL PRANKS ON THE SUBSTITUTE TEACHER.

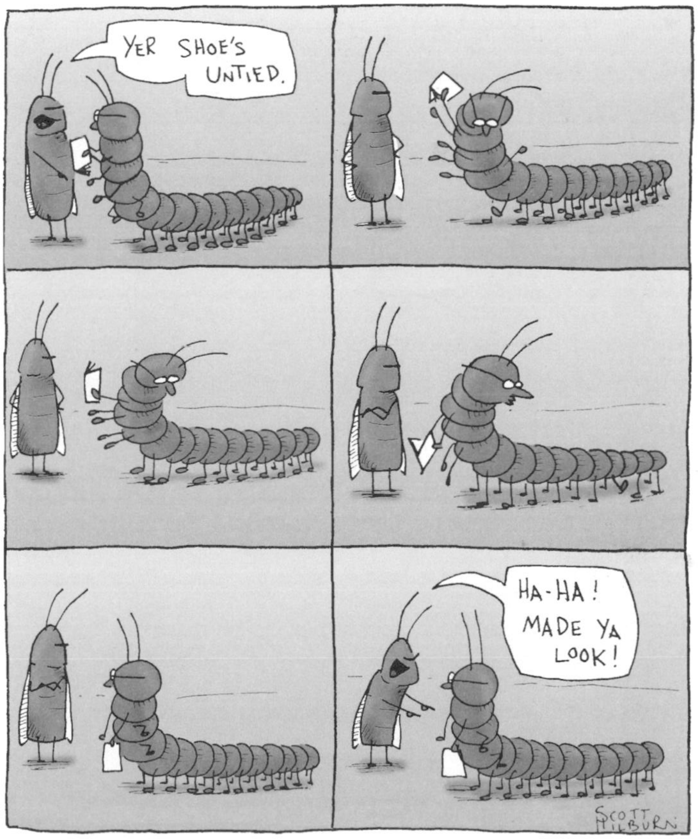
YER SHOE'S UNTIED.
HA-HA! MADE YA LOOK!
SCOTT HILBURN

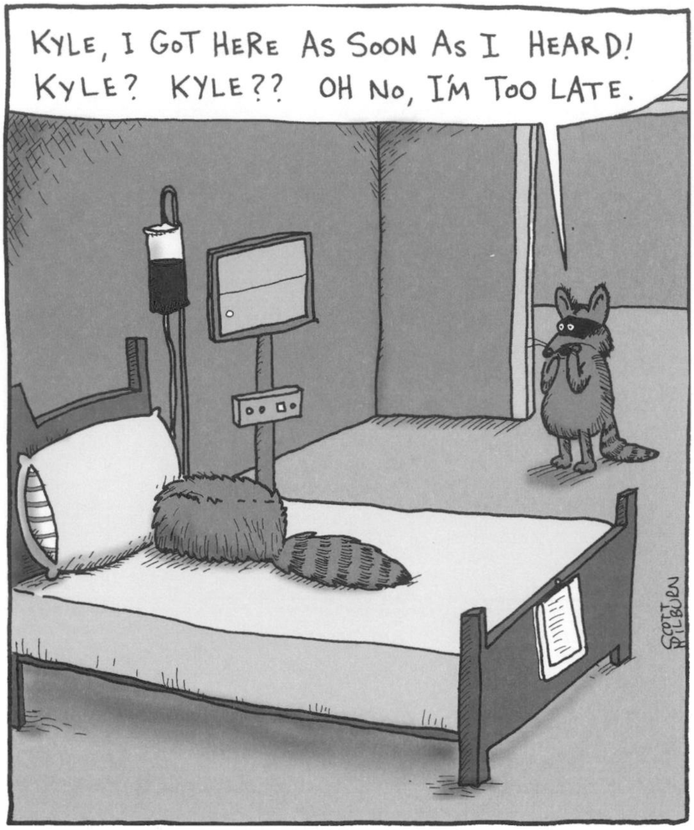
KYLE, I GOT HERE AS SOON AS I HEARD! KYLE? KYLE?? OH NO, I'M TOO LATE.
SCOTT HILBURN

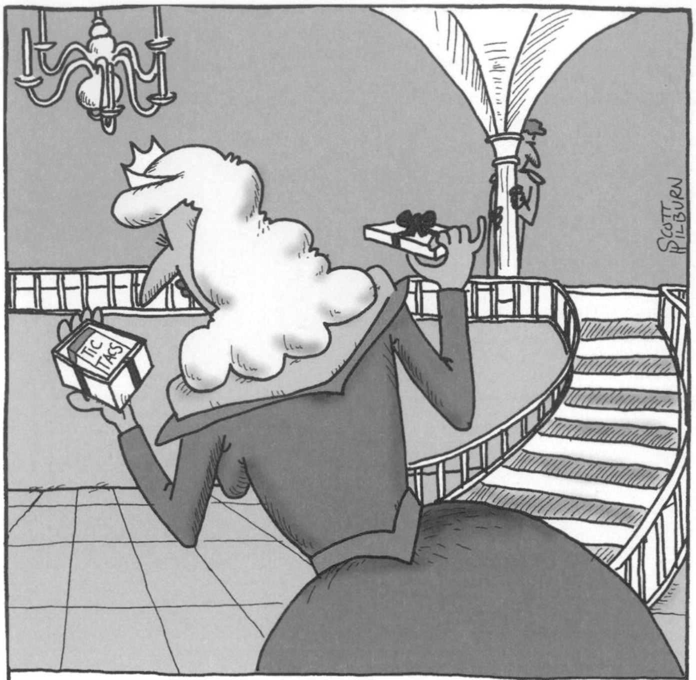
TIC TACS
SCOTT HILBURN
AFTER 100 YEARS OF SLUMBER, THE PRINCE AWAKENS SLEEPING BEAUTY WITH A KISS... AND THEN LEAVES HER A NOT-SO-SUBTLE HINT.

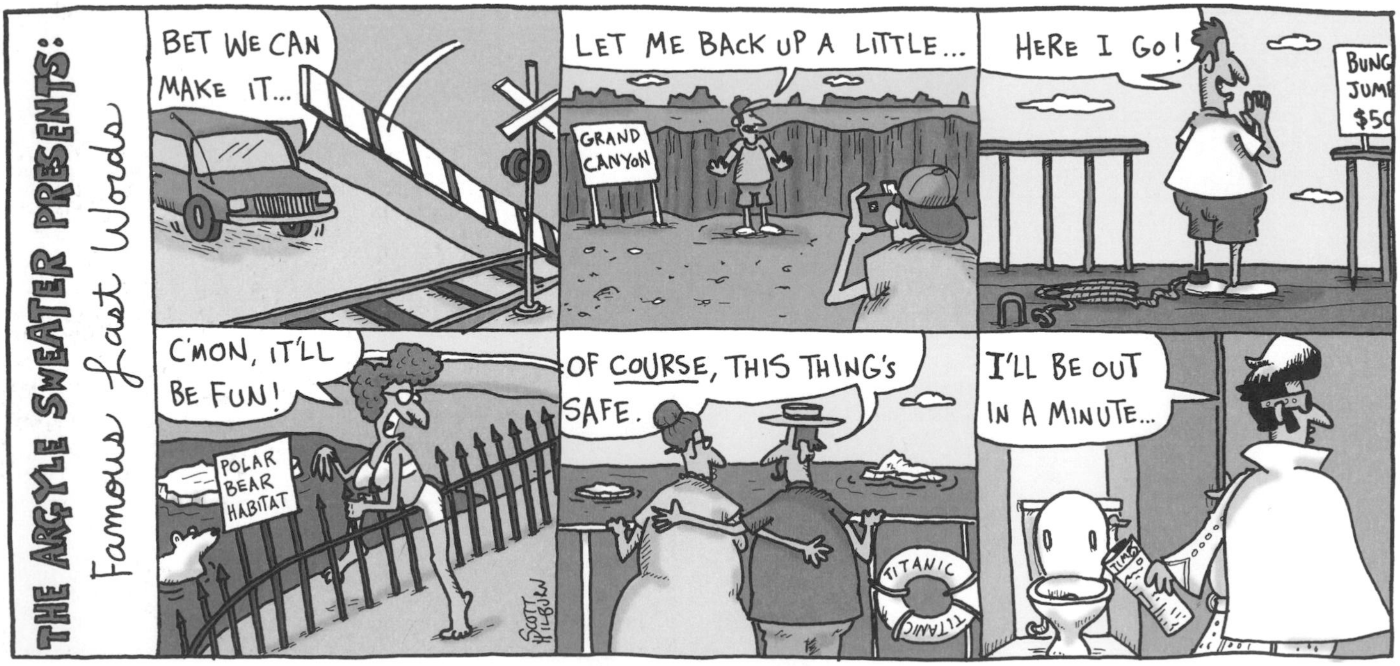
THE ARGYLE SWEATER PRESENTS:
Famous Last Words
BET WE CAN MAKE IT...
LET ME BACK UP A LITTLE...
GRAND CANYON
HERE I GO!
C'MON, IT'LL BE FUN!
POLAR BEAR HABITAT
OF COURSE, THIS THING'S SAFE.
TITANIC
I'LL BE OUT IN A MINUTE...
SCOTT HILBURN

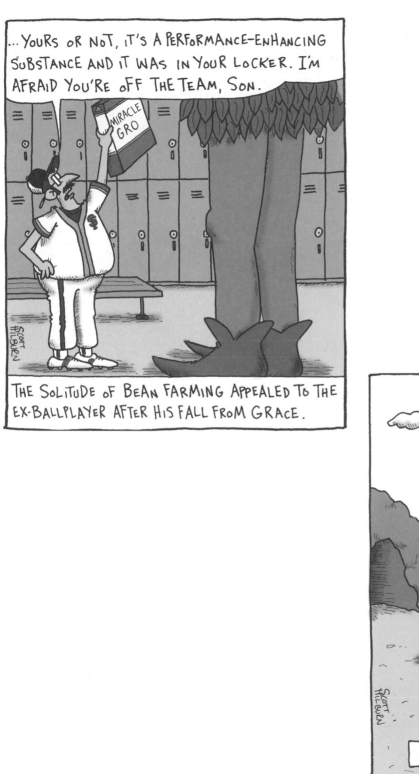

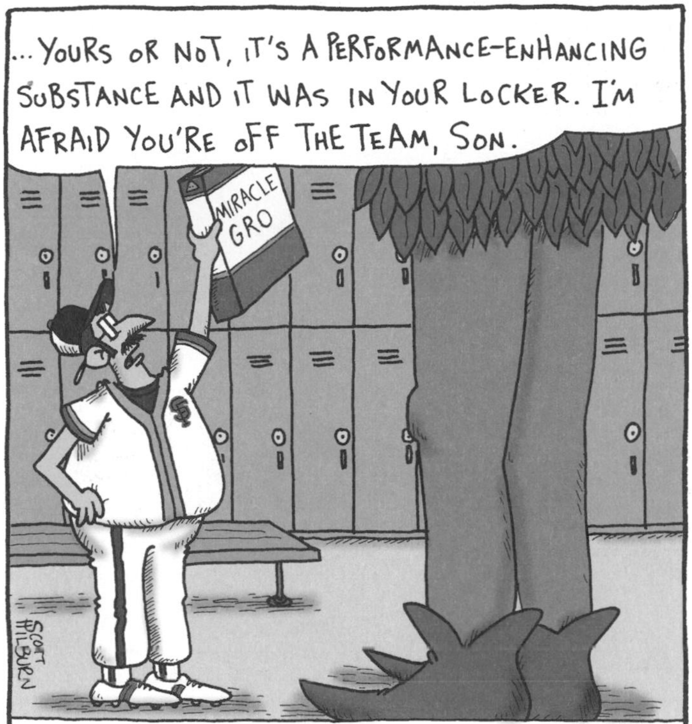
...YOURS OR NOT, IT'S A PERFORMANCE-ENHANCING SUBSTANCE AND IT WAS IN YOUR LOCKER. I'M AFRAID YOU'RE OFF THE TEAM, SON.
MIRACLE GRO
SF
SCOTT HILBURN

THE SOLITUDE OF BEAN FARMING APPEALED TO THE EX-BALLPLAYER AFTER HIS FALL FROM GRACE.

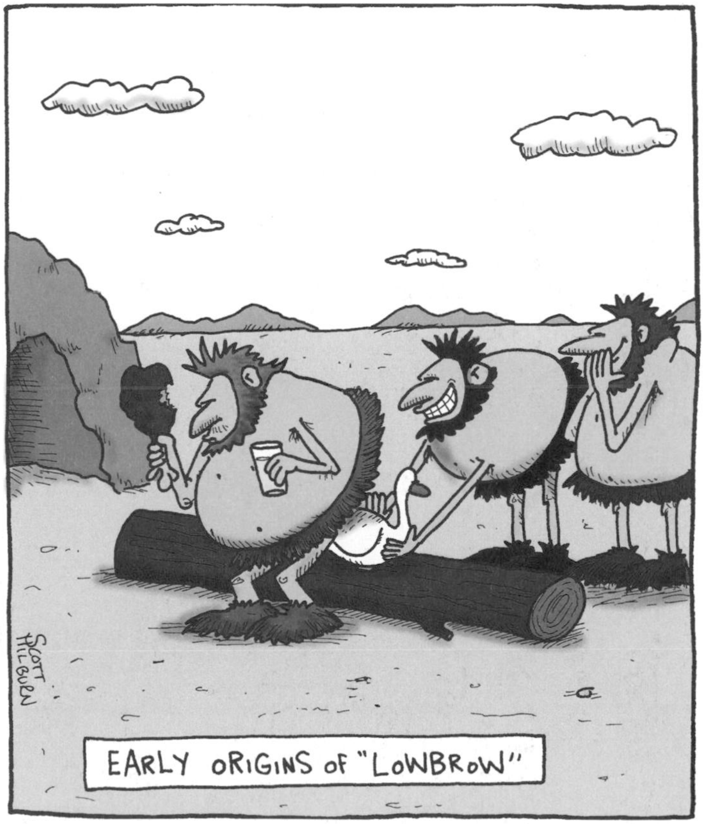
SCOTT HILBURN

EARLY ORIGINS OF "LOWBROW"

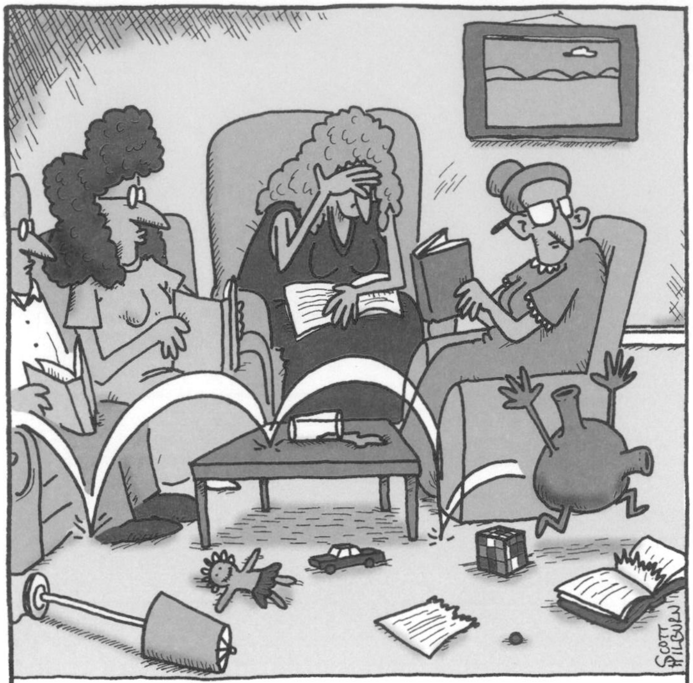
SCOTT HILBURN

AT HER WEEKLY BOOK CLUB MEETING, DONNA IS, AGAIN, EMBARRASSED BY THE INABILITY TO CONTROL HER BLADDER.

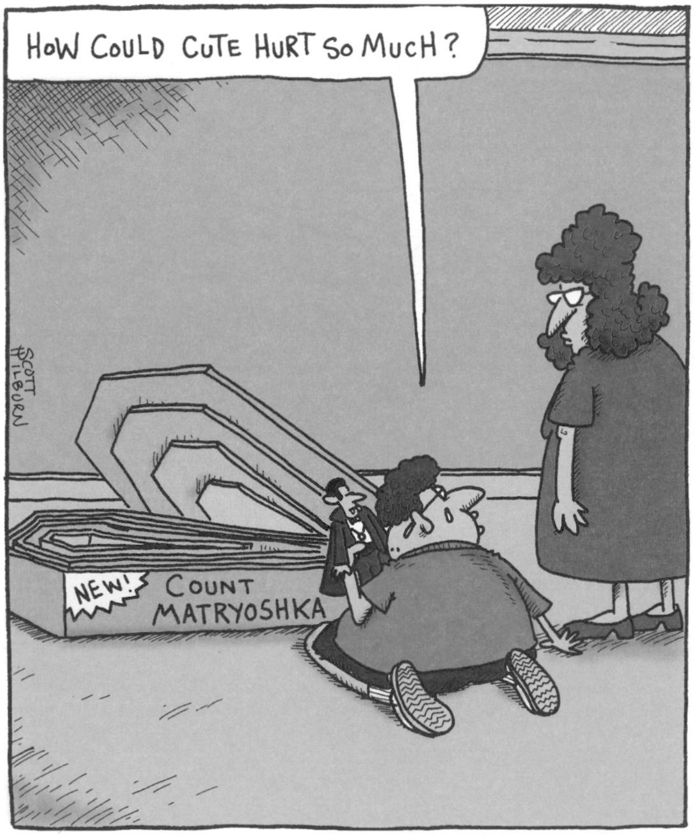
HOW COULD CUTE HURT SO MUCH?
SCOTT HILBURN
NEW!
COUNT MATRYOSHKA

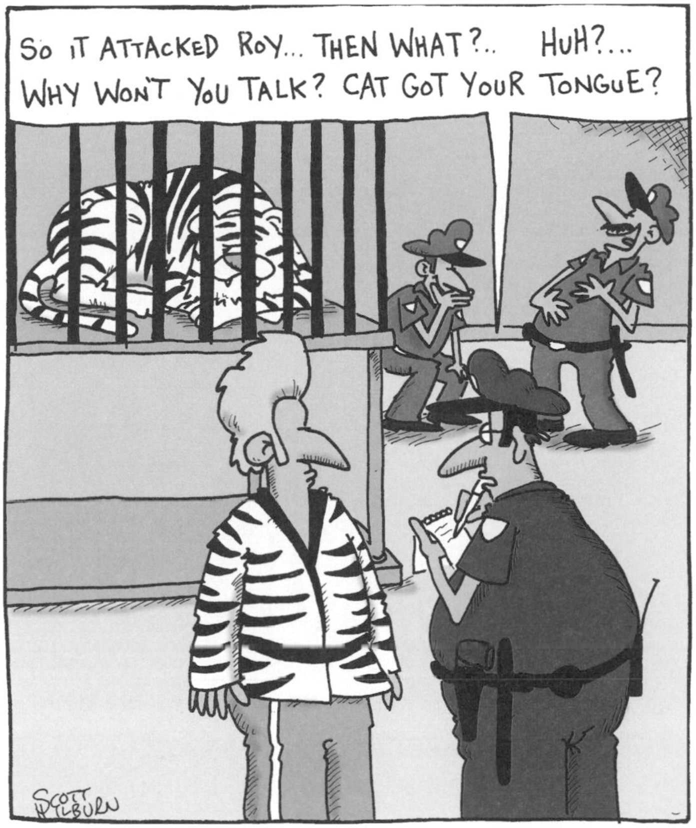
SO IT ATTACKED ROY... THEN WHAT?.. HUH?... WHY WON'T YOU TALK? CAT GOT YOUR TONGUE?

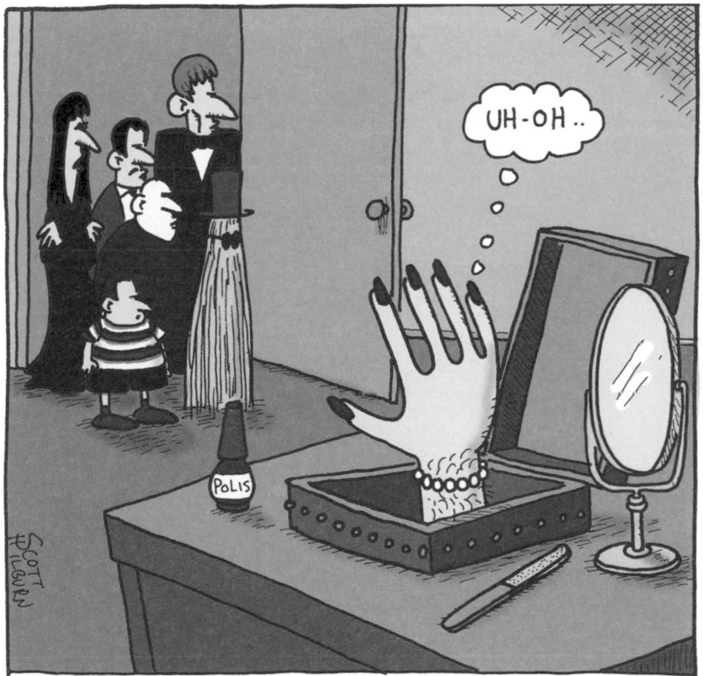
UH-OH..
POLIS

GOMEZ, MORTICIA AND THE REST OF THE FAMILY RETURN HOME SOONER THAN EXPECTED AND DISCOVER THING'S SECRET LIFE.

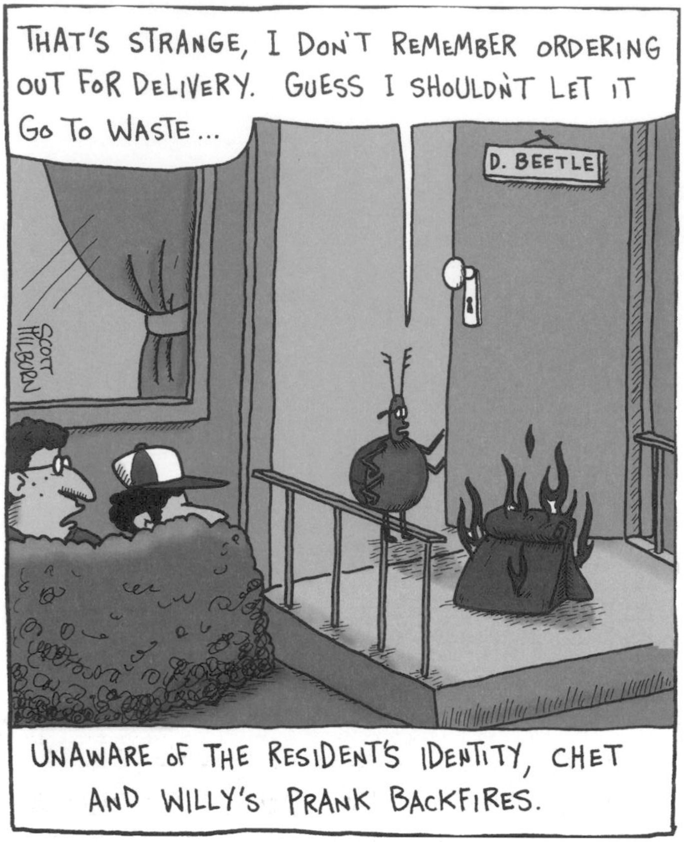
THAT'S STRANGE, I DON'T REMEMBER ORDERING OUT FOR DELIVERY. GUESS I SHOULDN'T LET IT GO TO WASTE...
D. BEETLE
SCOTT HILBURN
UNAWARE OF THE RESIDENT'S IDENTITY, CHET AND WILLY'S PRANK BACKFIRES.

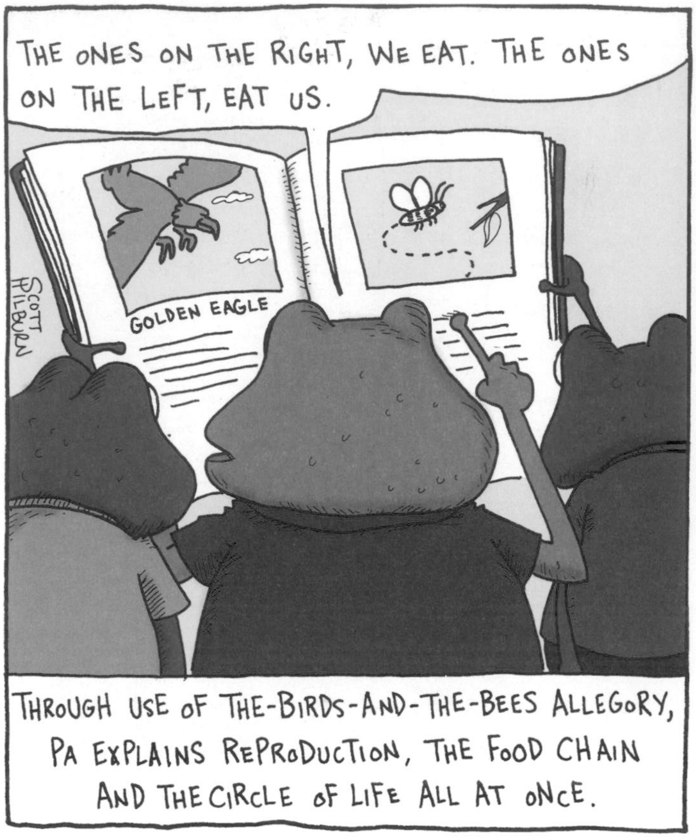
THE ONES ON THE RIGHT, WE EAT. THE ONES ON THE LEFT, EAT US.
GOLDEN EAGLE
SCOTT HILBURN
THROUGH USE OF THE-BIRDS-AND-THE-BEES ALLEGORY, PA EXPLAINS REPRODUCTION, THE FOOD CHAIN AND THE CIRCLE OF LIFE ALL AT ONCE.

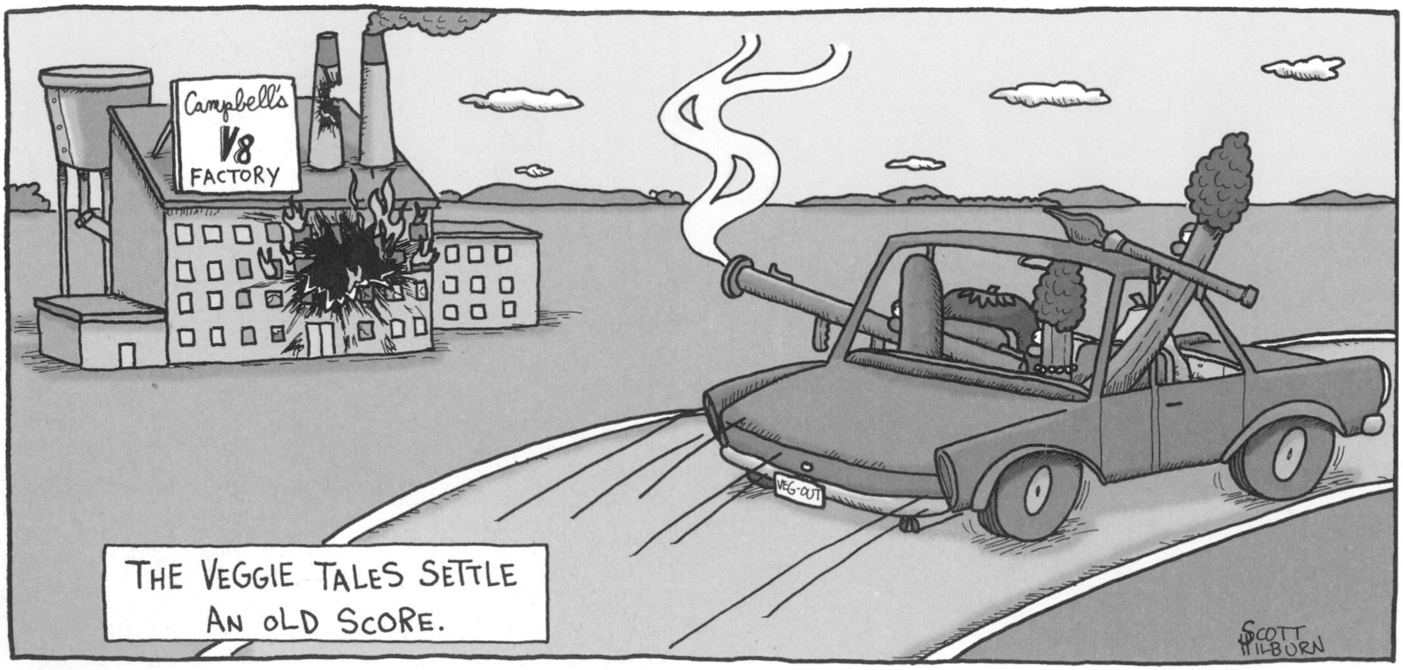
Campbell's V8 FACTORY
VEG-OUT
THE VEGGIE TALES SETTLE AN OLD SCORE.
SCOTT HILBURN

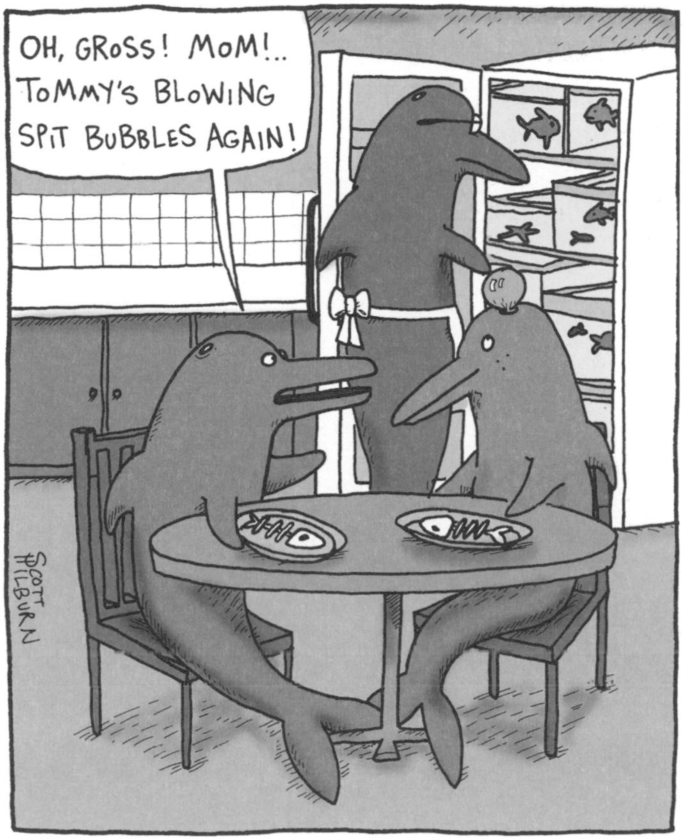
OH, GROSS! MOM!.. TOMMY'S BLOWING SPIT BUBBLES AGAIN!
SCOTT HILBURN

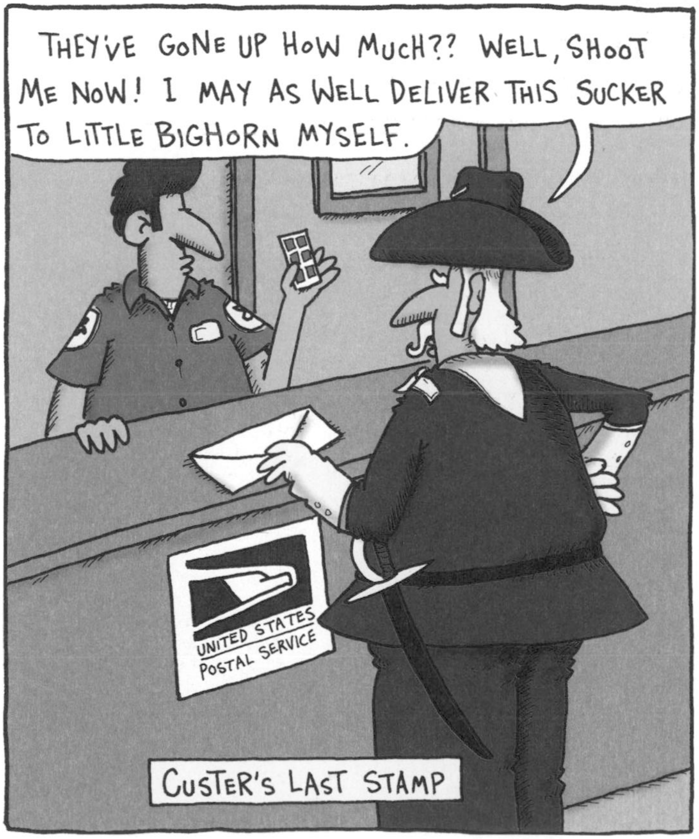
THEY'VE GONE UP HOW MUCH?? WELL, SHOOT ME NOW! I MAY AS WELL DELIVER THIS SUCKER TO LITTLE BIGHORN MYSELF.
UNITED STATES POSTAL SERVICE
CUSTER'S LAST STAMP

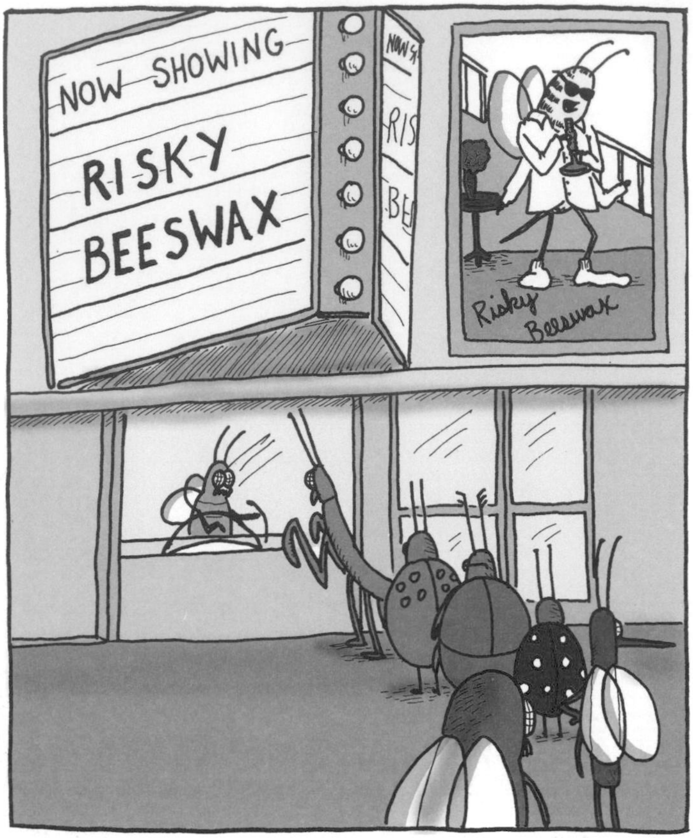
NOW SHOWING
RISKY
BEESWAX
Risky Beeswax

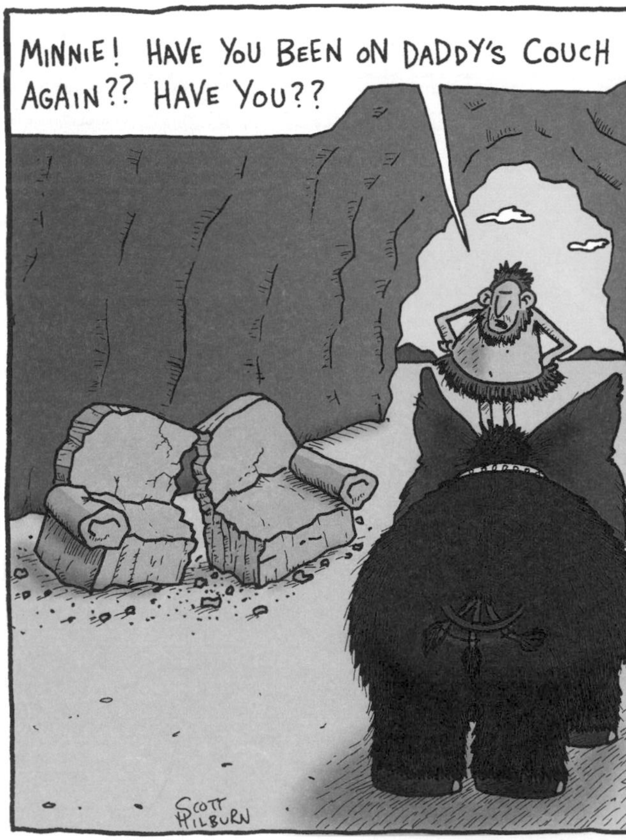
MINNIE! HAVE YOU BEEN ON DADDY'S COUCH AGAIN?? HAVE YOU??
SCOTT HILBURN

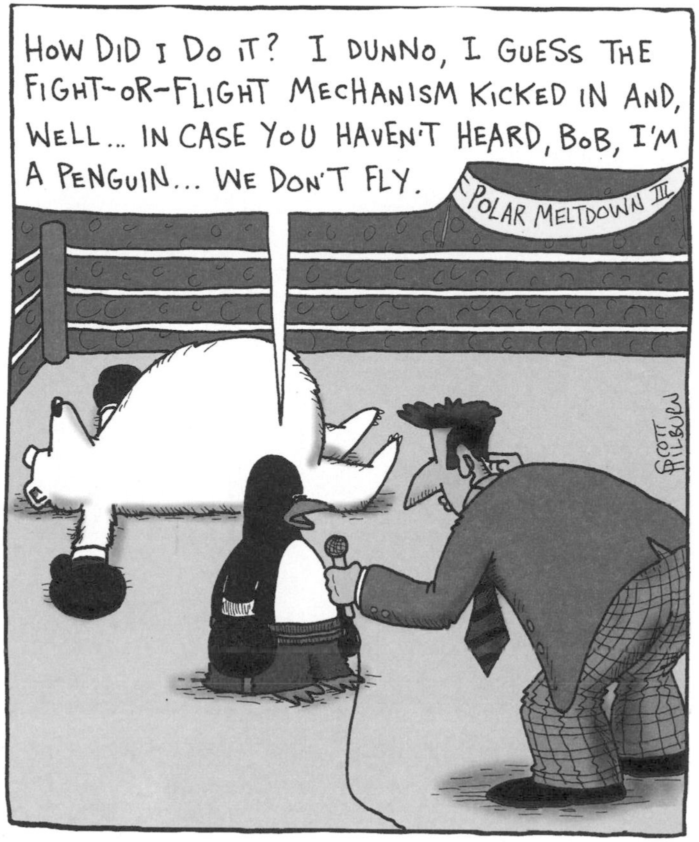
HOW DID I DO IT? I DUNNO, I GUESS THE FIGHT-OR-FLIGHT MECHANISM KICKED IN AND, WELL... IN CASE YOU HAVEN'T HEARD, BOB, I'M A PENGUIN... WE DON'T FLY.
POLAR MELTDOWN III
SCOTT HILBURN

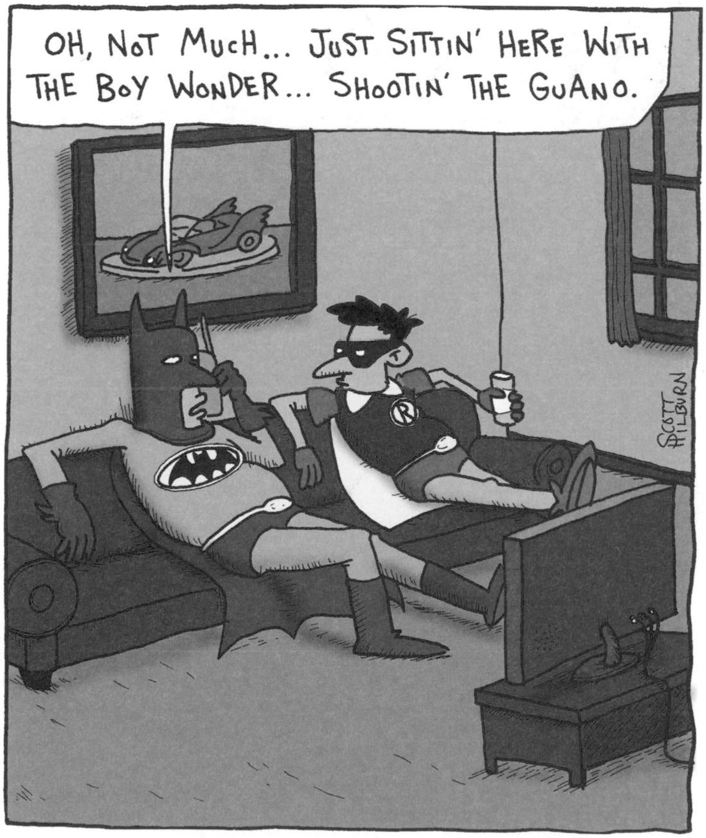
OH, NOT MUCH... JUST SITTIN' HERE WITH THE BOY WONDER... SHOOTIN' THE GUANO.
SCOTT HILBURN

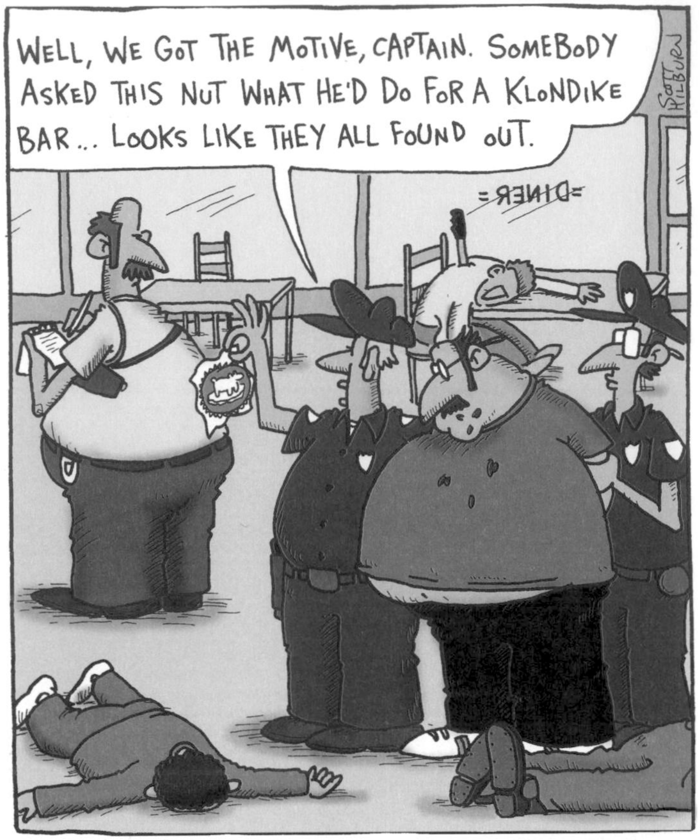
WELL, WE GOT THE MOTIVE, CAPTAIN. SOMEBODY ASKED THIS NUT WHAT HE'D DO FOR A KLONDIKE BAR... LOOKS LIKE THEY ALL FOUND OUT.
SCOTT HILBURN

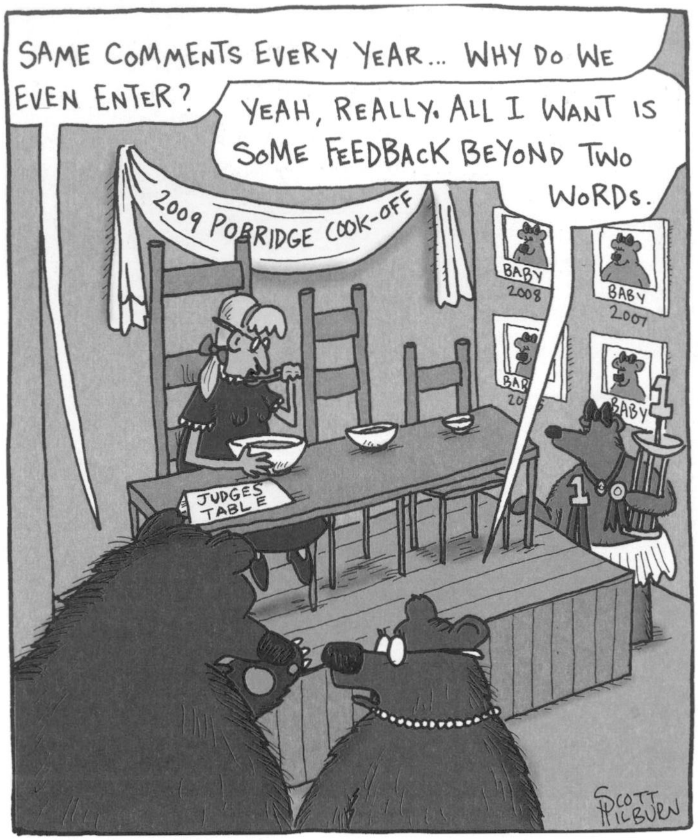
SAME COMMENTS EVERY YEAR... WHY DO WE EVEN ENTER?
YEAH, REALLY. ALL I WANT IS SOME FEEDBACK BEYOND TWO WORDS.
2009 PORRIDGE COOK-OFF
BABY 2008
BABY 2007
JUDGES TABLE
SCOTT HILBURN

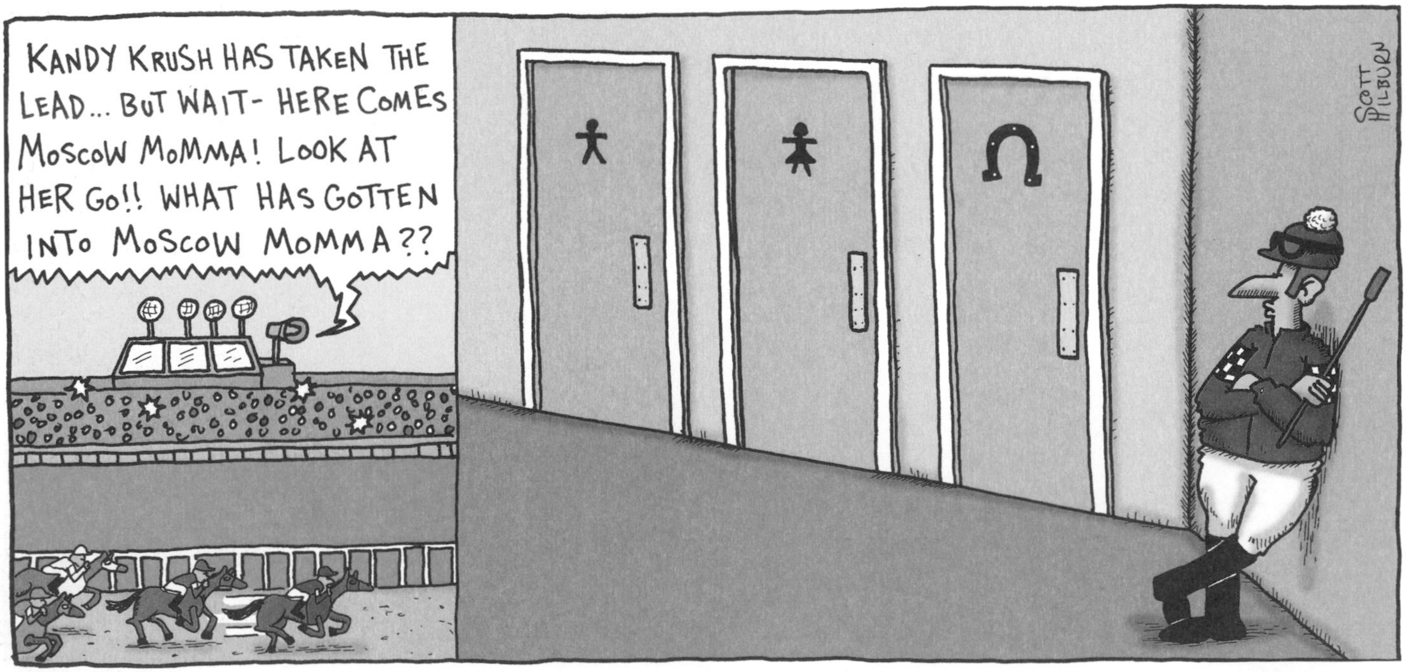
KANDY KRUSH HAS TAKEN THE LEAD... BUT WAIT- HERE COMES MOSCOW MOMMA! LOOK AT HER GO!! WHAT HAS GOTTEN INTO MOSCOW MOMMA??
SCOTT HILBURN

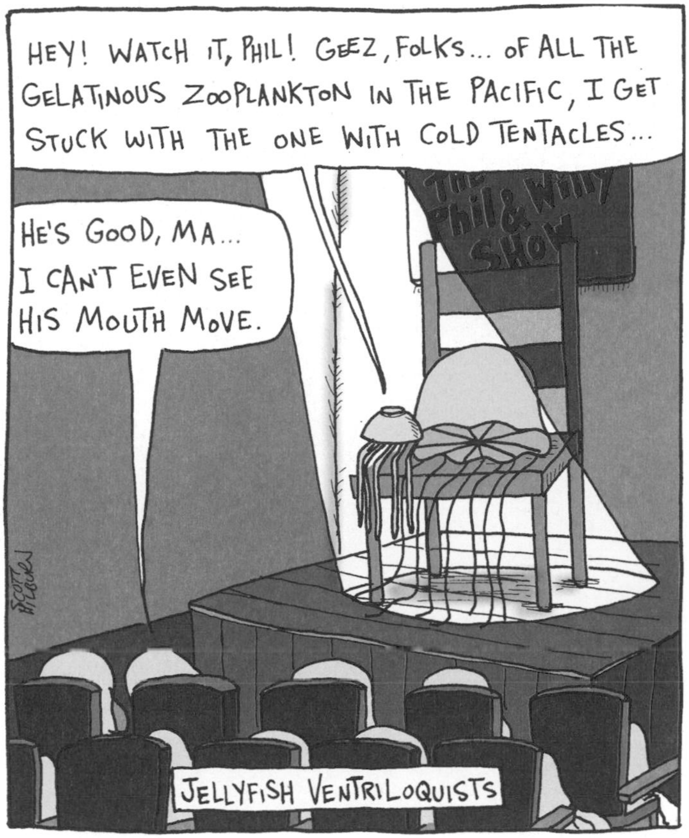
HEY! WATCH IT, PHIL! GEEZ, FOLKS... OF ALL THE GELATINOUS ZOOPLANKTON IN THE PACIFIC, I GET STUCK WITH THE ONE WITH COLD TENTACLES...
HE'S GOOD, MA... I CAN'T EVEN SEE HIS MOUTH MOVE.
The Phil & Willy Show
JELLYFISH VENTRILOQUISTS

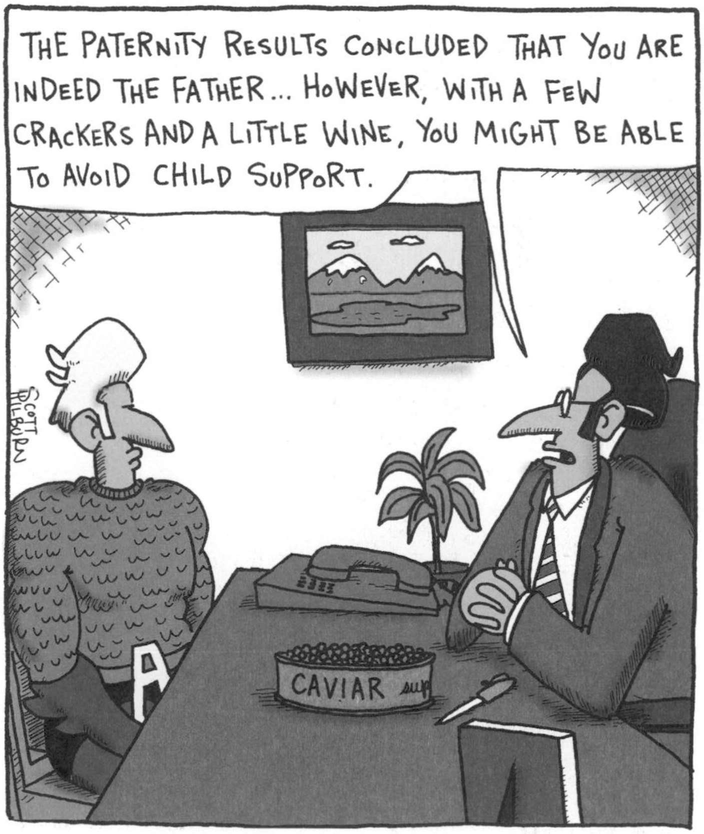
THE PATERNITY RESULTS CONCLUDED THAT YOU ARE INDEED THE FATHER... HOWEVER, WITH A FEW CRACKERS AND A LITTLE WINE, YOU MIGHT BE ABLE TO AVOID CHILD SUPPORT.
A
CAVIAR

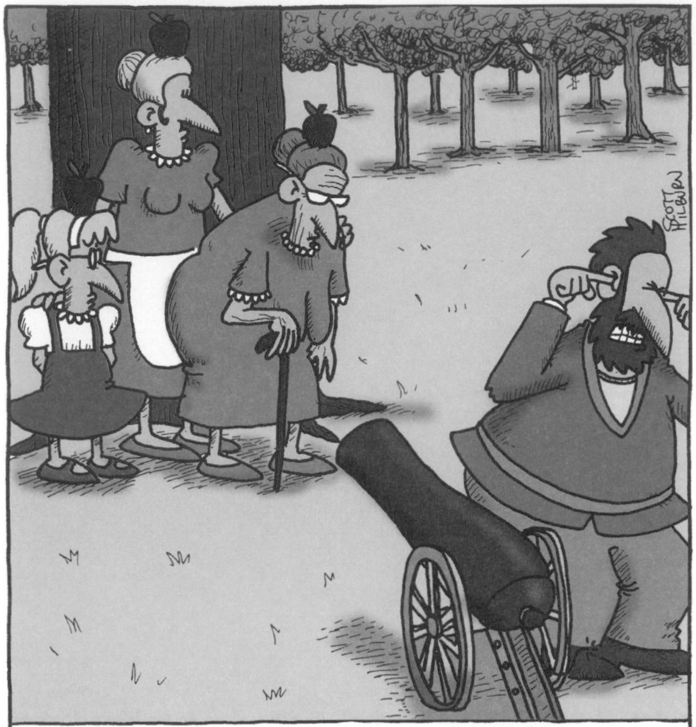
SCOTT HILBURN

BUOYED BY HIS PAST SUCCESS, WILLIAM TELL SOUGHT EVEN GREATER CHALLENGES.

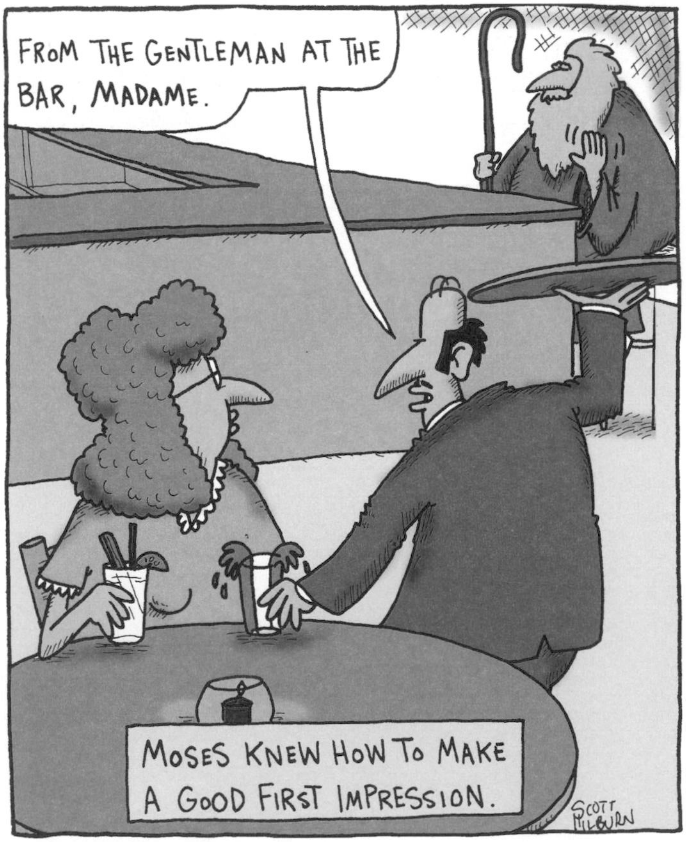
FROM THE GENTLEMAN AT THE BAR, MADAME.
SCOTT HILBURN

MOSES KNEW HOW TO MAKE A GOOD FIRST IMPRESSION.

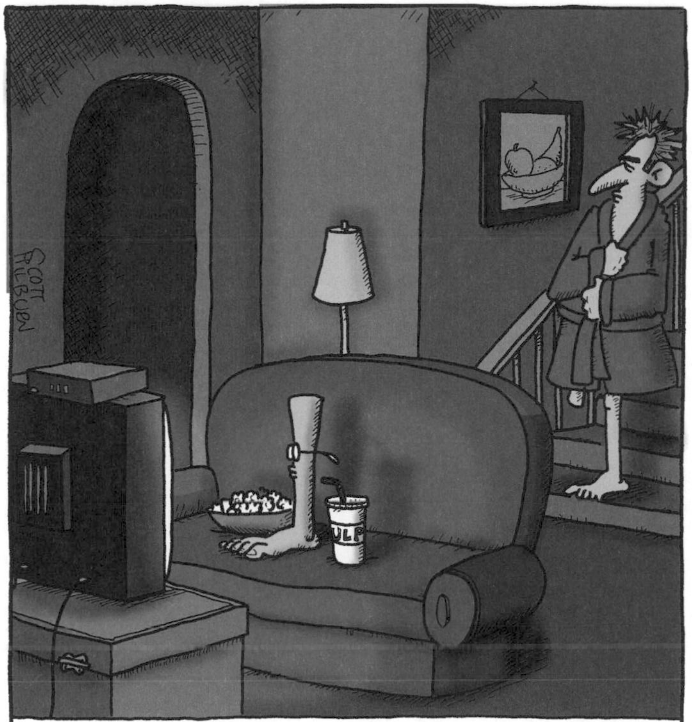
SCOTT HILBURN

FOR THE 5TH TIME IN AS MANY NIGHTS, HERB IS AWAKENED BY HIS RESTLESS-LEG SYNDROME.

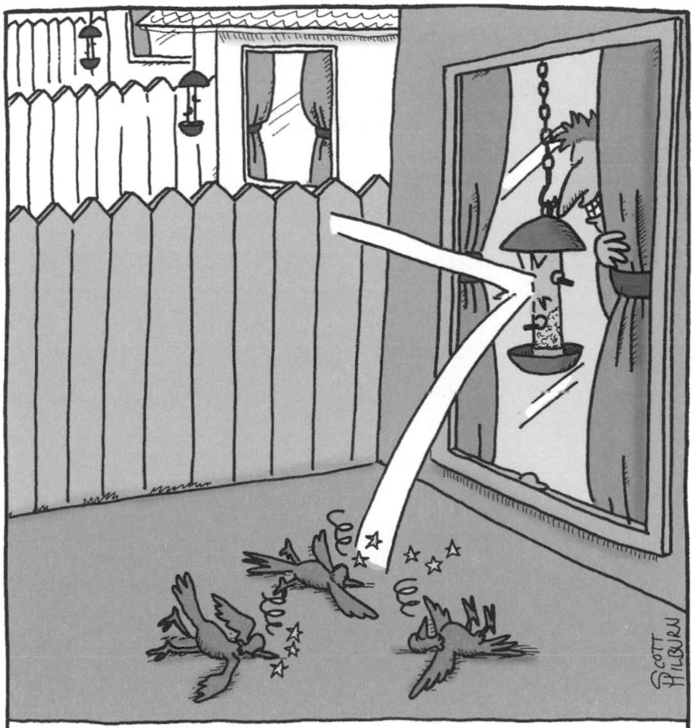
SCOTT HILBURN

THEY'D THINK TWICE ABOUT DEFACING ELLIOTT'S CAMARO AGAIN.

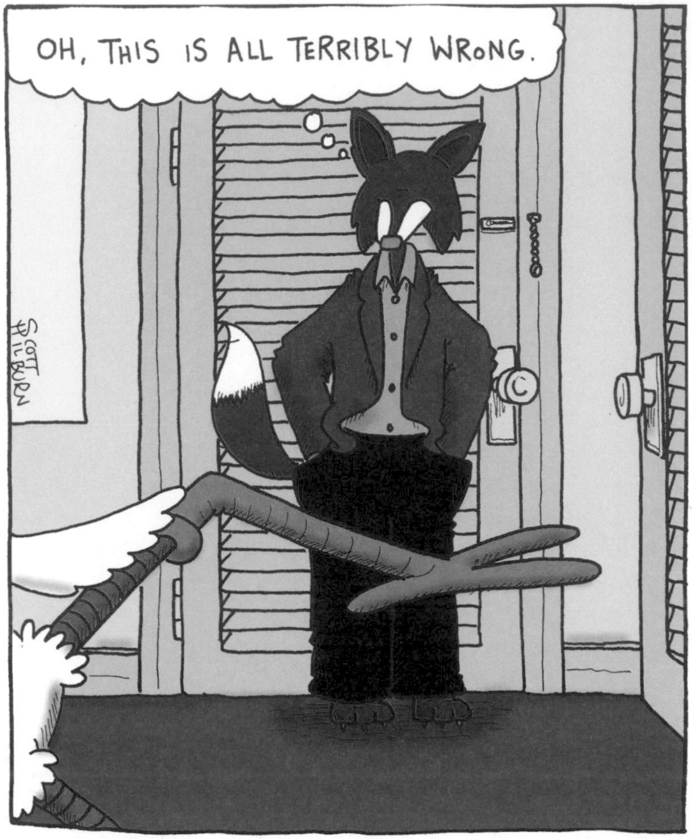
OH, THIS IS ALL TERRIBLY WRONG.
SCOTT HILBURN

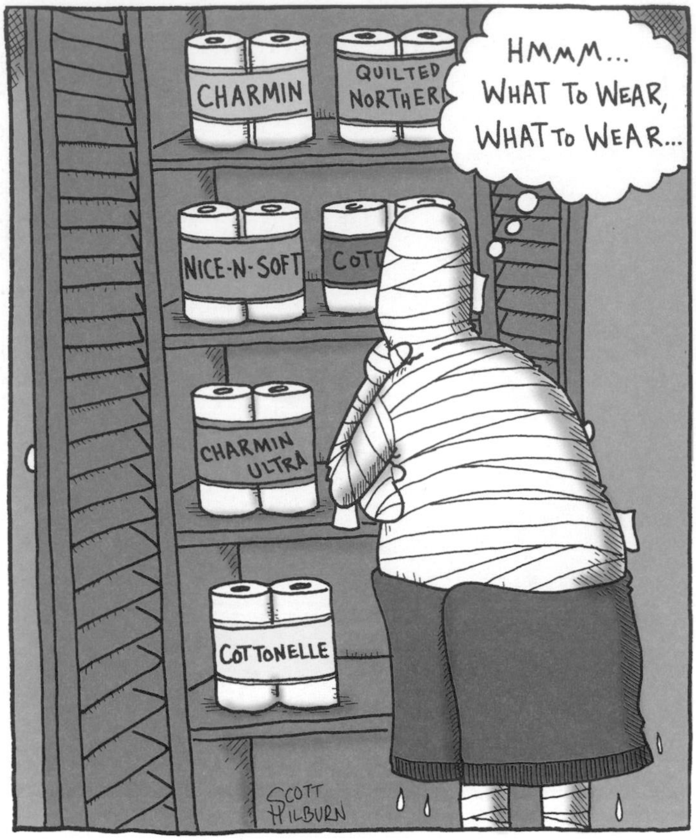
CHARMIN
QUILTED NORTHER
HMMM... WHAT TO WEAR, WHAT TO WEAR...
NICE-N-SOFT
COTT
CHARMIN ULTRA
COTTONELLE
SCOTT HILBURN

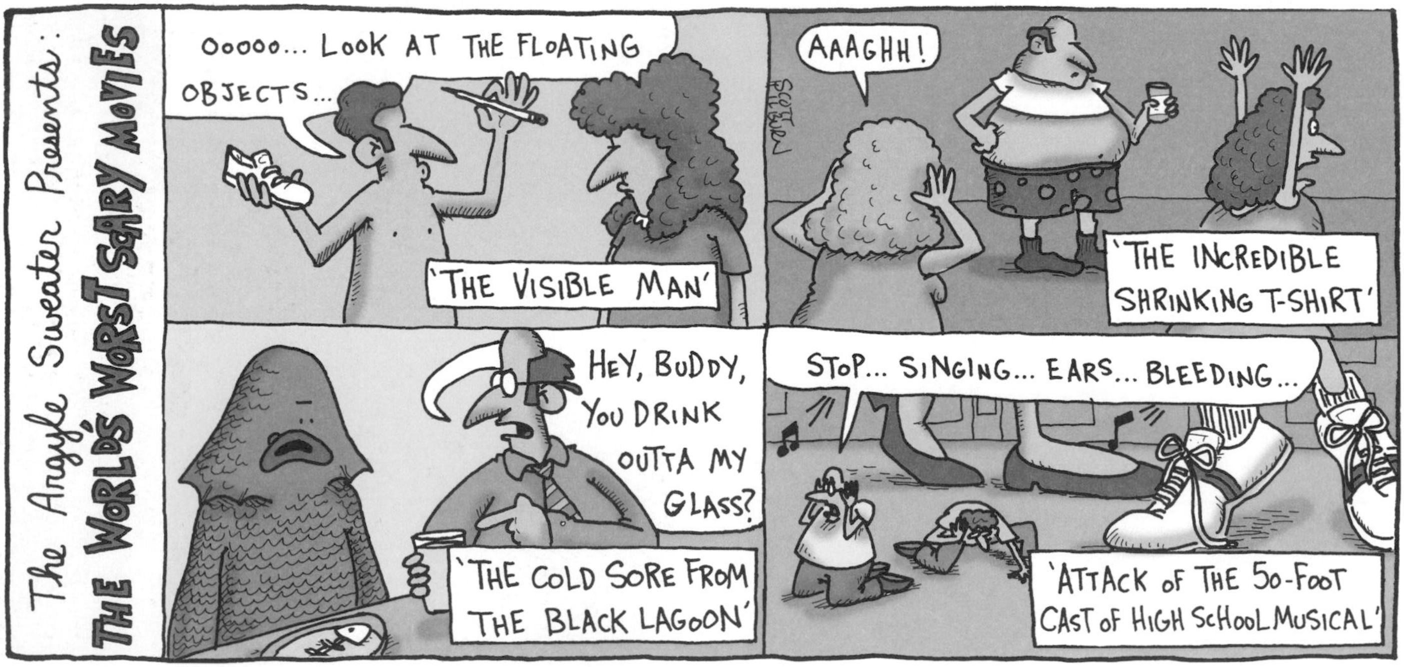
The Argyle Sweater Presents:
THE WORLD'S WORST SCARY MOVIES
OOOOO... LOOK AT THE FLOATING OBJECTS...
'THE VISIBLE MAN'
AAAGHH!
'THE INCREDIBLE SHRINKING T-SHIRT'
HEY, BUDDY, YOU DRINK OUTTA MY GLASS?
'THE COLD SORE FROM THE BLACK LAGOON'
STOP... SINGING... EARS... BLEEDING...
'ATTACK OF THE 50-FOOT CAST OF HIGH SCHOOL MUSICAL'

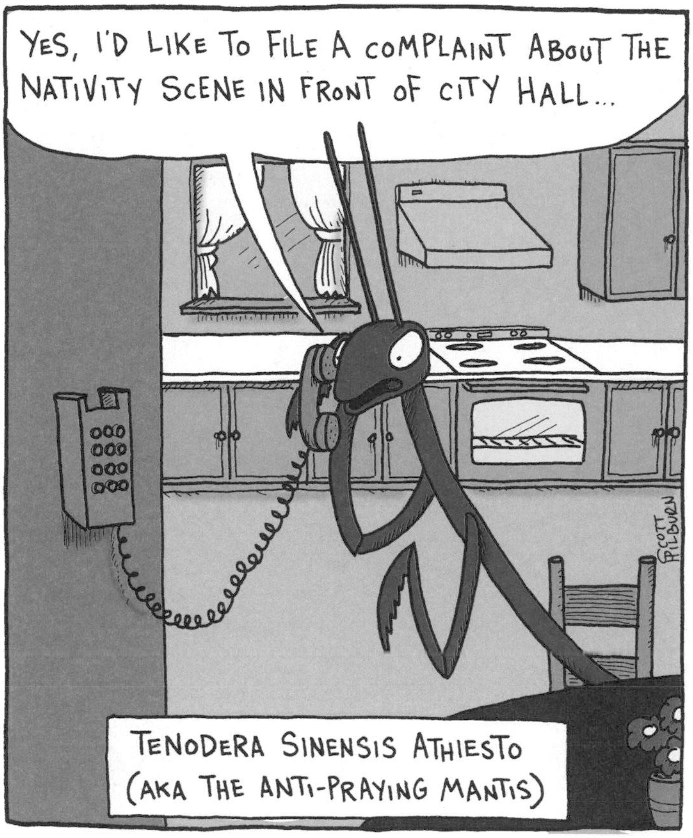
YES, I'D LIKE TO FILE A COMPLAINT ABOUT THE NATIVITY SCENE IN FRONT OF CITY HALL...
TENODERA SINENSIS ATHIESTO
(AKA THE ANTI-PRAYING MANTIS)

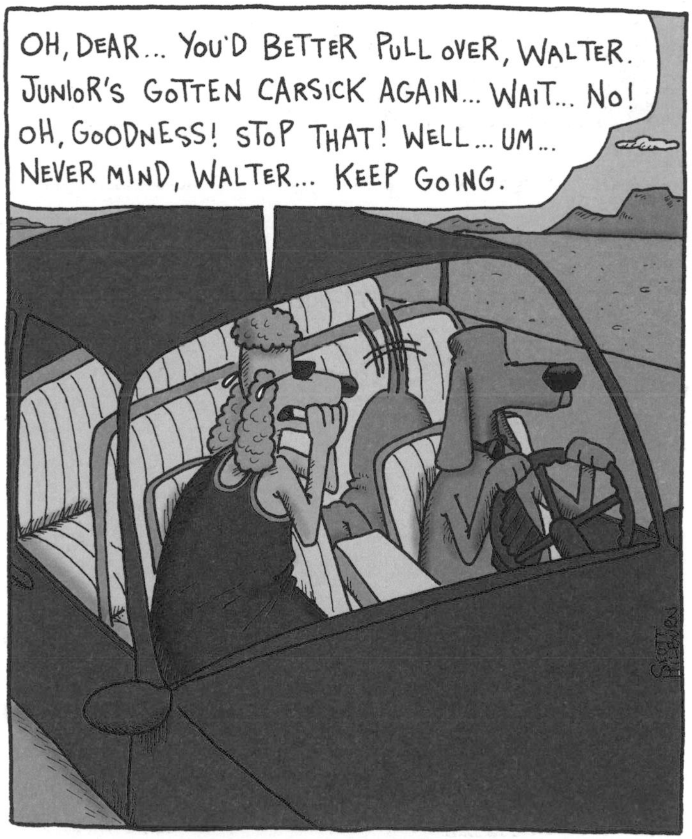
OH, DEAR... YOU'D BETTER PULL OVER, WALTER. JUNIOR'S GOTTEN CARSICK AGAIN... WAIT... NO! OH, GOODNESS! STOP THAT! WELL... UM... NEVER MIND, WALTER... KEEP GOING.

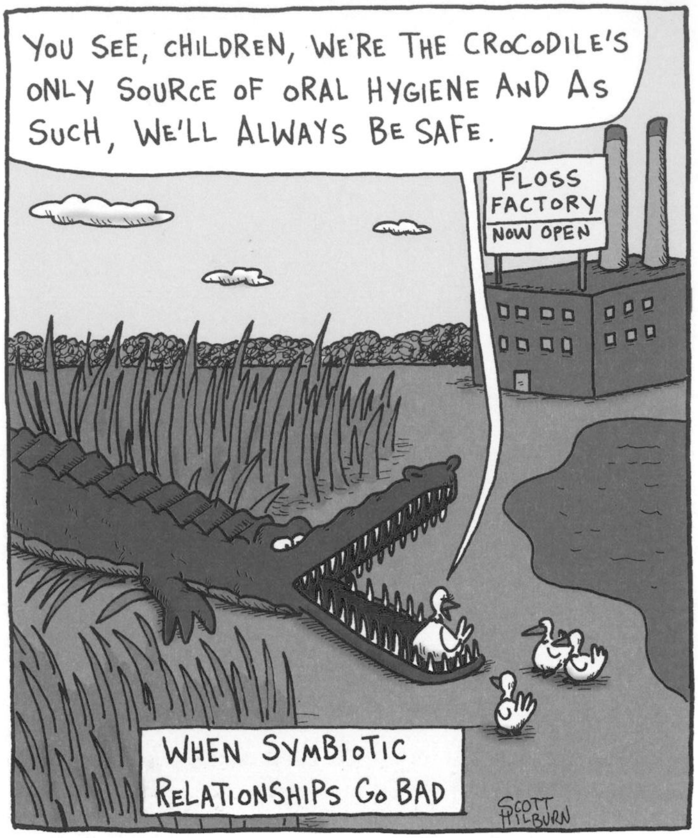
YOU SEE, CHILDREN, WE'RE THE CROCODILE'S ONLY SOURCE OF ORAL HYGIENE AND AS SUCH, WE'LL ALWAYS BE SAFE.
FLOSS FACTORY
NOW OPEN
SCOTT HILBURN

WHEN SYMBIOTIC RELATIONSHIPS GO BAD

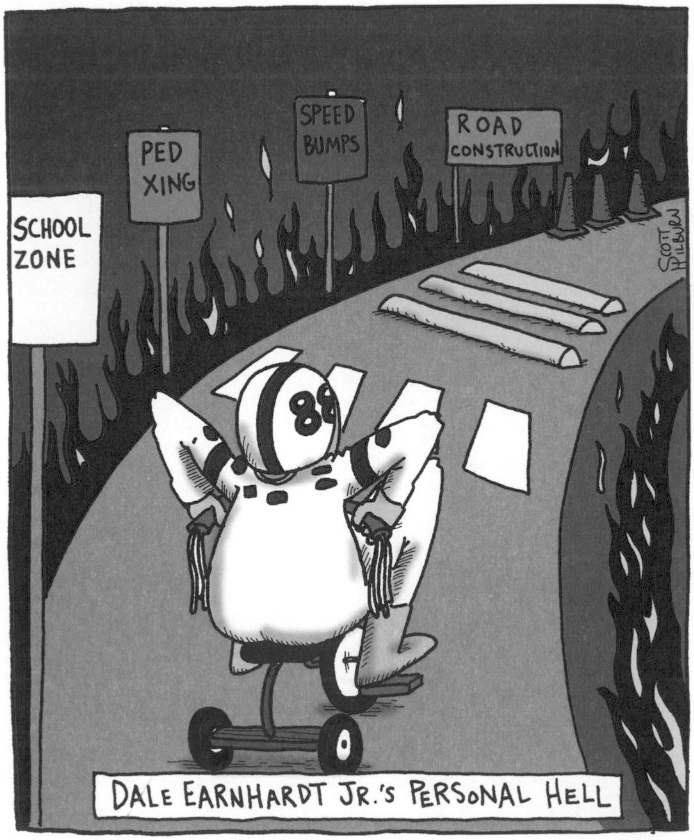
SCHOOL ZONE
PED XING
SPEED BUMPS
ROAD CONSTRUCTION
88
SCOTT HILBURN

DALE EARNHARDT JR.'S PERSONAL HELL

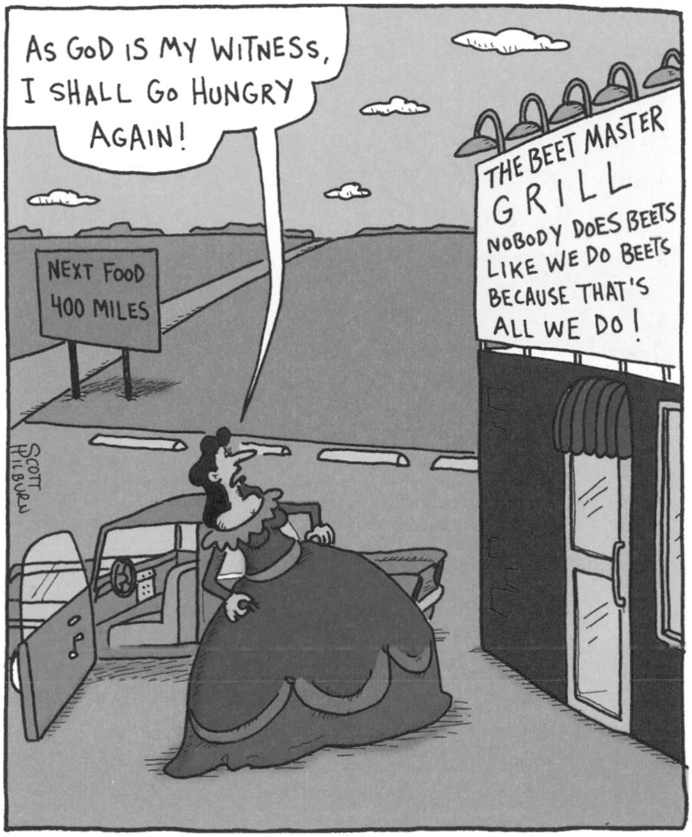
AS GOD IS MY WITNESS, I SHALL GO HUNGRY AGAIN!
NEXT FOOD 400 MILES
THE BEET MASTER GRILL
NOBODY DOES BEETS LIKE WE DO BEETS BECAUSE THAT'S ALL WE DO!
SCOTT HILBURN

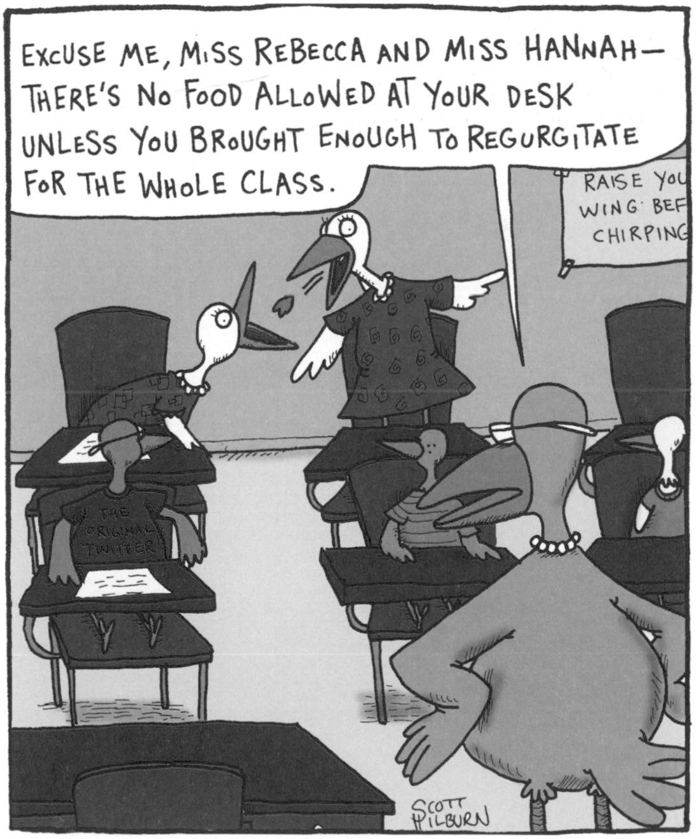
EXCUSE ME, MISS REBECCA AND MISS HANNAH— THERE'S NO FOOD ALLOWED AT YOUR DESK UNLESS YOU BROUGHT ENOUGH TO REGURGITATE FOR THE WHOLE CLASS.
RAISE YOU WING BEF CHIRPING
THE ORIGINAL TWITTER
SCOTT HILBURN

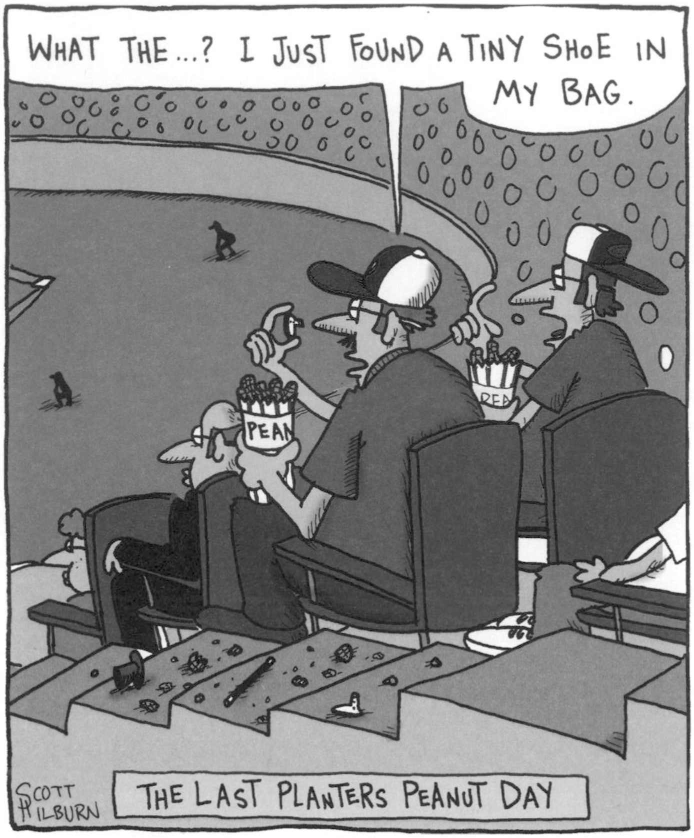
WHAT THE...? I JUST FOUND A TINY SHOE IN MY BAG.
PEAN
SCOTT HILBURN
THE LAST PLANTERS PEANUT DAY

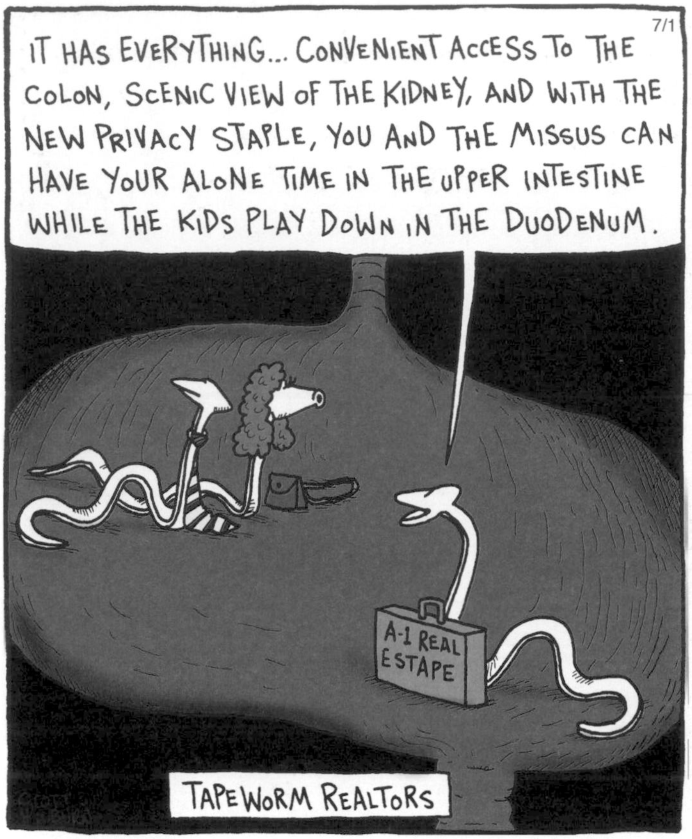
7/1
IT HAS EVERYTHING... CONVENIENT ACCESS TO THE COLON, SCENIC VIEW OF THE KIDNEY, AND WITH THE NEW PRIVACY STAPLE, YOU AND THE MISSUS CAN HAVE YOUR ALONE TIME IN THE UPPER INTESTINE WHILE THE KIDS PLAY DOWN IN THE DUODENUM.
A-1 REAL ESTAPE
TAPEWORM REALTORS

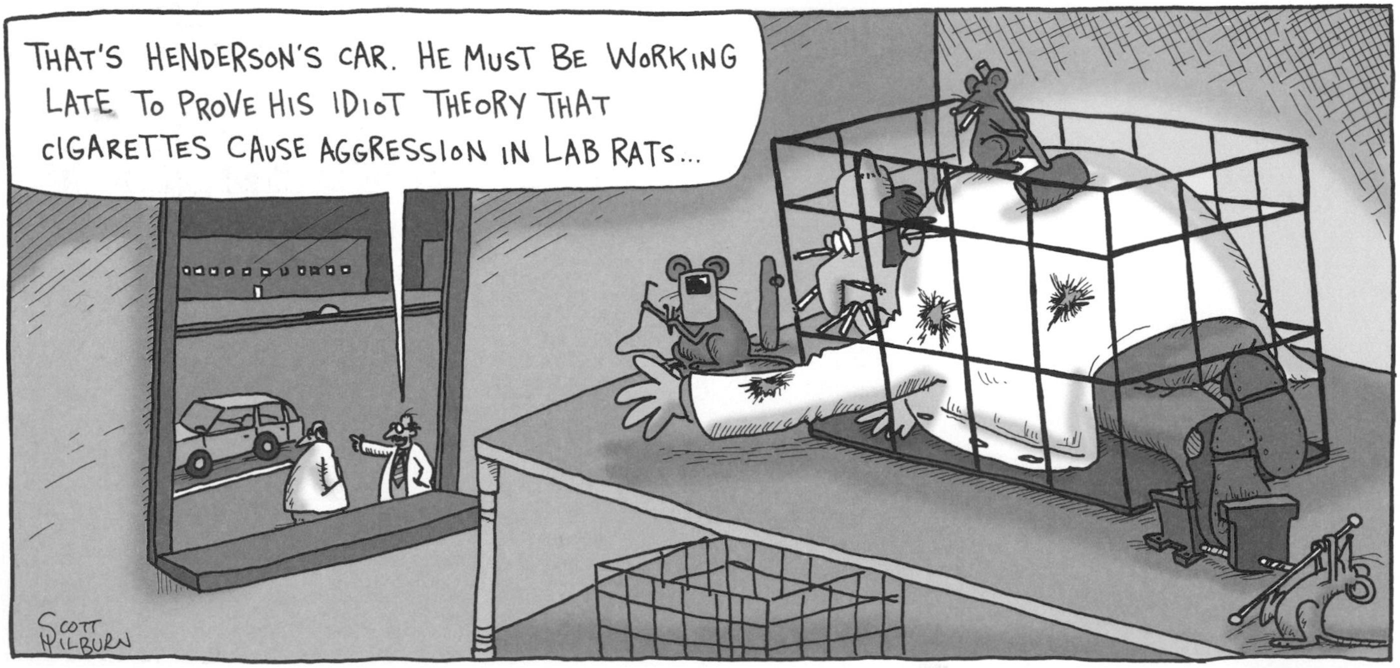
THAT'S HENDERSON'S CAR. HE MUST BE WORKING LATE TO PROVE HIS IDIOT THEORY THAT CIGARETTES CAUSE AGGRESSION IN LAB RATS...
SCOTT HILBURN

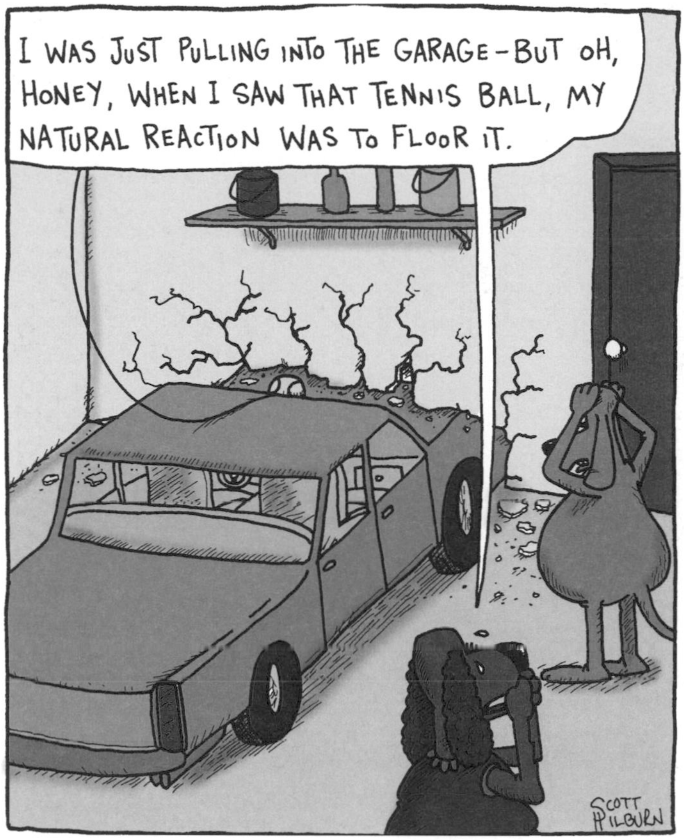
I WAS JUST PULLING INTO THE GARAGE - BUT OH, HONEY, WHEN I SAW THAT TENNIS BALL, MY NATURAL REACTION WAS TO FLOOR IT.
SCOTT HILBURN

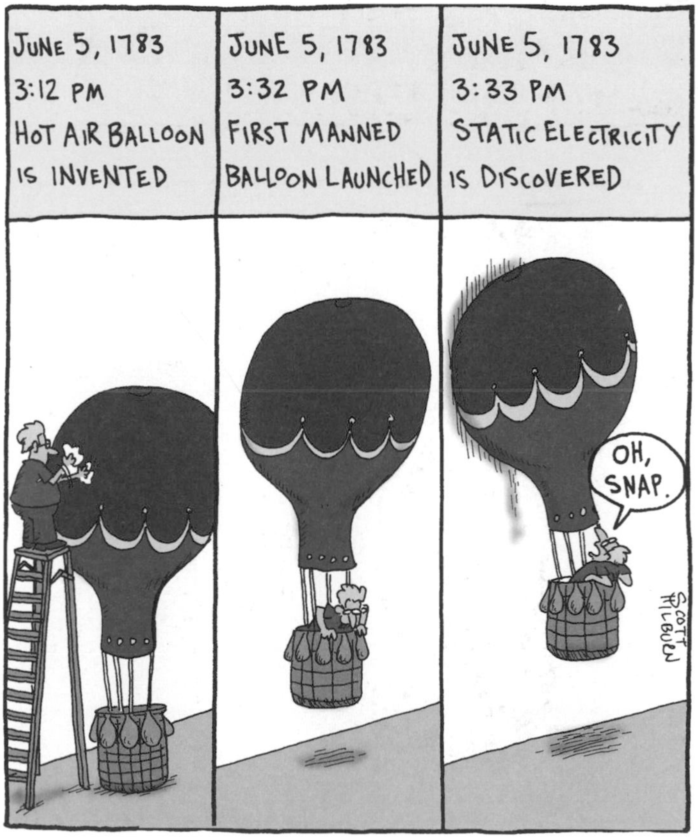
JUNE 5, 1783
3:12 PM
HOT AIR BALLOON IS INVENTED
JUNE 5, 1783
3:32 PM
FIRST MANNED BALLOON LAUNCHED
JUNE 5, 1783
3:33 PM
STATIC ELECTRICITY IS DISCOVERED
OH, SNAP.
SCOTT HILBURN

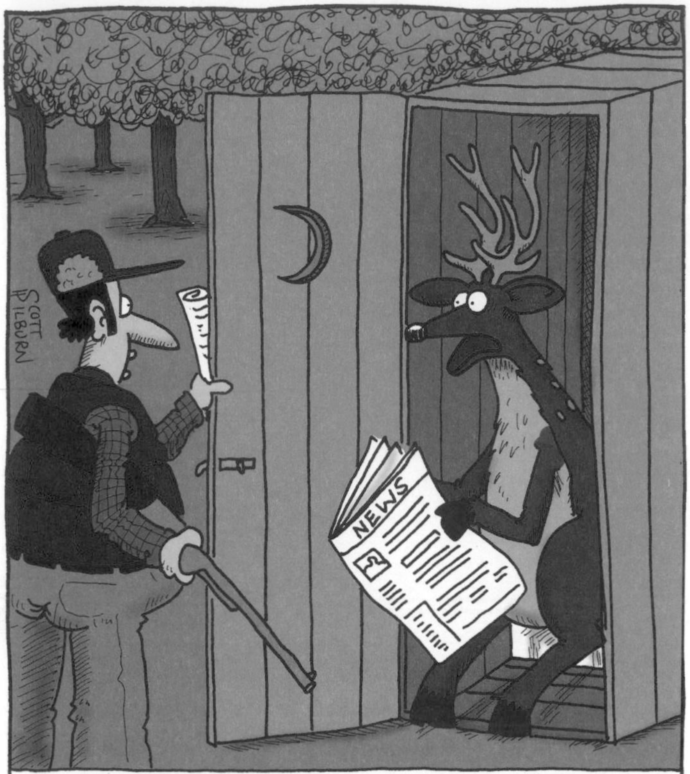
SCOTT HILBURN
NEWS

HOW POTLUCK MEALS CAME TO BE

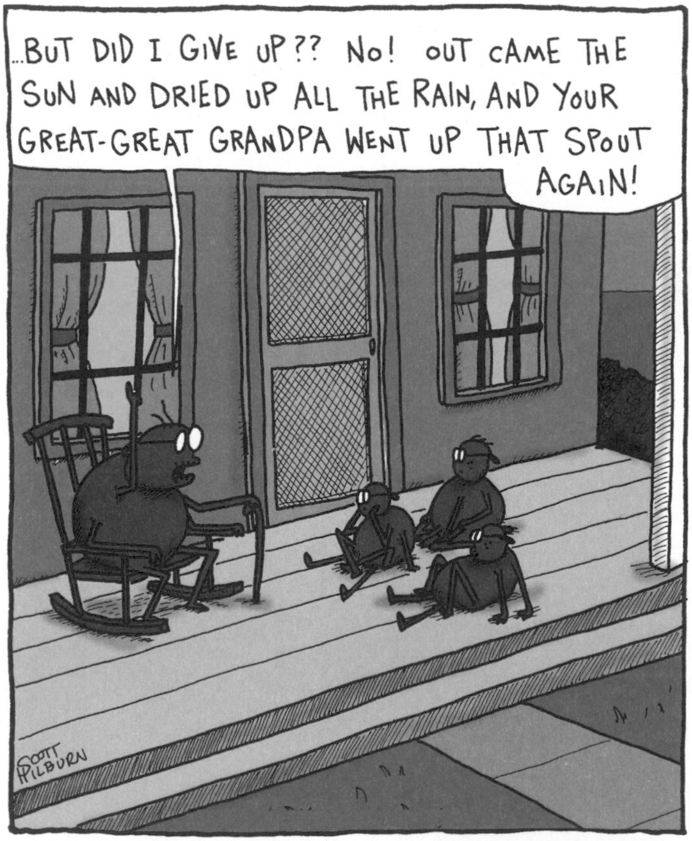
...BUT DID I GIVE UP?? NO! OUT CAME THE SUN AND DRIED UP ALL THE RAIN, AND YOUR GREAT-GREAT GRANDPA WENT UP THAT SPOUT AGAIN!
SCOTT HILBURN

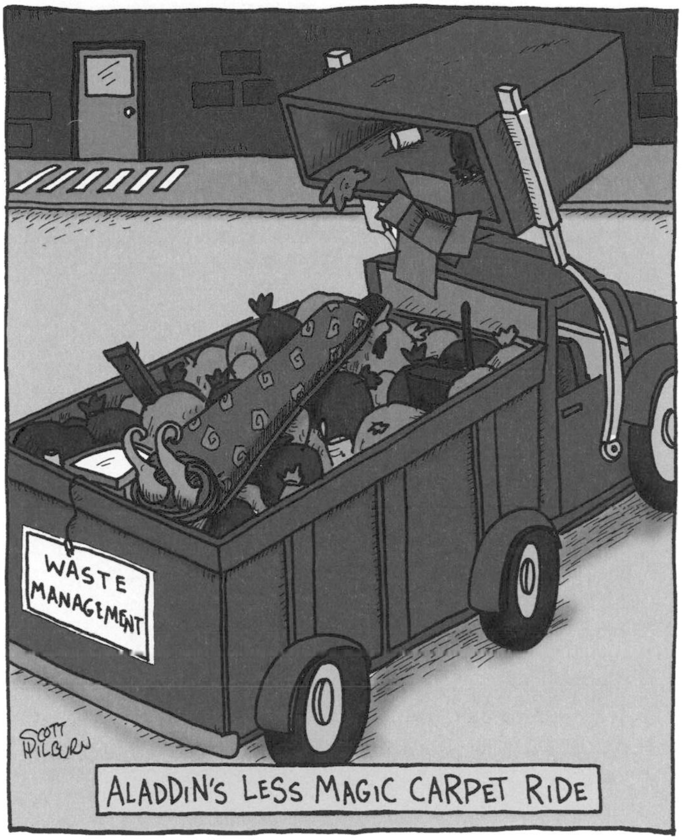
WASTE MANAGEMENT
SCOTT HILBURN
ALADDIN'S LESS MAGIC CARPET RIDE

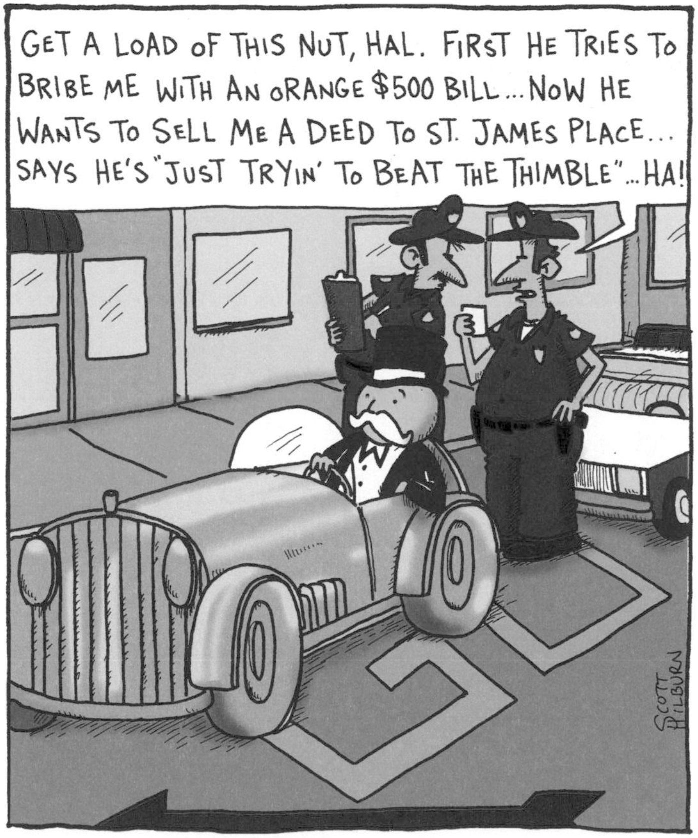
GET A LOAD OF THIS NUT, HAL. FIRST HE TRIES TO BRIBE ME WITH AN ORANGE $500 BILL... NOW HE WANTS TO SELL ME A DEED TO ST. JAMES PLACE... SAYS HE'S "JUST TRYIN' TO BEAT THE THIMBLE"... HA!
SCOTT HILBURN

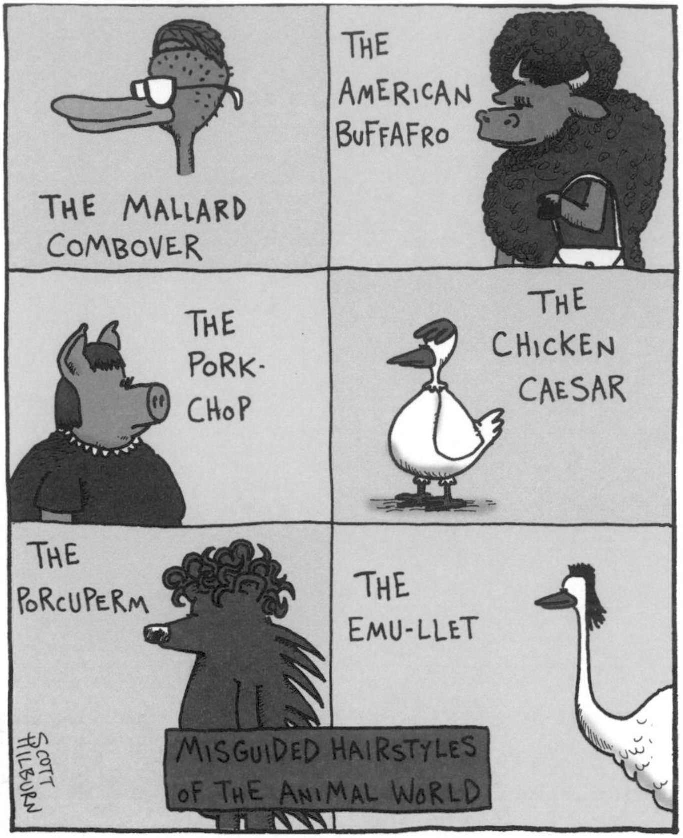
THE MALLARD COMBOVER
THE AMERICAN BUFFAFRO
THE PORK-CHOP
THE CHICKEN CAESAR
THE PORCUPERM
THE EMU-LLET
MISGUIDED HAIRSTYLES OF THE ANIMAL WORLD
SCOTT HILBURN

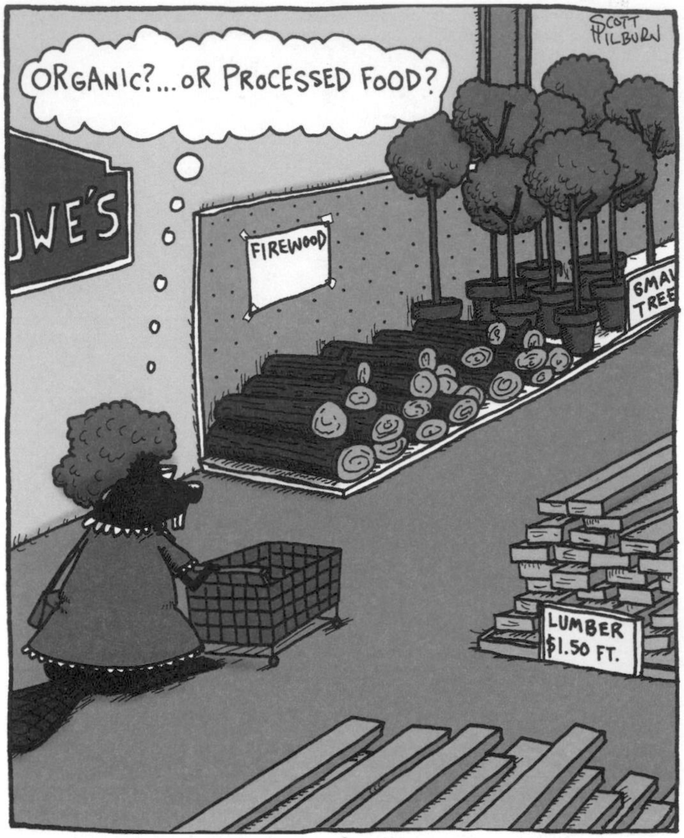
ORGANIC?...OR PROCESSED FOOD?
OWE'S
FIREWOOD
LUMBER $1.50 FT.
SCOTT HILBURN

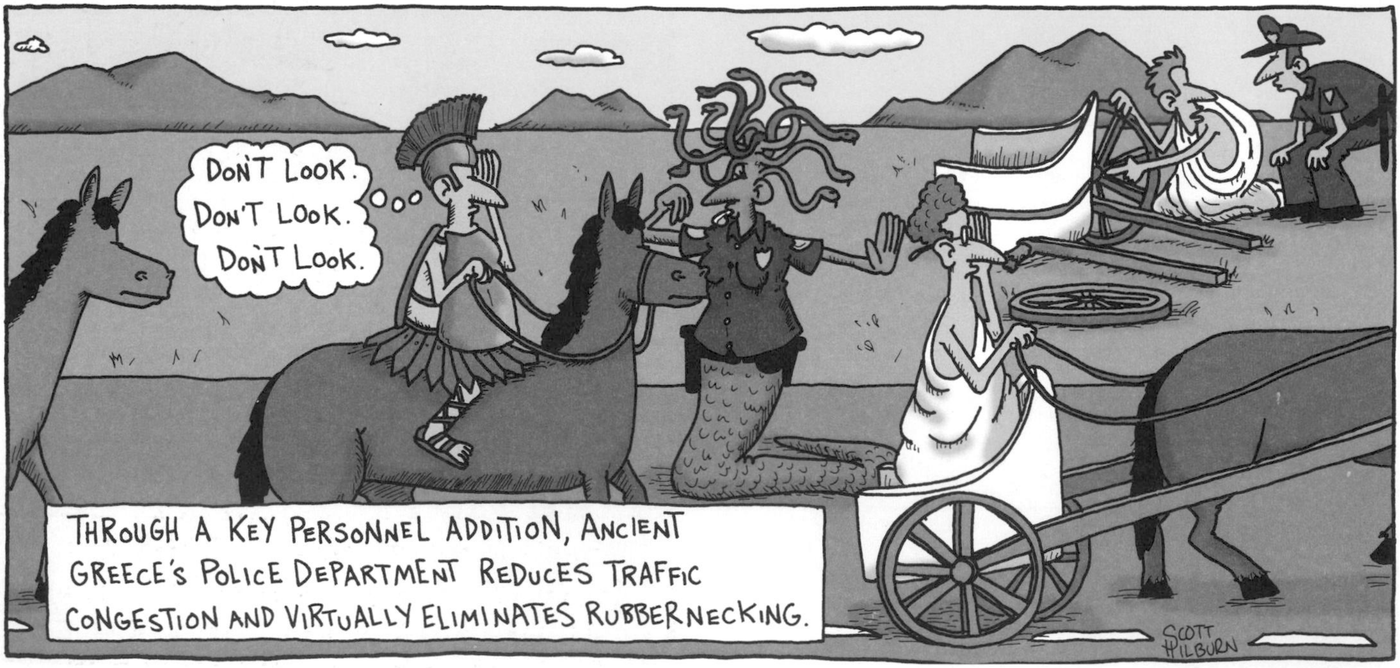
DON'T LOOK. DON'T LOOK. DON'T LOOK.
THROUGH A KEY PERSONNEL ADDITION, ANCIENT GREECE'S POLICE DEPARTMENT REDUCES TRAFFIC CONGESTION AND VIRTUALLY ELIMINATES RUBBERNECKING.
SCOTT HILBURN

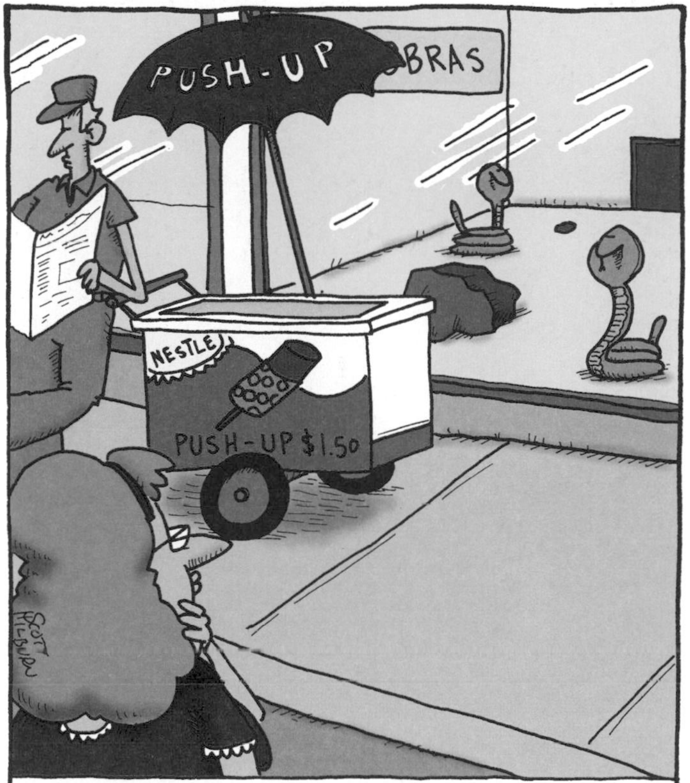
PUSH-UP
BRAS
NESTLE
PUSH-UP $1.50
SCOTT HILBURN

WHILE AT THE ZOO, VICTORIA GETS AN IDEA

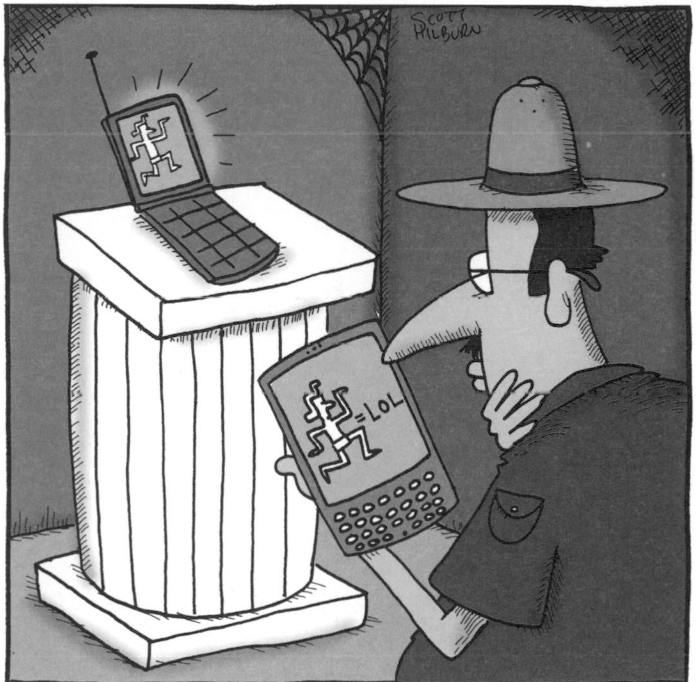
SCOTT HILBURN
=LOL

PREVIOUSLY INDECIPHERABLE, PROFESSOR WIGGINS TRANSLATES ANOTHER ANCIENT TEXT USING THE NEWLY DISCOVERED ROSETTA PHONE.

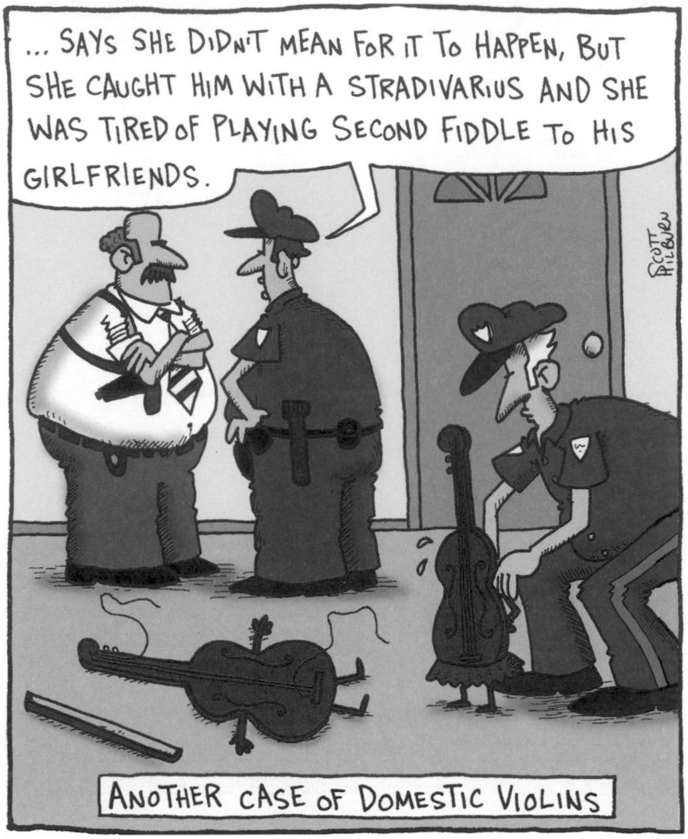
... SAYS SHE DIDN'T MEAN FOR IT TO HAPPEN, BUT SHE CAUGHT HIM WITH A STRADIVARIUS AND SHE WAS TIRED OF PLAYING SECOND FIDDLE TO HIS GIRLFRIENDS.
SCOTT HILBURN
ANOTHER CASE OF DOMESTIC VIOLINS

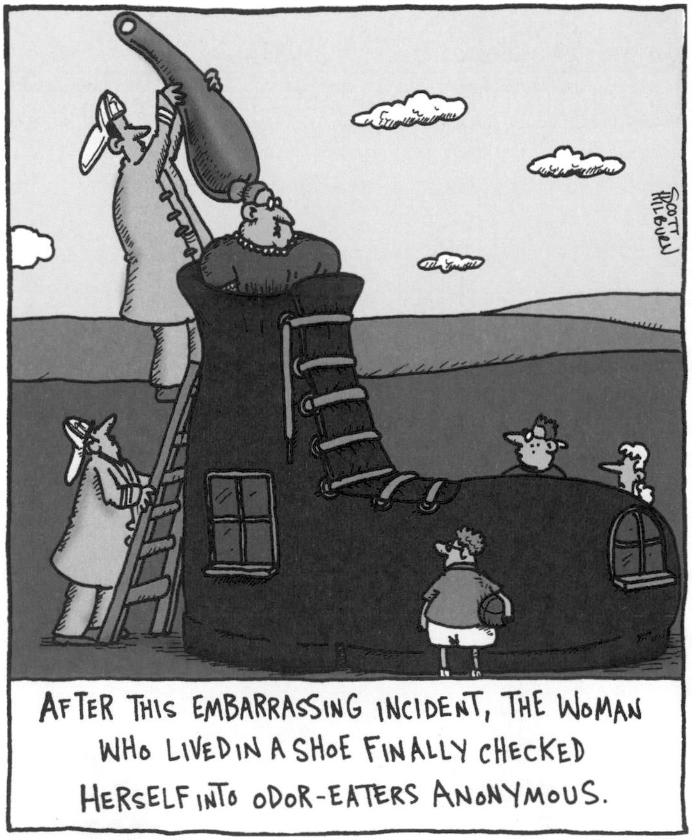
SCOTT HILBURN
AFTER THIS EMBARRASSING INCIDENT, THE WOMAN WHO LIVED IN A SHOE FINALLY CHECKED HERSELF INTO ODOR-EATERS ANONYMOUS.

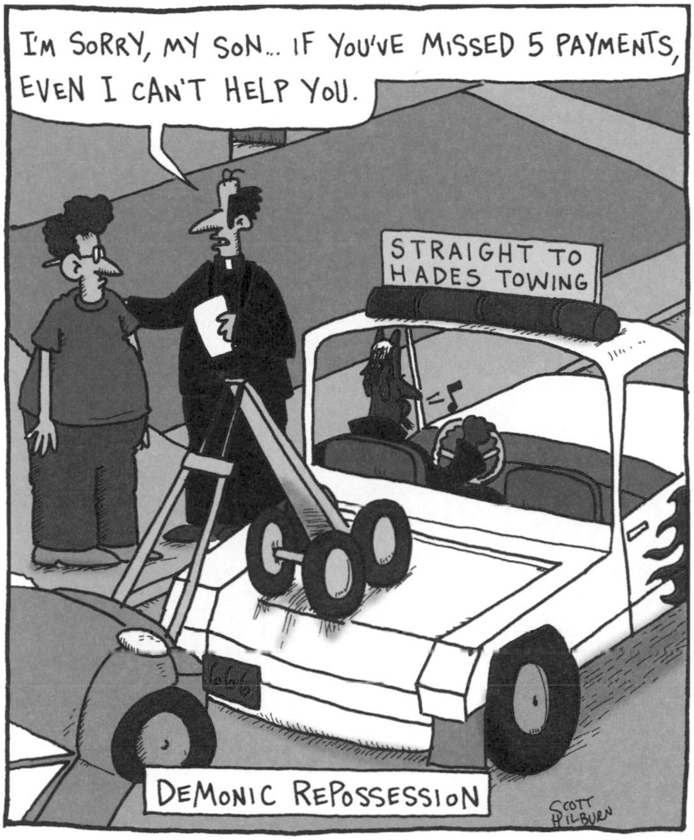
I'M SORRY, MY SON... IF YOU'VE MISSED 5 PAYMENTS, EVEN I CAN'T HELP YOU.
STRAIGHT TO HADES TOWING
SCOTT HILBURN

DEMONIC REPOSSESSION

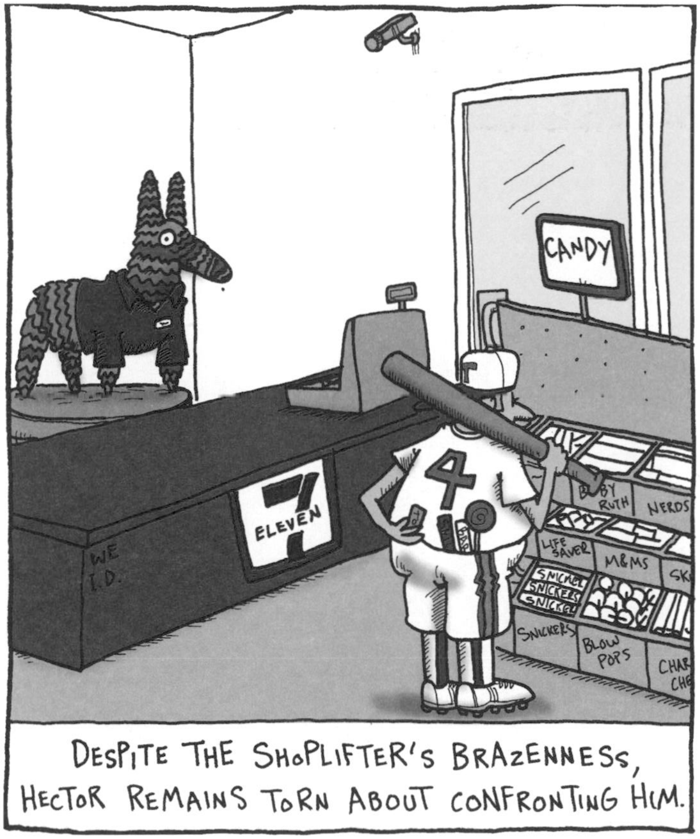
CANDY
ELEVEN
WE I.D.
4
NERDS
LIFE SAVER
M&MS
SNICKERS
BLOW POPS

DESPITE THE SHOPLIFTER'S BRAZENNESS, HECTOR REMAINS TORN ABOUT CONFRONTING HIM.

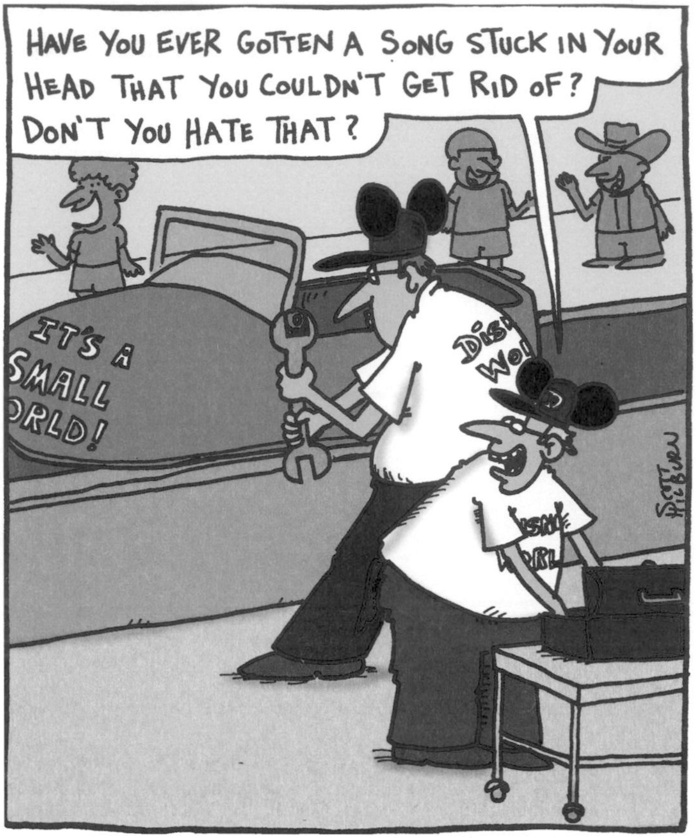
HAVE YOU EVER GOTTEN A SONG STUCK IN YOUR HEAD THAT YOU COULDN'T GET RID OF? DON'T YOU HATE THAT?
IT'S A SMALL ORLD!

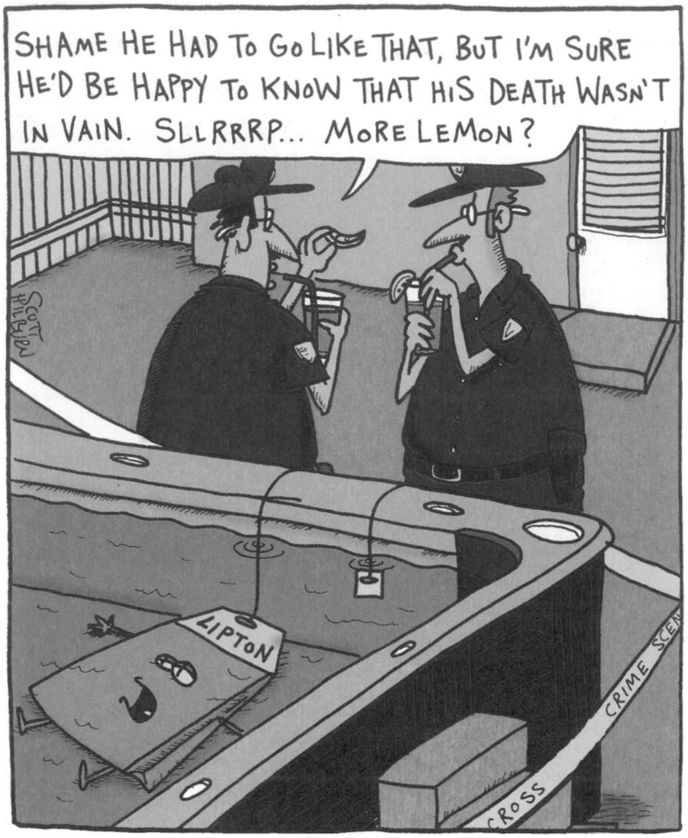
SHAME HE HAD TO GO LIKE THAT, BUT I'M SURE HE'D BE HAPPY TO KNOW THAT HIS DEATH WASN'T IN VAIN. SLLRRRP... MORE LEMON?
LIPTON
CRIME SCEN
CROSS

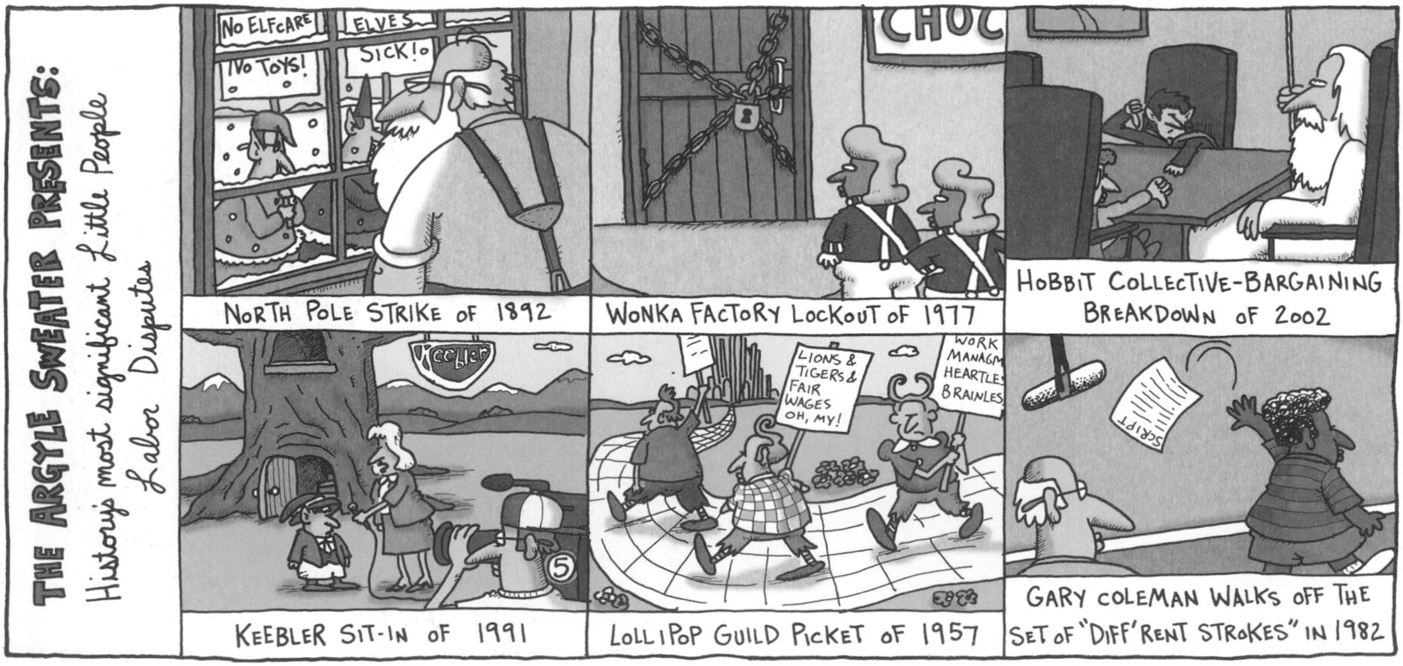
THE ARGYLE SWEATER PRESENTS:
History's most significant Little People Labor Disputes
NO ELFCARE
ELVES SICK!
NO TOYS!
NORTH POLE STRIKE OF 1892
CHOC
WONKA FACTORY LOCKOUT OF 1977
HOBBIT COLLECTIVE-BARGAINING BREAKDOWN OF 2002
Keebler
KEEBLER SIT-IN OF 1991
LIONS & TIGERS & FAIR WAGES OH, MY!
WORK MANAGM HEARTLES BRAINLES
LOLLIPOP GUILD PICKET OF 1957
SCRIPT
GARY COLEMAN WALKS OFF THE SET OF "DIFF'RENT STROKES" IN 1982

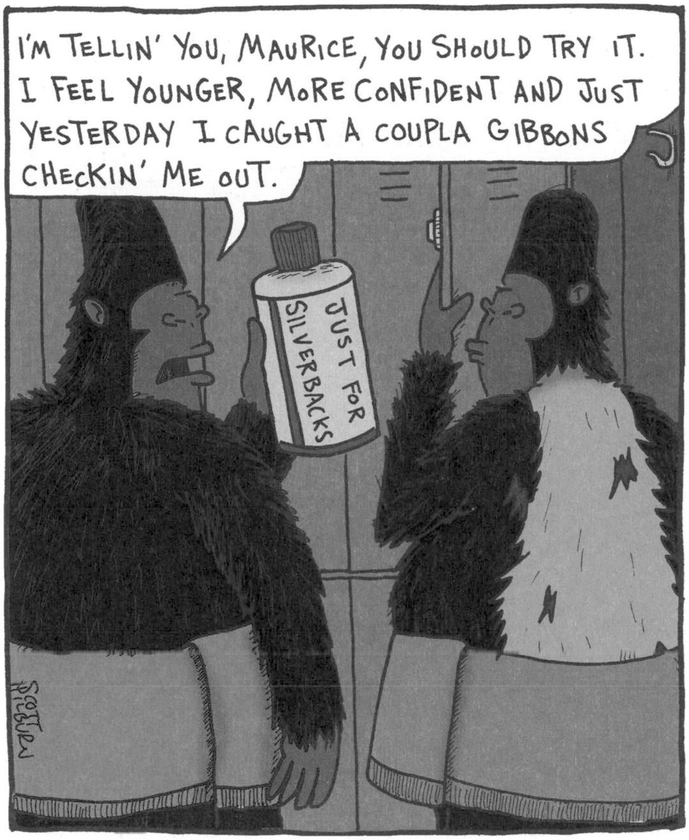
I'M TELLIN' YOU, MAURICE, YOU SHOULD TRY IT. I FEEL YOUNGER, MORE CONFIDENT AND JUST YESTERDAY I CAUGHT A COUPLA GIBBONS CHECKIN' ME OUT.
JUST FOR SILVERBACKS
SCOTT HILBURN

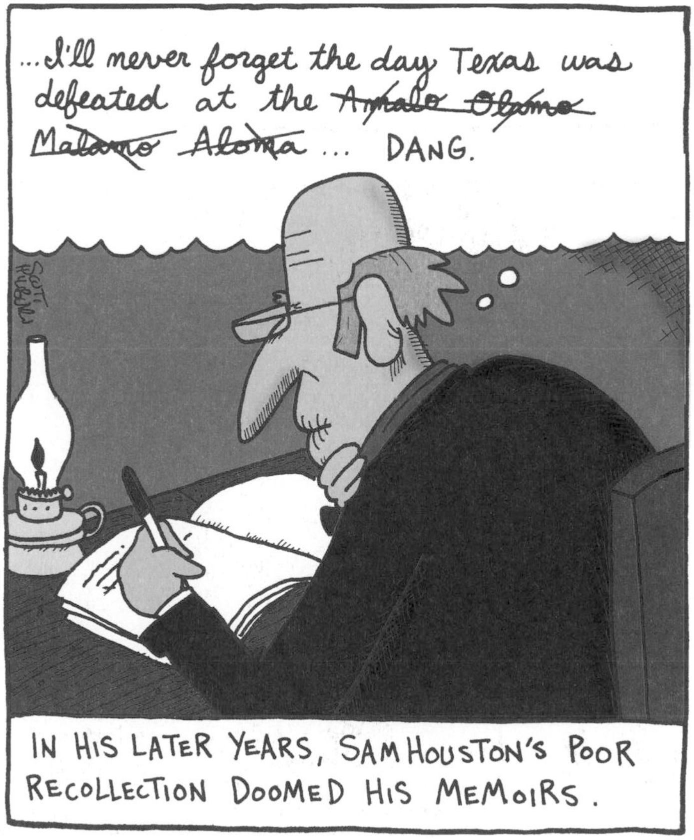
...I'll never forget the day Texas was defeated at the ~~Amalo~~ ~~Olamo~~ ~~Malamo~~ ~~Aloma~~ ... DANG.
SCOTT HILBURN

IN HIS LATER YEARS, SAM HOUSTON'S POOR RECOLLECTION DOOMED HIS MEMOIRS.

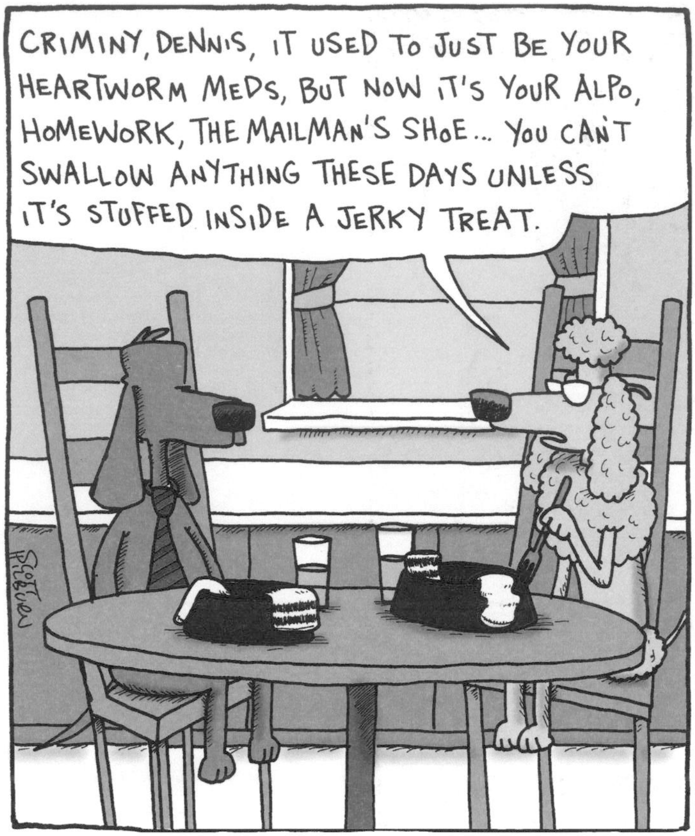
CRIMINY, DENNIS, IT USED TO JUST BE YOUR HEARTWORM MEDS, BUT NOW IT'S YOUR ALPO, HOMEWORK, THE MAILMAN'S SHOE... YOU CAN'T SWALLOW ANYTHING THESE DAYS UNLESS IT'S STUFFED INSIDE A JERKY TREAT.
SCOTT HILBURN

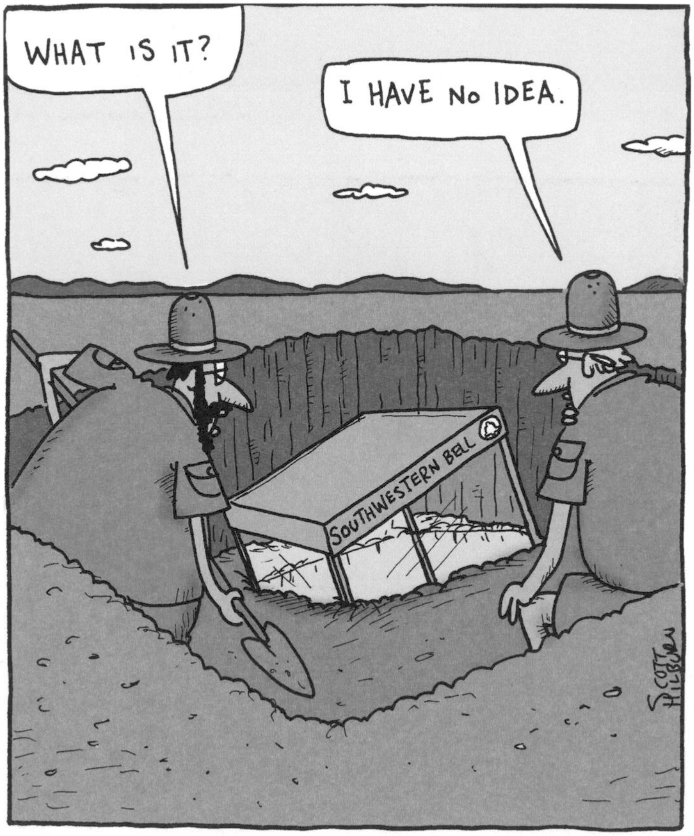
WHAT IS IT?
I HAVE NO IDEA.
SOUTHWESTERN BELL
SCOTT HILBURN

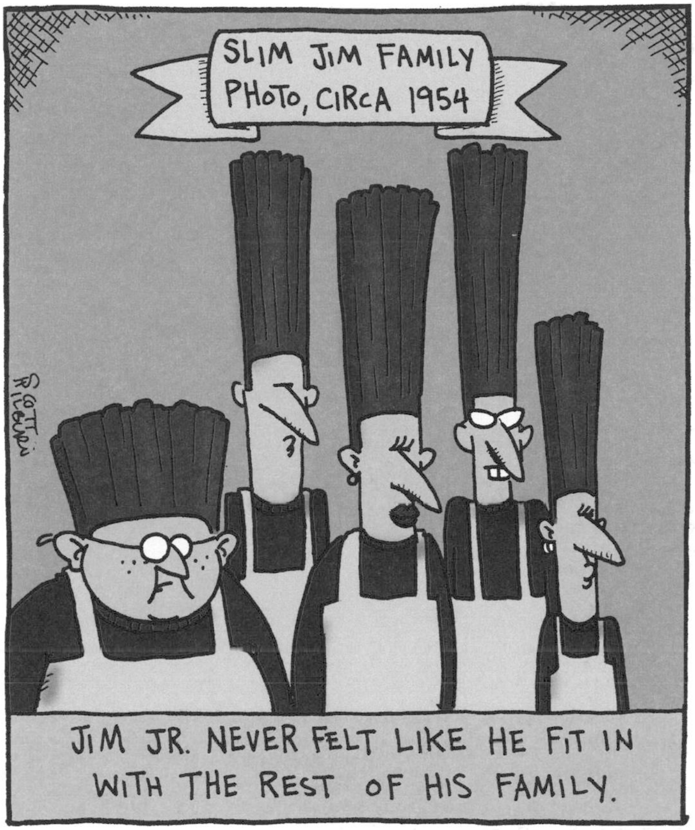
SLIM JIM FAMILY PHOTO, CIRCA 1954
SCOTT HILBURN
JIM JR. NEVER FELT LIKE HE FIT IN WITH THE REST OF HIS FAMILY.

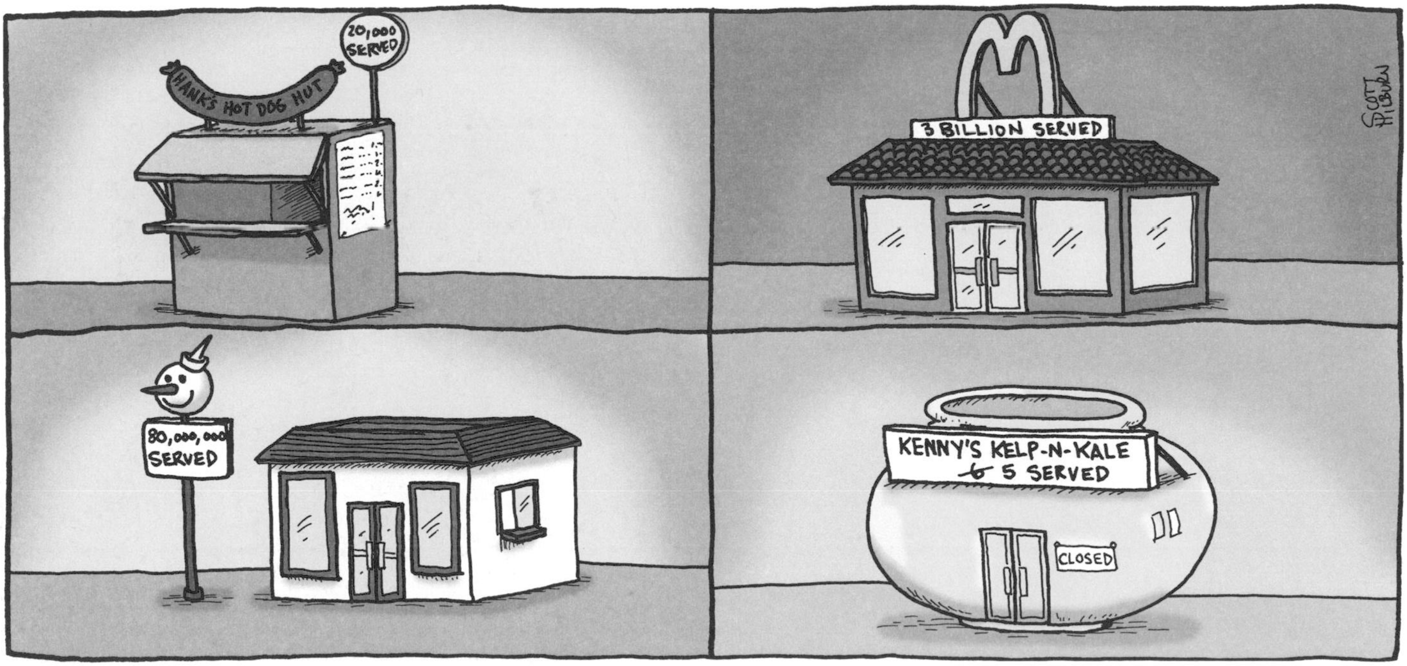
HANK'S HOT DOG HUT
20,000 SERVED
3 BILLION SERVED
SCOTT HILBURN
80,000,000 SERVED
KENNY'S KELP-N-KALE
6 5 SERVED
CLOSED